Roxbury Remembered

by Frederick Ungeheuer
with Lewis and Ethel Hurlbut

Authors Choice Press
New York Lincoln Shanghai

Roxbury Remembered

Authors Choice Press
an imprint of iUniverse, Inc.

For information address:
iUniverse, Inc.
2021 Pine Lake Road, Suite 100
Lincoln, NE 68512
www.iuniverse.com

Originally published by Connecticut Heritage Press

ISBN: 0-595-32940-3

Printed in the United States of America

Table of Contents

enstalled upon,
Just beyond this, on
the opposite side of
the Street, is a Methodist
Church, which has been
erected within the last
two years, for the worship
of the gospel, It has
been a great benifit.
It has been the means
of a number turning,
from the broad rode
that leads to distruction
J. the Straight and narrow
path that leads to
eternal life, Joining this
church, on the Same Side,
is the engine house, where
the fire company, meets,
to attend to their
nessary business.

Acrost the street, opposite
of this building, is the
resident of Copt. Amassa
Suthrs, Copt of said
company, persue your
a little farther, and you
come to B S Preston's
dry good store, situated
on the corner of main st,
and wheeler avenue, where
they do an extensive
business, in dry goods,
Such as neckties, cigars,
and plantation bitters.
in the opposite side of
the st, Situated between
the resident of Brigadier
General Nathen K Smith
and Beardsley & Leewises
extensive dry good
establishment, is the

Pages from Jeremah Decker essay describing Roxbury center in 1864.

2

Introduction

To the editors of the Roxbury Gazette.
Mr. Editors
Dear Sir

"As I have been for a long time a constant reader of your highly honored and extensively circulated paper, I feel it my duty as a citizen of this beautiful city and inmate of one of the most splendid edifices of learning this country affords to favor you with a short piece to help fill out the neatly arranged columns of your noted paper. Perhaps there is no place on the face of the globe that has greater facilities for acquiring learning & enterprise than the city we inhabit. Readers, if you doubt my words, just give one visit to this place and be convinse that I am telling the truth.

"As you enter main street, the first thing that comes to view is the Post Office Department, situated on the corner of main and Christian street, whare all the news of the city concentrates. On the opposite side of the street is the Episcopal church, one of the most splendid buildings for the worship of the Gospel that this country affords.

"The next thing that comes in view is a monument situated on the corner of main and Bradley streets erected in memory of Col. Seth Warner, one of the most noted heroes of the revolution, who fought sixteen hard and bloody battles to procure the freedom which we have enjoyed for over eighty years, and which we may as long as we hold to the same principles that his noted mind was enstalled upon.

"Just beyond this, on the opposite side of the street, is the Methodist church, which has been erected within the last two years for the worship of the gospel. It has been a great benefied. It has been the means of a number turning from the proud rode that leads to destruction to the straight and narrow path that leads to eternal life.

"Joining this church on the same side is the engine house, whare the fire company meets to attend to their necessary business.

"Acrost the street, opposite this building, is the residence of Capt. Amassa Lathrop, captain of said company. Persue your course a little further and you come to B. S. Preston's dry good store, situated on the corner of main street and Wheeler avenue, where they do an extensive business in dry goods such as neckties, cigars, and plantation bitters.

"On the opposite side of the street, situated between the residence of Brigadier General Nathen R. Smith and Beardsley & Lewises extensive dry good establishment is the Roxbury Chapel, the greatest emporium of learning in the world. It is here whare the young and tender mind is installed with usefulness. It is here whare we are taucht the way to science though the way may seem steap and rugged. But with diligence & perserverance we can assend it. And it is our duty to do all in our power to accomplish it, by so doing repay our parents for the pains they have taken in erecting this mansion and obtaining one of the best instructors this country affords.

"As I look around this room and see the nicely finished wall and neatly carved work on the desk it seems to me that all would try and see if we cannot repay for it in instructing our minds with usefulness.

"I will now leave the chapel and direct you to the Congregational church, where most of the young assemble on every Sunday morning and here the gospel preached. I have traveld in a number of different places in my short life, and have never found as steady a set of young men and ladies as there is in Roxbury. Readers, if you know of a steadier place than this please show it to me, and I will be convinsed. Otherways, I shall put Roxbury first in learning, first in enterprise, first in good morals, and above all esle first to defend her country."
Yours

Jeremah Decker

No. 101 Christian Street
Roxbury,
February 12, 1864

When Jeremah Decker wrote this touching eulogy to his home town, Roxbury was apparently a growing town, displaying signs of prosperity, and a place one could be proud of. It had first been settled by a group of families from Stratford in 1713, a hundred and fifty years before. Within one generation, or thirty years, it had attracted a sufficient number of additional settlers to be granted its own Congregational parish separate from Woodbury. By 1796 it was incorporated as a separate township, and in 1864, after two more generations, it had grown to nearly 1,000 inhabitants.

A few years later, in 1877, the Rev. Austin Isham, one of its well remembered church men, struck a similar note of civic pride when, in a retrospective prepared by M.L. Beardsley on the occasion of the Centennial of American Independence, he also referred to Roxbury primarily as a seat of learning. As early as 1834, Isham said, a private school had been established by a Mr. A.B. Campbell and a little later a second one by the Rev. George L. Foote, of which he said, "their reputation was so extensive that pupils from other places were frequently found here," and "the remark was frequently made by persons from abroad that our young people collectively were better educated."

Besides two private schools Roxbury then had seven public, one-room school houses scattered among the hills, where the children of its farmers, hat and saddle makers, gun and blacksmiths, or quarry workers got their primary instruction. The more talented went on to the school in the Congregational Chapel, where young Jeremah Decker wrote his letter to the editor of the "Gazette", while admiring the finish of its walls and the 'neat carving' on his instructor's desk. This school later became known as the Select School and functioned until the First World War. The building still stands - near the Congregational church.

One may wonder how Jeremah came to write this paean to his home town. The first thing it tells us is that, unlike today, Roxbury had its own newspaper. Could it be that its editor did not have enough local material to fill its pages? Since there was no radio or television then, it probably was the only source of news. More likely the instructor, perhaps a friend of the editor, asked his students one day to put on paper what they thought of their town. He may just have wanted them to think of it as a contribution to the Gazette.

Young Jeremah was a good reporter. He wrote down what was most obvious to him. The praise with which he padded his observations were probably what he had heard at home around the dinner table. It is a little surprising that he made no reference at all to the war, then entering its fourth and final year. This must have been the assignment on some other occasions. The Hurlbuts have four more samples of such Select School compositions. These were written by A. F. Squire in 1862 and 1863. In these Squire complains bitterly about what the war has done to his nation and its government.

"I am afraid we have seen the best days that we shall ever see as far as this nation is concerned," he writes in the last one dated February 26th, 1863, "I am sorry that the inhabitants were foolish enough to cause a war for the sake of party," a line he defends in each of his compositions. They are filled with patriotic fervor. "I am not ashamed to stand up to uphold this government and Constitution, if the whole school was against me." And he pities the "thousands (who) have given their lives on the battle field, and thousands more are waiting in their camps for it, seemingly to no purpose."

A lot of Roxbury's young men had gone off to fight in the war on the Union's side--as many, in fact, as were to join the Armed Forces in World War I. Many deserted, most likely because they could not accept the idea of having to shoot on their own countrymen. A lot did not return from the war at all and left the town more thinly settled as a result.

In 1850, a decade before the outbreak of the war, Roxbury's population had been 1,114, according to an official census held that year. By 1870, five years after the war, the number of residents was down to 920, or nearly 200 people less. What had happened? There may be several explanations other than the fact that 63 young men had gone off to war and only a few returned. The Western Reserve in Ohio was, of course, attracting more and more farmers from Connecticut's stony hills, although the exodus from eastern Connecticut is said to have been bigger than from its northwestern parts. The period after the Civil War, however, was particularly unsettled and unsettling. A stepped-up thrust westward was only a part of it. Many northern states complained about a rising exodus to the cities, as well. The refrain of a popular song enjoined them to, "stay on the farm, stay on the farm, though the profits come in rather slow. Stay on the farm, stay on the farm, don't be in a hurry to go."

Young Jeremah also claims that he had been to many other places in his short life, a sign that people were beginning to move around a bit. Perhaps his naive insistence on Roxbury as first in just about every imaginable endeavor reflected the local drive to keep young people at home. But Connecticut Yankees had always been great itinerants, both as peddlers and preachers. A century earlier, Roxbury's most illustrious sons, Ethan Allen and Seth Warner, as well as Remember Baker, had all sought their luck in the Green Mountains of Vermont.

A simpler explanation for the decline in the number of residents may be that Chalybes was counted separately. This growing part of the town, named after an ancient Asian tribe of iron miners, had sprung up around Mine Hill. By the early 1870's more than 200 men were working there and another 140 in garnet and silica quarries in Roxbury Falls. In 1872 the Shepaug Valley Railroad opened a spur to Chalybes. Today what remains of the place is known as Roxbury Station.

There was also disease. It is often forgotten how it could ravage a population as late as the last quarter of the 19th century, and even after World War I, when more people lost their lives in a flu epidemic than had been killed in the fighting. In 1902 the town's health officer Dr. Louis Pons wrote that "chills and fever of the tertian variety have been very prevalent the past three years, but more especially the past summer, when probably 40% of the population residing in Shepaug Valley have been affected." How much the mosquito was responsible for these outbreaks of malaria, he wrote, was "still a mooted question." But he had no doubt that "some mosquitoes are capable of conveying malarial germ from a sick person to the well." He also noted that, "very little improvement has been made to the disposal of garbage and sewage."

It is doubtful that people still died of malaria in Roxbury then, but perhaps some moved out of the more infested areas to nearby towns such as Bridgewater and New Milford. The fact remains that until urban dwellers, especially from New York, started seeking second homes or places of retirement in Roxbury, the town never again attained the population it had in 1850. By 1950, a full century later, it was down to 750 people, counting everyone in Roxbury Station and Roxbury Falls.

Jeremah makes no mention of the mines or the railroad, either. Neither was in operation yet. His is a schoolboy's perspective. He seems aware of little more than the houses on the street he saw as he walked to school every morning and of some of the values his teachers and parents were trying to 'instal' in him, as he would say. It is amazing how enduring some of these values have been. Freedom was writ large. It has remained the basic tenet of the American ideology. Usefulness and enterprise were also valued in connection with any form of learning, while the purer pursuit of science was considered a "steap and rugged path," emulated more perhaps as a test of a student's perseverance than as a goal in itself. Steadiness of character was prized, as well as good morals.

One may ask what he associated with the latter: honesty, most likely, and obedience to the rules of his religion and church, rather than sexual discipline with which it tends to be chiefly associated today. Roxbury then (as now) was a 'dry' town, the public consumption of alcohol having been prohibited in the state in 1854, long before national prohibition. Dancing was also frowned upon.

Janice Law Trecker writes in her historical sketch of Connecticut in the early 19th century Preachers, Rebels, and Traders that "early Connecticut devoted an amazing amount of time to religion and religious observances. This was especially notable among the Congregationalists who emphasized the strict observance of the Sabbath. Well into the 19th century, Connecticut laws prohibited not only work but almost all manner of recreation and frivolity on Sundays, even including such innocent pastimes as walking in the country."

Old Roxbury records show that people were excommunicated for not observing their family prayers at home. Houses of worship then, as now, served as a town's social center. Clergymen provided spiritual guidance and comfort, but also educational and intellectual enrichment. The church, Trecker writes, "was the visible embodiment of the community, its gathering place and symbol of unity." But people also had fun in their way. The great events of family life: christenings, marriages, and funerals, provided the occasion for convivial gatherings with great dinners, bowls of punch and flip, music and dancing. There were turkey shoots and picnics with wrestling and running contests and quilting bees for the women. We shall see that Roxbury's families had additional ways of getting together for social evenings outside the standard family occasions.

There are nevertheless a few minor incongruities between Jeremah Decker's brief description of Roxbury on the eve of its 'industrial revolution' and other surviving accounts. Readers may also be surprised that Roxbury had a fire station then. As the town lost much of its population in the first half of the present century, the fire department also disappeared. It had to be resurrected by the modernizing First Selectman Allen Hurlburt in 1935, after more and more second home owners began to settle in Roxbury. But by then - as we shall see - many of its finest old houses had already burned to the ground.

Jeremah also mentions the existence of a Methodist church in 1864, which by other accounts did not have a building of its own until 1867, when the Congregational church split over the abolition of slavery. (Lewis Hurlbut believes Jeremah meant the wagon shop where meetings of the Methodists were held before the church was completed. It had a porch which indicated that it may have served some other purpose earlier.) Jeremah clearly states, however "...the Methodist church, which has been erected within the last two years." It would have been difficult for him to mistake the meeting room above a wagon shop for a church erected two years earlier. Because the scission in the church started before the outbreak of the Civil War, it also seems more likely that it was built before the end of that war.

Connecticut had abolished slavery in 1848 and the venerable Rev. Austin Isham himself recalled that in 1847, a year before abolition, the first Methodist society had been organized in Roxbury. In the spring of 1862, he says, Rev. Spencer H. Bray commenced preaching in a house then occupied by a Rev. Jones and a Mr. Gillette. It was the General Ephraim Hinman house that is now the home of Geddes and Leonie Parsons. Later, Methodist services were conducted for a while in the upper room of Mr. H.W. Trowbridge's wagon shop. Isham said this is where services were held, "until the present church edifice was erected in 1867." Could this temporary arrangement be what Jeremah meant? The riddle about the date remains.

To us the year 1864 seemed a good point of departure, because it stands at the parting of an earlier agricultural past that has already been amply described by others, especially William Cothren, the first historian of the region and still the one on whose work all other histories appear to be based. Roxbury was entering a new age, the age in which machines

8

replaced handcrafts, and industries were organized that called less for manual skills and for more organization, when modern communications such as the telegraph and railroads and eventually the automobile broke the isolation in which small New England towns like Roxbury had lived for so long.

A few years later Jeremah Decker would probably not have been able to write of his town in the same manner anymore. His confidence in Roxbury as the center of the universe and apogee of culture would no longer have been so total. To Jeremah, Roxbury offered just about everything the average lad could possibly desire: two dry good stores in which you could buy "anything you want," even plantation bitters. Roxbury boasted a post office, three pretty churches, and the best schools anywhere. Farmers and artisans were not alone. The town had lawyers and doctors and politicians. Prominent Roxbury families like the Smiths and Bakers had already brought forth judges and men who held high federal offices. (See Norman Hurlbut's sketches.)

The basics required to lead a full life could be procured through the efforts of any family. People then were less dependent on the outside world than they are today, and also more self-reliant as a community. Besides the food on their tables and in their pantries or cellars (food they grew themselves), farmers wove their own cloth, fashioned their own furniture, tanned their own leather for shoes and harnesses, and made many of their implements. More complicated ones such as saddles, rifles or plows were made in local workshops. They did not have to be imported from some other town. People raised their own barns and houses with the help of neighbors, and tapped plenty of water power to run grist and saw mills. Their only contact with a national industry was through a number of small hat shops, where three to five workmen blocked beaver and later felt for factories in Danbury, the country's chief hat maker.

"Towns like Roxbury were like states are today," Lewis Hurlbut says. All of this was to change after the end of the "Great Rebellion," as the Civil War was called here. Roxbury, hitherto a community of nearly self-sufficient farmers, was about to get its whiff of industrialization, however brief.

To this day the roughest work, relegated to the least developed regions of the world, is mining. In a sense it is really a pre-industrial activity. Rather than transforming materials it means scratching, or stripping the soil for the minerals embedded in it. This kind of work had been tried in Roxbury's Mine Hill for nearly a century without much success. Only the granite in the hill had been carved out regularly, serving as a handy foundation stone for almost all houses and barns as well as hearth and chimney stones. The quarry began to be worked industrially in 1850 and was in full operation at the time Jeremah Decker gave us his description of what he saw around him in Roxbury.

There had been earlier efforts to get at the ores which were known to be abundant in Mine Hill. The first diggers had been after gold and silver. Four of the oldest Roxbury families were involved in this effort: Moses Hurlbut, Abel Hawley, and Abraham and Israel Brownson. They bought tracts on the hill in 1751, sold stock in a company, and hired a German expert named Feuchter to drive a shaft into the hill. Apparently, little if any silver or gold was found. Town lore has it that Feuchter made off with some ingots of silver, however. A second attempt was made by a group of New Yorkers to whom the Brownson brothers leased their tract in 1764. This time they were looking for lead with the help of another outside expert, Daniel Feuter, who at one time had 33 mine workers and one blacksmith in his employ, tunneling into Mine Hill laterally instead of vertically down.

Why none of them ever had the idea to exploit the iron ore, which they must have encountered in abundance, is still something of a mystery. Iron ore had been mined successfully in other parts of New England, especially in northwestern Connecticut, since well before the Revolution. In fact, its village forges were known as the 'arsenal' of the Revolution. They produced more iron than all of the forges in England and Wales. Salisbury, in the northwestern corner of Litchfield county, started making iron in 1730, Lakeville in 1762, and Kent had a blast furnace which it converted to 1/4 use of anthracite coal in 1854, eight years before Roxbury's smelter was fired up for the first time -- with charcoal.

Usually, when iron deposits were found in colonial times, furnaces and forges were quickly built to make cooking pots, end irons, tools such as hammers and axes, hinges, and door latches, as well as fire arms and, when needed, cannons and cannon balls. By the time Roxbury finally got around to exploiting its own iron ore, there were more than a dozen such blast furnaces in operation in northwestern Connecticut and just across the border in Massachusetts. If the original 'diggers' and entrepreneurs had not realized that they were sitting on a rich lode of iron, it was certainly known to a lot of other people for almost half a century, before serious mining for iron ore actually began.

Some have conjectured that they missed the ore at first, because it was siderite, which is tied to carbon rather than magnetite, an iron oxide found everywhere else in New England. But in 1816 Benjamin Silliman, a geologist at Yale University, reported that siderite lay about in great discarded heaps of rubble outside the old Roxbury mine shafts. He described its iron ore potential in the most glowing terms. In parts of Europe this ore was known as spathic iron, he said. It only required special puddling techniques to separate the carbon from the ferrous mineral to produce steel from this kind of ore.

In 1824 David Stiles of Roxbury began to buy up tracts. It took him more than 30 years to assemble all the titles to Mine Hill. His effort provides an insight into one other aspect of the Yankee character. Like Americans today the people of Roxbury were a litigious lot. Holders of older titles and or leases fought Stiles every bit of the way. There were many old titles like those of the Brownsons perhaps, and one that went all the way back to Jabez Bacon of Woodbury and Ethan Allen, who had tried their luck sometime before the Revolution, when Mine Hill was still known as Spruce Hill. By 1856 he had won the battle. All titles were finally cleared and in his hands. Nine years later, in January 1865, he found a company willing to exploit the deposits.

The newly established Shepaug Iron & Steel Co., backed by $300,000 in outside venture capital, paid him $100,000 for the entire property. It made Stiles one of the richest men in Roxbury, if not the richest, and compensated him very well for 40 years of stubbornness. In his history of region, two years earlier, the Woodbury lawyer William Cothren had described the Mine Hill iron ore deposit with familiar hyperbole as, "the richest in the United States, and as good as any elsewhere on the face of the earth, so far discovered." He was probably echoing the views of another Yale geologist, Charles Upham Shephard who, at Stiles' behest, propagandized the untapped riches of the spathic ore as early as 1831 and 1837. Cothren also pointed out that the hill had "been alternately worked and litigated for more than 150 years."

Extraction of iron ore began late in 1865, and smelting in 1867, two years later. It lasted only until 1872 through some dramatic ups and downs: bankruptcies and re-organizations that have been well documented by Richard L. Kruse of Roxbury Land Trust and a team of Yale researchers, Michael Bell and Diane B. Mayerfeld, in a study entitled <u>Time and the Land: the Story of Mine Hill</u>. Both conclude that the venture was probably doomed from the start, because it came too late. The technology of steel making on the site was never fully mastered, and blast furnaces of the type constructed were already obsolescent.

The only real beneficiary, aside from David Stiles, was Albert Hodge, a prominent citizen of Roxbury, who was hired as supervisor and manager for a salary of $1,200 a year, then a handsome income in a small town. After the mine's last of several financial failures, Hodge bought the defunct property for $1,000 and assumption of a $3,000 mortgage in

1894. His descendants eventually sold the hill to the Roxbury Land Trust for $360,000 in 1979.

Perhaps it was just as well that this great industrial venture never got off the ground. The heavy use of charcoal was an ecological disaster. It prompted local farmers to denude their forest land in order to provide the wood. The furnace poured out eight to ten tons of pig iron a day when it was operating at full blast. It took three cords of wood to make the charcoal to produce one ton of pig iron. So the furnace consumed between 24 and 30 cords a day. Since a dozen blast furnaces were already operating in other parts of northeastern Connecticut, the state was fast running out of this basic fuel. Richard Kruse reports that as the local supply dwindled, "charcoal was brought by train from Vermont, New Hampshire, and Maine: and later the Virginias and the Carolinas." But it was not only the iron forges. Waterbury's brass factories were also heavy users of charcoal.

Ironically, the spur of the New York & New Haven Railroad from Hawleyville to Litchfield, which became known as the Shepaug Valley Railroad, was finished in 1872, the year the iron mine and smelter finally closed down for good. The railroad subsequently carried a lot of stone from the quarry, where more and more granite was mined with industrial methods and exported to other towns in the region. According to Richard Kruse, Roxbury granite was also used to build the 1,350 foot long retaining walls of the New York Central & Hudson River Railroad from 67th to 72nd Streets. The wall reached a height of 58 feet and a width at the base of 21 feet. Roxbury granite went into the 16,000 feet long retaining wall and numerous bridge abutments of the New York, New Haven & Hartford Railroad line running through Bridgeport, which averages 20 feet in height and 12 feet at the base. The railroad also allowed Roxbury to ship its silica and plows to more distant markets, and later its milk and cream.

While the great iron and steel making venture may have failed, it nevertheless changed Roxbury in many respects. For one, it brought hundreds of new residents to the town. Most of the miners settled in Chalybes, near the mine. Doubtless, many continued to work in the granite quarry after the iron mine was closed down. Most were immigrants from Poland, some from Sweden or Germany, but a lot were Irish. It may have taken a little while before the older citizens, who were primarily of English stock, began to accept the newcomers in their midst. Thus, Roxbury absorbed a small part of the influx of new immigrants that so profoundly changed the population of Connecticut after the Civil War from one of primarily native born people to 41% immigrants by 1900.

Nearly all the workers in the mine were foreign born. While the older families lived in clusters near the fields, which their ancestors had cleared for cultivation, or near each other in the center of town, the newcomers settled around what today is Roxbury Station. A map of Roxbury in 1874 (see front page) shows three Leavenworths, where Tophet and Painter (then Planter) Hill Road meet today, five Castles and four Tyrells at Warner's Mill, and four Beardsley homes along Good Hill Road. For a time, Chalybes, or Roxbury Station, became a thriving village with its own post office, general store, a school, lumber yard, coal yard, creamery, grist mill, hattery, a cigar factory, brass factory, hotel, several boarding houses, a bar, the railroad station, mine and quarry.

As previously mentioned, other industries sprang up at about the same time. On the other side of Roxbury, at Warner's Mill, near what is known as Roxbury Falls today, two quarries began to be worked for garnets. A mill to grind silica, which farmers found in large outcroppings of distinctive white rock on their fields, was one of the first sources of cash for many.

Tobacco was the other. As early as 1830, Connecticut farmers had begun to make broad leaf tobacco, which proved a better cigar wrapper than the former 'shoe string' variety, and by 1890, Connecticut was producing ten million pounds of tobacco leaf, much of it from small plots its farmers had reserved for this "cash crop." In Roxbury the plain east of Mine Hill, along the Shepaug River, was almost solely given over to growing tobacco. In town Colonel George Hurlbut, a successful hatter who had bought one of the large houses across from the Episcopal church, as we will hear from his great-granddaughter Sarah Houck, planted tobacco in neat rows on eight acres right behind his house. In recent years the grounds were planted to other crops. They were acquired in 1988 by the town to provide room for expanded town facilities.

We shall also learn that to distinguish herself from the Hurlbut family, who were still farmers, the Colonel's daughter insisted on inserting an 'r' in her name. The family gravestones have only Colonel George Hurlbut's name chiseled into it without an 'r' but their son's with one. Allen and Everett Hurlburt adopted their grandmother's spelling. They were, however, descended from the same Joseph Hurlbut, who was one of Roxbury's original settlers in 1713.

The end of the Civil War brought with it other new conditions to which Roxbury farmers, like their kin in the rest of Connecticut, had to adapt. Ruth O.M. Anderson writes in her historical monograph, From Yankee to American that in that period "dishonesty and corruption were rampant in business and politics." It was a time of inflation in which the rich grew richer, and the poor had difficulty surviving. Although there was full employment, hours were long, wages were low, and prices high. The Connecticut farmer, still relatively isolated and self-sufficient, had to rethink his position in the economy. First, she writes, he had to take account of the fact that he could not compete with western cattle raisers after 1877, when Gustavus Franklin Swift successfully shipped the first refrigerator car load of fresh meat to the east.

This left him only dairying as an alternative, and perhaps cheese making. Goshen turned this to advantage. Elmer Worthington, a retired New Milford banker who lives on South Street and has researched various aspects of local history, says that for a decade or so Goshen became the "cheese capital" of the United States, turning out thousands of tons of fine cheddar cheeses. Connecticut's farmers could at least turn their proximity to New England's booming city markets to advantage. In Roxbury, as we shall see, Col. George Hurlbut & Son was the first to open a permanent trade link with New Haven, shipping farm produce there to his brother, who had established himself as a wholesaler. They brought back dry goods for distribution here. Later, the railroad helped bring other cities closer, but the battle was never won. It became harder to make any kind of living in this small, remote hill town as industry sought out towns mostly along the coast, and along the shores of the Great Lakes.

In the following pages we will try to trace how it happened, and how local people reacted to the changes. This is not meant as a historical study. Nor can it pretend to any kind of completeness. It is a work of selective memory to give a glimpse at how things were a generation or two ago. It is based largely on interviews with a few people, who remember how they and their parents lived in the old days, when Roxbury was still primarily a farming community.

The effort to put down such memories began with Norman Hurlbut, who served as town clerk for 46 years from 1900 to 1947 and who, in his spare time, began to write a rudimentary history of his own, including revised and expanded portraits of its three most famous sons: Ethan Allen, Seth Warner and Remember Baker. His son Lewis continued his father's work by saving many newspaper clippings that dealt with Roxbury's history. He also interviewed the 94-year-old Clayton Squire shortly before his death in 1976.

Squire's memory, as we shall see, went back to the time right after the Civil War, when young Jeremah Decker was attending school. The span of his memory became our time frame. Through it we will try to show what has changed, how the town lost its struggle with industrialization

14

and with richer, more extensive farms in the west, but also how much its people retained of their character, and how their love of the town survived. This love, it seems, also affected newcomers. In many respects it remains as strong as that of the young Jeremah Decker in 1864. At a meeting of townspeople in 1986 Roxbury was variously described as "our garden of Eden" and "paradise" and by playwright and resident sage Arthur Miller simply as "my fields."

Jeremah thought of Roxbury as a town that had everything. It even had a surplus. Town records show that in his day Roxbury exported $21,000 worth of hay a year, followed by flour ($6,000), Indian corn ($5,000), and butter ($4,000). The people must have felt that a great expansion lay just ahead. Somehow the modern era passed them by. But let's hear it first from Lewis Hurlbut, as he dips into his and his family's memory to describe how the town settled by their ancestors entered its second century.

Old Roxbury Post Office and store until 1936. Beyond it is the home of Mr. and Mrs. Allen Hurlburt, built in 1784.

Congregational Chapel built in 1844 for "prayer, exhortation and other attainments," including "academical studies."

W.L. Hobson.

Monument to Seth Warner, Revolutionary hero and the Episcopal parsonage which was once a tavern.

Home of Amassa Lathrop, Captain of local fire company in Decker's letter in 1864. Now 8 Church Street.

W.L. Hobson.

Former home of Brigadier General Nathan Smith, Connecticut Judge and U.S. Senator. Pillars on house were drawn by oxcart from a New Haven Church that had burned. Now 12 Church Street.

Present Congregational Church built in 1838 at 24 Church Street, the fourth meeting house of that society. The first and second were built in 1732 and 1733 in the old Roxbury Center.

17

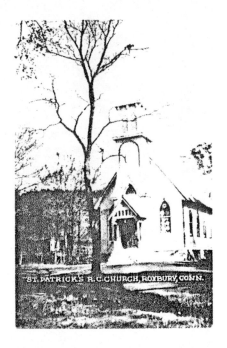

Christ Church Episcopal was organized in 1740. Its first church building was contiguous to the First Congregational Church. This present building was first built in 1807. It was turned and renovated in 1861. Now at 4 Wellers Bridge Road.

St. Patrick's Catholic Church, dedicated in 1855, was remodeled in the early 1950's. Now at 25 Church Street.

Methodist Church (on left) was built in 1867 and dismantled in 1940. Town Hall (on right) was built in 1872 and is still standing at 7 South Street.

Oldest house in Roxbury is at 112 Sentry Hill Road at corner of Route 67. It was built circa 1733 and is known as the Remember Baker House.

W.L. Hobson

The Remember Baker house before modernization. This was at one time the home of Treat Davidson.

Home of Ephraim Hinman, eccentric town leader, was built in 1784. It is now #1 Church Street.

19

I.
The Oldest Farm

The Hurlbut family has farmed in Roxbury continuously since the early 1700's, and is generally credited with the first settlement of both the Shippauge (Shepaug) district of Woodbury and the Judea Society area, a few miles up river. (Judea and portions of Litchfield, Kent and New Milford were set off as the Town of Washington early in the War of Independence.) But first they had built a sawmill on Moosehorn Brook. Joseph Hurlbut & Sons built a log cabin and a small fort on Sentry Hill overlooking the Shepaug Valley. Their first unfortified house on what is now called Hurlbut Corner, behind the present Maple Bank Farm outlet, was built about 1730 by Jonathan Hurlbut, a son of the first settler, and was lived in by three generations of Hurlbuts. The present house, higher up, was finished in 1830 and became the home of five more generations of Hurlbuts. In 1980 Lewis Hurlbut passed it on to his daughter Cathleen and her husband Howard Bronson Jr. For the first time in 180 years, no male Hurlbut was ready to continue in the family's tradition.

Lewis and his brother Alden had joined their own father somewhat reluctantly, as we shall see. In a brief portrait of Lewis and his family in 1977, Arthur Miller predicted that "the farm will probably vanish with him--it makes little sense to work this hard."

The book, entitled In the Country with photographs by Miller's wife Inge Morath, shows Lewis at a sheep shearing and his wife Ethel at the produce stand. Ethel comes from the Frost family of Bridgewater whose roots in New England also go back to the early 17th century. They agree that the hilly, rocky slopes of northwestern Connecticut have never been very rewarding to farm. But they gave sustenance to him and Ethel and to their eight children and allowed those who wanted higher education to go on to college. It was rough going to feed and clothe and educate such a large family, Ethel says, but there were even larger families in Roxbury then. "The Lincoln Smiths had nine," Lewis said. "We wanted four," said Ethel, "and got eight. It always bothered me, when people said farmers' families were so large because more hands were needed."

When Lewis married Ethel he and his brother Alden were still helping to work off a heavy debt incurred by their grandfather. Before his death in 1910, Henry Hurlbut, had added another 34 acres along Ranney Hill Road, which brought the farm to 114 acres but saddled it with a $3,300 evergreen mortgage, the kind that carried only interest but no provision for amortization.

"We paid it several times over, before finally paying it off more than thirty years later," Lewis said. His grandfather, Henry, apparently thought the farm needed more land, after seeing the size of Midwestern farms on a reconnoitering trip to Illinois. What the Hurlbut farm produced had not changed much since 1766, when Henry's great-grandfather Gideon Hurlbut was taxed for 44 acres of which only ten were under the plow. He had a couple of oxen to pull it and one horse, next to seven head of cattle for which he kept eight acres of clear pasture and eight acres for mowing.

"Our ancestors did what all farmers did," Lewis explained, "they had a couple of pigs. They had sheep. Later they raised a little tobacco. They grew some flax, and just enough wheat to sustain their families. They had very little money." But they did not give up. "They kept adding to their land all the time."

Henry's stint in the Midwest was cut short. "Around 1890 he went out to Illinois," Lewis was told by his father, "if things were good, the Hurlbut family intended to move to Illinois. He was not far from where Chicago is now. But in 1893 we had a big depression. The family was writing and pleading with him to come home. They wrote him how they had nothing to eat but potatoes. So he came back, and resumed his office as town clerk, which he had first assumed in 1872, and stayed in it until 1910. When he died my father took over. My father was there from 1910 until 1957. Then it went to my brother Alden, then to Alden's wife Elinor, and then to their son Peter." So, except for the year or so that Henry Hurlbut went west, the post of town clerk has been in the Hurlbut family for better than a century. The work also suited Lewis and Alden's father better than farming, he said, although "in his early years my father was going on with the milk. Down where the stand is there was a spring. They used to put the milk cans in that spring. It was still a little bit of a dairy farm. But my father was not exactly a farmer. He wanted to get out of the milk business. I remember he had problems with it. He wanted to go into the production of market products. He went into poultry. He did a little of it when we were young. But we did not get very heavily into it until we were older."

The boys, it seems, were drawn into working the farm more out of necessity than choice, just before another depression foreclosed all other options. "Our father had started a route to supply eggs in Danbury. And he used to take some poultry along. We found more and more demand for it. I went on the route with him when I was quite young. Then we built it up. We grew fresh vegetables and fruit. We did not have any local market, yet. People here were all growing their own then. I handled the

Waterbury end of it. We got to where we had as many as 3,300 poultry layers for eggs, and we raised broilers and turkeys and geese, and ducks. We got up to dressing as much as 125 poultry a week. At Christmas time and Thanksgivings we had a large bunch of turkeys."

A roadside stand, which has since become one of Roxbury's landmarks and was much enlarged by Howie and Cathy Bronson, was started in 1963. In the beginning they used it mainly for selling apples and eggs. "The vegetables and plants we sold were surplus from our fields. We had only a very small greenhouse," Ethel said. At first the stand was only a table across the street from the one Alden still has in front of his house on Church Street. Lewis and Ethel and their children lived between the old firehouse and the Congregational Church then, but eventually moved into the old farmhouse with Lewis' father after his wife, Clara, died. Following their father's death in 1957, Lewis and Alden continued the farm partnership for about 20 years. Then they "retired," each to work his own holdings as previously deeded to them by Norman. Lewis owned the old homestead house and earliest acreage. Alden had his house on Church Street and the land on Ranney Hill Road for which his grandfather had mortgaged the farm, and also the former Trowbridge chicken houses and land thereon. Norman felt that Alden should have a piece of the original farm, too, and left him an acre on Good Hill Road.

In 1977, Arthur Miller remarked on the "amazing range of crops: sweet corn, potatoes, many varieties of apple, pear, cherry, peach; chickens and eggs, duck, capon, geese, pigs, and sheep." Cathy has since added her own washed - and unwashed - homespun wool at the stand, as well as flower and vegetable seedlings in their season, but--except for the wool--the Bronsons have eliminated all animal produce. The jar full of change on the counter, which Lewis and Ethel kept on a table inside the unlocked stand, has also disappeared.

Arthur Miller wrote of it, "When everybody is too busy to tend the roadside stand, Lewis leaves a jar on the counter full of change; the customer helps himself and drops what is owed into the jar. The unguarded money dumfounds foreigners and most city people, yet is rarely stolen, although produce occasionally disappears."

Lewis recalls that they built the stand, "after we had levelled the ground and set it up." They even had some help from a visiting agricultural agent from Ghana. Both Lewis' and Alden's families tended the stand at first but later Ethel was manager. "We found that it steadily grew. When we started, you couldn't sell a zucchini squash for nothing. We owe that to the Italian influence. Another was leeks. No one would buy leeks in those days. People bought squash and turnips, potatoes and lettuce, and carrots. It seemed to be the kind of food that the English ate. In time the type of things we grew changed."

A stop at the Hurlbut roadside stand became a must for weekenders, and others who had found country retreats in Roxbury. Most of the dressed chicken, however, were sold directly to households in Danbury, New Milford, and Waterbury. "Some of the eggs went to a store and restaurants," Lewis said. Roxbury's oldest farm has not vanished; it just changed as it passed from one generation to the next.

Not Steel but Stone

By the time Lewis Hurlbut was born in 1909 the town's experiment with the iron and steel industry had come and gone. The iron works at Mine Hill on which so many hopes had been pinned in the latter half of the 19th century were only a memory. In one lengthy interview at his home in Roxbury in the summer of 1985 Lewis recalled, "After all, the time the work in the iron mines was going on was a very short period. It was between three and five years. The activity there was very intense."

"But there was something else going on there, which was the real business that started before 1800 and continues to the present day. That was the quarry. The quarry was then going full blast. They had a spur of the railroad that went right in. According to Clayton Squire, who was a small boy then, there were about 140 people working at the quarry long after the mine closed. The people at the iron works had been English, Polish, and German. But when that began to fall apart the quarry was still running and kept running. The railroad kept the quarry going. A great deal of building stone went straight to New York. Passengers, of course, also went to New York by the railroad." Lewis believes the iron mine may have failed, in part, because "they found that it was very hard getting that ore out of the rock."

In their history, Time and the Land: the story of Mine Hill, Michael Bell and Diane B. Mayerfeld put the emphasis on faulty and obsolete smelting and steel making techniques. "In the latter half of the 19th century," they write, "Mine Hill was no island of nature, but a busy, noisy, smoky industrial center...Where Highway 67 now crosses the Shepaug River a small community formed around the mining and quarrying activities."

The Shepaug Iron and Steel Co., which started the extraction of the ore in 1865 with $300,000 in capital, relied heavily on the know-how of a German-born steel worker named Henry Kolbe, who had persuaded the owners that Mine Hill ore resembled the spathic iron deposits in Prussia and Austria. The Shepaug Iron and Steel Co. had to be refinanced with $1 million and was renamed the American Silver Steel Co., when the smelter formed a 'salamander' at its first firing in the spring of 1867. But the 'puddling' technique did not produce the kind of steel Kolbe had promised. He and some German workers he had brought to the mine were dismissed. The American Silver Steel Co. moved the steel making to conventional facilities in Bridgeport. It had to reorganize once more in 1872, when it changed its name to the Shepaug Iron Co. Colonel A. L. Hodge, who served as general manager for all three companies, left no clue in his diary why the steel making technique had failed. The Bridgeport facility actually used another German open hearth technology, "the first American Siemens-Martin furnaces," according to Bell and Meyerfeld.

Why smelting lasted only from 1867 to 1872 is much clearer. For one, as we mentioned earlier, the Roxbury smelter still relied on charcoal when less expensive and more heat efficient petrified coal was becoming the prevalent fuel elsewhere, including Connecticut. "Seen from the perspective of events in the U.S. iron and steel industry from 1865 to 1872, the operation at Roxbury was some ten years out of date," Bell and Mayerfeld wrote, "The coal and coke burning furnaces had capacities ten or more times greater than that of the Mine Hill furnace." An attempt to improve the efficiency of the smelter by changing from cold to hot air blasting also failed. "Instead of rising, the output of pig iron fell, and the furnace began to malfunction."

The authors speculate that this may have been because of the smelter's "experimental design; it was constructed in the form of an ellipse rather than the traditional circle." The oval form was so inefficient that it was installed in only four United States furnaces.

But Lewis is at least partially right. Bell and Mayerfeld write that "contrary to all expectations, the main vein narrows out in depth," which must have made the ore harder and harder to reach, even though to this day, "a great deal of ore remains in the hill."

Finally, the railroad came too late. In 1872, when the spur to the quarry and iron mine was complete, the smelter had become unusable. By that time much larger deposits had been discovered in Michigan and Minnesota. If the land title had not been contested so fiercely, the researchers concluded, "and if the iron mining had begun a decade earlier, Mine Hill might have played a more significant role in the history of the American iron and steel industry. Instead, Mine Hill remains a monument to the many small rural industries of New England."

Luckily, the farmers of Roxbury and the Shepaug Valley in general were spared cutting down more of their lumber to feed this behemoth. They turned back to dairy farming. "There was a lot of milk production in the Roxbury area," Lewis recalled, "They had one creamery there (at Roxbury Station or Chalybes while the mine was operating), and they had another creamery about three miles and a half down at Roxbury Falls and one at Judds Bridge. There were four right around the railroad. Everybody was producing milk. People had a few cows, and they had three or four cans of milk a day. They had a spring that they set the milk cans in to keep it cool, and they took them right down into the creameries, where the milk was separated into cream and skimmed milk and was put on the railroad and went to New York. The surplus milk helped to fatten pigs. That held things together for a while."

Gradually the area around Mine Hill lost its population, and it was no longer referred to as Chalybes. "As long as I can remember," Lewis said, "my father always called it Roxbury Station. Albert Hodge, the father of Charles Hodge, who never married, was able to buy it for something like $1,000 (in 1894), because no one else wanted it. They just wanted to get rid of the whole hill. Albert wanted to clear the books. He knew when he bought it that it would never bring any money." But it did. "Charles Hodge's niece's husband, Bill Matthews, really went to work on the Roxbury Land Trust to have it acquire the 300-odd acres," Lewis said, "The idea was to bring back those relics and keep them for the future. It's the impressive granite of the furnace, and how they were laid. They show that Roxbury had stone cutters and masons that were really good."

Lewis also recalled that Gino Perone, who once worked the quarry, told him that it would take some big equipment to keep it going as it did formerly. Perone had only worked it with a hand drill, so he could not get the big slabs out. "They really went into the scrap piles from the old mining days. Now you can still get mining blocks there." Bell and Mayerfeld report that the upper quarry closed down around 1905, and when the Shepaug Valley Railroad stopped operating in 1935, Rockside Quarry was also closed. Then, in 1952, Charles Showalter obtained permission from William and Adelaide Matthews to cut and sell stone from the lower quarry. Soon afterwards, he moved his operation to the upper quarries, where the stone is easier to work. He and his son worked the upper quarries until 1961, when Gino Perone, a stone mason from Southbury, took over the business of salvaging building stone from the Mine Hill quarries. The quarry is still being worked.

In the Hurlbuts' files there is also an old newspaper clipping about Michael Callahan, who worked as a stone cutter in the Roxbury quarry.

By the 1940's he had become a "sort of a dean of stone cutters" the interviewer, Villette Young, said. He was then 82 years old. Callahan said that in his day the town had five hatting establishments, two small factories for forming hat bodies, a grist mill, ten saw mills, and two foundries. Tobacco was a big crop, he said, and many of the old buildings still standing were used to store tobacco. The town had a real saloon, complete with swinging door, and a hotel which was more like a big boarding house. Mabel Bernhardt Smith, who taught school in Roxbury Station in the early 1920's, says it was still standing then on a stretch of the road called 'the row' leading up to Mine Hill. There were two stores near the railroad depot "catering to the few wants of the people." Most, he said, "lived off their own land, buying staples such as flour, sugar or tea. A hundred dollars a year would usually cover this, and the stores trusted everyone until pay-day, even when it came but once a year as it did for the tobacco farmers. One suit of store clothes sufficed and that was seldom used except on a man's wedding day or his funeral."

Callahan also described work at the quarry, which had been leased by A.L. Hodge to a couple of brothers named Moore. In his day, which must have been about 1890, it employed about 50 people. Although stone cutting had been mechanized, he said, "the stone cutter is still the most valuable 'machine' because much skill is needed to find where the rock will separate most easily. The 'plug and feather' method is the one used most frequently, when working by hand."

"Holes are drilled a few inches apart along the line where they want the stone to separate and in each hole is placed two feathers (flat pieces of steel rounded to fit into the hole). A plug, or narrow wedge, is driven between these feathers and each plug is then struck a blow hard enough to break the rock. This same method is used in quarries to separate large blocks after they have been cut vertically by channeling machines.

"A 'channeling machine' is a small locomotive which travels back and forth upon a short track attached to the solid rock. As it travels, long chisels set at different angles, strike on one of both sides of the track and cut a channel about two inches wide and four to ten feet deep. Later, this rock must be lifted from its bed by blasting or by the plug and feather method."

At the time of the interview Mike Callahan lived with his wife, his son Leo and a small daughter, three-year-old Kathleen, in Roxbury Station. He also revealed that Roxbury quarry stone was seldom used for monuments or grave head stones, because of its heavy iron content, but much for bridges, viaducts, walls, and fireplaces.

For a while, Callahan took his skills on the road, and worked in quarries in 17 states, as well as in the Klondike. By the time he returned, Roxbury had changed, and even he noted that "the majority of the old houses have been bought by city people to be used as 'our place in the country.' Many are artists, sculptors or writers and more and more of them stay in Roxbury the whole year instead of just summers," Callahan said.

On Their Own

With both the iron mine and the quarry gone as a potential industrial base, the farmers were back on their own. "Prior to 1850," Lewis said, "in fact, ever since they first came here, the people were poor. The only way to reach another village was by foot or by horse or oxen. They supplied themselves first. They had the wood, and they brought a few pigs and a few sheep with them. They had looms and made their own clothes. It finally got where they had a tin smith and gun smith. They tried to have in a little village practically all the things they needed. They were not in any kind of mass production whatsoever. If you wanted a gun, you went down to the gun smith, and you told him you were six foot tall and you wanted a gun that was so many feet long and the stock the way you wanted, and they made it. Everybody's gun was different before they got into the Revolutionary War. In that time the boundaries of a town were almost like boundaries of the state were later."

From his father Lewis inherited a rather large collection of rifles, which Miller described as going back "to King Philip's War and down through every war Americans have fought." The first Hurlbut in this country, Thomas Hurlbut, who lived in Saybrook and Wethersfield and died in 1671, actually fought in the war against the Pequot Indians but, says Lewis, the guns were not as valuable as they had hoped, when they sold the whole collection to raise money for a town scholarship fund. One of them Lewis took to Boston to have it appraised by a scrimshaw expert, from whom he learned, "usually when a war was finished, they would put out these guns for sale cheap. The farmers used to buy them, because they could buy them cheap and do something with them. Sometimes they cut back the stocks, or take six or ten inches off the gun. He told me, if this gun had not been fooled around with, we could have got $2,000 for it. He said, 'I can give you $100 just for the parts.' That's what happened."

"But there were some I hated to give up," Lewis granted, "One was a seven-shot repeating rifle introduced at the end of the Civil War. This gun

27

was made in Connecticut: a Spencer 50. They took it down to Washington. Even Lincoln is said to have used it. But they could not get the Union Army to take it. They finally got a company to buy them Spencer rifles. They said they now had seven shots, and they could kill one person every day of the week with one load. After the war it was used as a Buffalo gun. It was now a long rifle, seven shot, and 50 calibre.

"Then we had some that had been given to my father. We had muzzle loaders, cap and ball guns, where you put in the powder, put in the cap, then pull the trigger and hear it bing but it might not fire within another second. If you took it down, it might come back and hit you on the head. We had a 20 gauge shot gun, a 16 gauge, and a 10 gauge, which was really like a cannon, and an old flintlock from revolutionary times.

"Of course, a lot of mills were started before 1800. By the time of the Civil War you had around 1,700 and 1,800 people here. Those people had come to the mines and the quarry. Besides the iron mine there was a silica mine and a garnet mine. But the saw mills and grist mills came first. Every town that had water power had them, because people did not want to take their grain to the next town. In 1850, they had ten saw mills.

"Then, when the railroads came, that really widened things out. The Squires, I remember, produced beef cattle all across that valley down there. But when the railroad was built across to the Northern Pacific, the beef business here dropped right out of sight. There was no beef raised here to any great extent after that. They brought it in from the West on the Northern Pacific Railroad. And it was much cheaper.

"But we also had hat shops here. The biggest change was the railroad, though, which allowed people to reach out beyond Roxbury, and that came right after the Civil War. Thanks to the creameries a family could be held together on a farm with ten or fifteen cows. That lasted until pretty close to the Second World War. But then milk production went up in New York state, as well. They had much better farming country than Connecticut up in New York state. So they started to bring milk to Connecticut in very large quantities. Then refrigeration came and you had to build a cooler in your milk house. The people from the extension service were preaching to the farmers that they had to have a milking machine so that forty cows would be as easy as fifteen. But they also had the cost of cooling the milk. And the standards were set by the state. On top of that they had a big fight about milk coming across state line from New York.

"Finally, it got down to where it got out of the hands of the farmers and their milking association. Milk quotas were put up, because of the New York surplus that was allowed in. Many farms here were too small to handle the required volume of production. They did not have the land for forty cows. Our land was too hilly. One answer was to rent more land.

"Many farmers had another cash crop in tobacco. There were many plots of tobacco in this town. There were tobacco barns in the flats along the Shepaug River. And people had their own looms in their houses. A lot of times when they had a house, they built a loom right up in the attic. When a child reached about six years, they had it right on that loom, because the loom took a lot of time. You could not take the looms out of the attic. They were built right in. Children would come home from school and go right on to the loom.

"By the Second World War people went into all walks of life from these little hill farms. When I was a small kid every house between my house and the Woodbury line was a farm. By 1920 farming was still prevalent. Land was cheap. People from New York and other places were not coming to Roxbury in great numbers. Nobody came here. People then lived where they worked, and they could not go very far from there. People might have an old car with which they drove into Woodbury or Waterbury. But they did not get very far until it got to the Second World War.

"By 1920 the hat shops were done. We still had the creameries. We still had plow making. That was in its glory from 1910 to the 1920's. D.G. (Gaylord) Bronson had bought out the Wakely Plows of Southbury, and they were shipping plows all over New England.

"The farms had pork, and lamb and milk. The farmers would have an extra beef that they would dress themselves and sell for cash. By the time the Second World War came, the dairy men that were left had bigger farms. Farms also used adjacent property to make it profitable for them to continue to operate. You needed 40 to 50 cows."

People Changed

"But then, after the war, land values began to rise. Cars and trucks became plentiful so that the population began to move, as well. People went to wherever education would take them. You also had better schools. Roxbury was getting more people from New York, who wanted weekend homes. They were professionals, bankers and lawyers. These people came in by car. I've heard people here say after World War Two, 'You know, there really is not anything to come back to in Roxbury. There is nothing that can give us the kind of living that we want.' My own children went away. Even food-growing was not a really good business on these small, hilly farms. So many people would say they would love to farm in here, but they had to have money to live on. It always had been hard to make a living here, including the very first people who came here. They had hard work right up to the present time. Now people began to say, 'We ain't going to work like that, anymore.' No one wanted it. Life became easier.

"Companies, after the war, started to confer benefits. Producing became very well organized. It went in a very short time from where you had a person's ability vested in a very small area, like making saws or rifles by hand, to mass production. In the years before 1900, it seems to have been a glorious time. People began to have something. In the time from the Civil War to about 1900, people started to go out and be gainfully employed. They would get paid in cash instead of a side of beef or pork. It must have been great to have the extra cash, because at home they were still providing themselves with the basic needs of life."

"People changed," Lewis recalled, "They had grown up in very sheltered circumstances here. For the first eight years of your education, you went to the same school house. There were seven one-room school houses in Roxbury. Each had its own woman teacher. She really led our lives through eight years." A few people, who were successful in making money elsewhere, came back to this shelter. The best known of these was Allen Hurlburt, who served as the town's First Selectman for 29 years. "Hurlburt came back from the war when he nearly 50 years old," Lewis remembered, "He owned a factory out in Hartford. He sold it and devoted the rest of his life to this little town. But he was a man who had financial means even before he went into the war. For most others here there was little difference between rich and poor. People could talk shop, because they were all in the same boat. Everyone had to strive to live. And so they helped each other out. In that kind of life you have much less quarreling. But when you got into Mine Hill, you had people with expertise in certain areas, people who were good at the smelter pot and would not do anything else, men in the ore mine and that is all they did. Their level would be set by where they were. On the farm there wasn't any level. Of course, there was some quarreling, some scrapping, and suits, but not much among farmers. New England Yankees are not always docile."

Who were some of the other prominent people in town? "Everett Hurlburt was probably the richest man in town then. Everett had gone off to Glastonbury and worked for J.B. Williams Co., which became important in men's shaving lotions. Like his brother Allen he had been to Yale. He rose by leaps and bounds in those years, as cosmetics became more important. Finally, he became president of the company. He introduced Aqua Velva shaving lotion. The family already had money when he was born. Col. George Hurlbut, his grandfather, had made money owning hat shops, and later the Hurlburts handled produce back and forth to New Haven. So they were well off as young men. There was probably not anyone in town better off than Everett. This also had a bearing on people in the town. You had reasons for being competitive. You had people who were in different categories all the way up the ladder. It made people more restless.

"And the people who came up from New York liked to come here especially in the summer. They could buy a place for not much money. We got some prominent people here. There was Dr. Williams, for instance, a plant pathologist, who was known all the way to the West Coast. And another man, who did the engraving on dollar bills. My father took me up there one night and he did a little sketch of a monkey holding up a cup to get change, which I found most interesting as a boy."

Among prominent but not necessarily wealthy people within our time frame, Lewis also mentioned the Rev. Austin Isham, the Congregational minister who read the "Historical Sketch of Roxbury" prepared by M.L Beardsley on July Fourth 1876 in which the first 200 years of the town are recounted, beginning with the frontier explorations in 1673. "He was really an outstanding person. He was a great speaker and a great leader of the Church. Then there was the Rev. Walter Downs Humphrey, the father of John Humphrey, who was a rector of the Episcopal church for 39 years. He was on the Board of Education, the town's Treasurer and, together with Everett Hurlburt, started the Library of Roxbury in the back room of the town hall in 1896.

"Then there was Nathan Beardsley, who was a real character. He was someone you just could never forget, once you had talked to him and listened to him. He was a state representative from here, and a famous raiser of Devon oxen." Perhaps, if the example of Nathaniel Beardsley had been followed, Roxbury might still be a farming community today. He was an innovative farmer with a fine, if sometimes biting wit, who knew that to survive against the farmers of upstate New York and farther west, you had to do something better, add more value than they did. Instead of just producing milk, you had to make a fine cheese, and instead of beef cattle you had to produce prize steers.

The Beardsleys chose the latter. In 1938 when Allen Raymond of the "New Milford Times" interviewed him, Nathaniel Beardsley, then 70 years old, gave vent to his opinion that mechanization may have been the ruin of many of his neighbors as well as farmers in general. "If more of these farmers bought oxen and fewer bought tractors," he said, "you wouldn't have so many farm mortgages and folks wouldn't talk so much about a farm problem." Of course, tilling land with oxen is much harder work than it is with a tractor.

Nate, as he was known to his friends, had a 200 acre spread on Good Hill Road then, where he grazed 52 head of red Devon cows and steers. He also had a cellar full of 20 barrels of cider of which he and his son Percy drank a barrel a month. He refused to install electricity until the end, and never learned how to drive a car. But he drove the largest team of red oxen to country fairs anyone had ever seen and had won 5,000 prizes with them.

Raymond spent only an afternoon at the Beardsley farm sipping cider. He described Nate as "tough as a pine knot, with only a sprinkling of gray in his brown hair, and appetite enough to eat big steaks for breakfast.

"The barn swallows twittered and fluttered in the doorway, the sun shone bright on the old stone steps," and, "across the dirt road, between two broad barns of gleaming white, half a dozen of the likeliest red calves a man ever saw were grazing contentedly."

The Beardsleys had been in Roxbury for several generations then--almost as long as the Hurlbuts with whom William Beardsley had first settled at Stratford--the starting point for the original Woodbury colony. "There's been four Nathans on this farm," Nate told the reporter.

His wife died shortly after his son Percy came home from France, where he was with Sergeant Alvin York who, together with sixteen other men in his platoon, captured 100 Germans "single-handed" in the Argonne forest.

Percy never made much of it but before the film based on Sgt. York's famous exploit was made with Gary Cooper, it did become generally known that York was not alone. The "Waterbury Republican" first published the real story in 1927, based on an account given by Sergeant Bernard Early of New Haven who was in command of the platoon, and subsequently he and Percy were given Distinguished Service Crosses. York received the publicity, according to Beardsley, because he took command of the platoon after Early was wounded, but he and the sixteen other members of the platoon accounted for some of the 25 Germans killed and 132 that were eventually taken prisoner.

Beardsley himself received a citation from his brigade commander immediately after the action at Chatel Chehery which said, "Mechanic Beardsley with a detachment from his company surprised and captured a number of Germans, who were delivering a flanking fire on the attacking lines." Three other members of the platoon were also belatedly decorated.

In an interview with the "Waterbury Republican," Percy Beardsley pointed out that York was armed only with a pistol, while he was armed with a French Chauchat, a sub-machine gun. Although his two ammunition carriers were killed, he continued to work his gun until the Germans surrendered. York had the reputation of being a dead shot from his practice of shooting off the heads of moving, wild turkeys in the Tennessee mountains, but Beardsley had quite a reputation as a hunter in the Roxbury woods. Nate said of his son, "I'd back Percy's shooting against York's any time."

While Sgt. York may have fit the image of the lone captor better, and served wartime propaganda because of his background as a conscientious objector, Beardsley gave credit to the whole platoon and its wounded leader. He personally rescued Early, after he had been wounded, and helped carry him back, after the Germans surrendered. The entire episode lasted less than half an hour, probably 15 minutes, he said.

The detachment had gone so far that the Germans were on three sides of them. The first Germans encountered, probably 30 or 40, thought a large force was approaching and surrendered without firing a shot. The rest of the Germans, realizing that the American force was small, started firing. The Americans took cover, either behind trees or lying down. Then they started using their arms, and captured the major in command of the German battalion. The Germans, firing from three sides, were not only hitting those who had already surrendered, but also their own troops on the opposite side. So the major, who had been made a prisoner, shouted to them to surrender. About 100 did. On the way back the Americans encountered two more machine gun nests, which were either eliminated or made to surrender by command of the German major. By that time there were only seven of the original sixteen Americans. Six had been killed. Beardsley was carrying Sergeant Early and others of the detail were carrying the remaining two wounded.

Asked why he and other survivors allowed him to get sole credit, Beardsley said, "Well, York was always a pretty good fellow for letting everyone know how good he was. He never missed a chance." Arthur Miller once asked him how they got so many Germans to surrender. Beardsley said, "Well y'know, they'd started fighting way back in nineteen-fourteen, and we only came over in seventeen, so by that time they were pretty tired."

For a time, after his return, father and son had a housekeeper on the farm, but Nate sent her off, when she became too covetous of Percy. Or so he thought. Nate was also a bit of a tyrant. Percy finally did marry, but he upheld the masculine priorities of the household. Mrs. Beardsley told another reporter in 1966 that once, "there was a time when the installation of a furnace threatened to upset the quality of the cider in the cellar. For a moment we thought that either the furnace or the cider had to go. And if the furnace went, I went." Percy figured out a way to keep all three: the cider, the furnace, and the wife "in that order," she said.

"I bought this farm from my father," Nate said, "It took me twenty years to pay it off. You've no idea of the hardships. I'd like to get a little more land, and then there's some I'd just as soon sell."

Percy eventually took it over and was still raising his father's favorite Devon, when he was visited in the 1960's by Senator Wayne Morse, who raised the same breed on his farms in Maryland and Eugene, Oregon. Percy's brother Paul was another famous breeder, working as foreman to C.T. Crocker's Wachusetts Farm in Princeton, Massachusetts. He had one of the finest herds of Shorthorn milking cattle in the country.

Nate sold many of his prize-winning Devon to gentlemen farmers, who liked to decorate their pastures with them. On average he got $500 a pair, but twelve times he got $6,000 a pair. He walked his teams to fairs in Woodbury, Watertown, Washington, Newtown, Danbury, Mount Kisco, Lincolndale, Orange, Savin Rock, Monroe, Huntington, Middlebury, Meriden, Berlin, Hartford, Wolcott, Plymouth, Guilford, Torrington, Bristol, Beacon Valley, and New Milford. Sometimes he drove as many as sixteen matched pairs at a time, calves, yearlings, two-year-olds, three-year olds, and up.

"The farmers came to the fairs to see me beaten," he recalled, "You know it's the champion everybody wants to beat." Driving his cattle, he said, "I've walked to Hartford in a day." The pace of the oxen is perhaps three miles an hour, slower if there are many pairs. Driving, he said, was an art, an art of few commands, of calling 'gee' and 'haw' and 'whoa' and 'back,' plus a flickering whip on the neck and rump of the off or near ox.

Once Nate was taking his cattle down to Danbury Fair. He had one pair he was taking through Danbury's center. A policeman stopped him and said "You can't go through here." Nate said, "Yes, I can." So he gave the policeman his whip to hold and said, "Here, you take them where you want. I'm going into the saloon here and get a drink."

When he was getting along in years he asked his next door neighbor Thomas Lilly and his son Percy to come to the cemetery with him to level the stone for his grave, which had already been selected. They got it all level so that it was just about right to his satisfaction. Nate looked at it for a while, and said, "No it's got to be changed." They asked him why, and he said, "You see the bevel on the stone is cut so the water will drip off right on my face."

The Hurlbuts went visiting him one night and noticed that he had all of his clothes hung on a line in the kitchen. He said his daughter had given him a new vest. It hung there, too. He said his old vest was still good enough to wear. But it was much too small for him. "To hold it together he had connected the button holes to the buttons on the other side with pieces of string at least two inches long," Lewis recalled.

"And there was another thing that was really interesting about Nate Beardsley's house. For all the years he had the farm, he said he never carried fire insurance. If you were careful about it, you would never have fires, he said. The amount of money he saved was terrific. He used to have a lot of dances there. He was terribly set against cigarettes, though.

"One night at a party at his house the revellers were sitting around drinking coffee, after the liquor. Nate would walk around to refill cups as the good host he was. Two fellows sitting there had empty cups. So Nate said, 'Would you wish more coffee?' They nodded. He picked up the cups to go into the kitchen to refill them, and he noticed a cigarette butt in the bottom of each cup. He poured the coffee right over the butts and went back and placed them on the table in front of the young men. They looked at the cups with the butts floating on top of their coffee and said, 'There are cigarette butts in the coffee.' Nate said, 'I know, but I did not put them there.' That was the kind of humor he had."

Actually, Beardsley's barn eventually also caught fire, but by then it belonged to his son Percy. Lewis did not remember whether in the meantime Percy had insured it. But it never burned so long as Nate Beardsley owned it.

Though a widower, he could still be romantic at the age of seventy and recalled with pleasure the time the actress Norma Talmadge came to the farm with a troupe of other movie actors to make a picture with his oxen. "I was forty-nine the day she arrived, and I'll say she certainly looked pretty good to me," he said. She left a pair of gloves in the cider cellar, on a barrel. They were never removed so long as Nate lived, and remained there for many more years after his death.

Years later Marilyn Monroe, then married to his neighbor Arthur Miller, also came for a visit and Percy treated the prints left by her high heels in the cider cellar with the same kind of reverence. "I never let anyone walk on her heel prints," he said, "and when an old drover scuffled them into non-existence, our friendship was never the same."

Although a life-long Democrat, Nate voted against Workers Compensation in 1911 as a representative in the state legislature in Hartford. He considered the New Deal and any form of government welfare a horror. At that time such views were considered eccentric.

His famous "ruby red" oxen were often called into service by the town, for a fee, of course, when roads had to be snow-plowed or scraped and also when anyone was stuck in the snow or mud. The last pair were sold in 1964, when there was no one left to carry on after Percy.

The Beardsleys are a large clan, but now most live elsewhere in the state and in other parts of New England. Nellie Beardsley Holt, a sister of Percy and Paul, called them all together in Stratford in 1936 to celebrate three centuries of Stratford's and their family's history, and received permission to place a boulder with an inscription in a town park to commemorate William and Mary Beardsley, who started this notable Connecticut family.

Another prominent, and eccentric person, in his day was Harvey Minor Booth, who gave the town its school, the Booth Free School. He was quite an eccentric, but was also described in 1892 as "one of the brightest members of the class of 1843 at Yale," in another newspaper clipping from the "Waterbury Republican" kept by the Hurlbuts.

"Mr. Harvey Minor Booth," the report said, "is one of the plainest sort of New England farmer. And there in an old, weather-beaten house on a lane or back road he has lived for fifty years, in good financial condition, yet satisfied perfectly with the exhausting toil of cultivating a New England farm. His only recreation is solving the most abstruse algebraic problems known to science. His only light is a tallow candle, and his fare is of the most frugal kind.

"In all these years his only human companion was a spinster sister, who died a few years since. He and his sister inherited a good farm, and by careful investment had amassed considerable wealth at the time of her death. He was in the habit of walking from this farm to New Haven, a distance of thirty miles, during his college days, and until very recently he has been in the habit of walking to this city (Waterbury), a distance of eighteen miles, rather than hitch up one of the horses which he has in his barn.

"For a time after graduating he tried teaching, but gave it up in disgust, as he could not understand girls. Nor did he ever fathom the peculiarities of the fair sex to all appearances. He did marry, but the very next morning, he gave the bride a handsome sum with which to get a divorce from him and she complied.

36

"Summer and winter he wears brown jean trousers with a coarse jumper, and heavy army brogans on his feet in winter and none in summer. He is a familiar object to the villagers as he goes to the Post Office for the large checks that he periodically receives from his different investments. One day he carried home on a hand sled two miles and up hill 150 pounds of pork rather than to take one of his horses.

"Some years since Mr. Booth lost quite a sum in an investment on the recommendation of a Waterbury Sunday school superintendent. Since that time he has had a bitter aversion to all church people, and if he learns that a man with whom he is about to do business is a church member it is said that he immediately drops the transaction.

"The methods of his sister were not so strict as his as the following story will show. After her death he told a friend to inquire at a Waterbury savings bank for a deposit his sister had said she had there. The friend found no deposit, but fortunately happened to recollect that she had been interested in the settlement of the estate of a Waterbury man through whom the Booths lost considerable money. His theory proved correct. The books had been given to Miss Booth but had never been transferred in the bank. As the President of the bank was an old college mate of Mr. Booth's, the matter was set right. The sum with interest, which had been accumulating, was more than $2,000.

"Two years ago Mr. Booth gave to this town $10,000 to establish and maintain a select school, where boys and girls could fit for college or for business life. As the only expense was the salary for a teacher, the sum has proved ample, and the school is prospering."

According to Roxbury lore Mr. Booth established the school so that youngsters would not have to walk the thirty miles to New Haven to attend secondary school and college the way he did. The school is now a grammar school, but still bears his name. As the town and neighboring towns grew, their high school students started to go to joint schools, and finally the Shepaug Middle High School, which today sends more students to Ivy League colleges than the private Gunnery School in Washington.

Land Values Rise

Not only people changed, of course. Land values also began to rise, and conflicts over zoning began as a result of the influx of outsiders. Rules had be established on how much acreage was needed to build a house, and on how much frontage was required, and on the drainage of sewage.

"I know that the first kind of zoning was instituted in 1932," Lewis remembered, "The two brothers, Allen and Everett, got together. They drew up some of the first zoning regulations in the state. The interesting thing was that it just was not accepted at all well. At that time the regulation was an acre and a half. They were just trying to get a skeleton of zoning, but they knew it would not be accepted easily. The idea was to be able to plan the development of the town.

"Before that many times people would not even ask for a permit to build something. They owned the land and no one was going to tell them what they were going to do with it. So what Allen would do was to come running with an application in his hand, the moment you started any new structure. He asked people to sign it, saying it was 'just to give us a notice.' That went on for years.

"When we got into the 1940s, we became more stiff. We went out and got outside expertise. There was more building going on, and we wanted more control about how the town was going to grow. We had meetings in the hall and instituted changes in the regulations. People would fill the hall. And we had all kinds of arguments against that whole set-up." Then, somewhere around 1950, a petition came in to do away with zoning. That night the town hall was full. As I recall the argument in favor of zoning was to control the size of lots and how close they are to one another, and that in future we would not have problems with septic systems. We knew that we needed at least two acres, and we changed from the smaller acreage to the two acres. The people who were against it did not want any organization in the town of Roxbury to tell them what they were going to do with their land. Also, we wanted the new structures to be in keeping with the kind of colonial village that we had in Roxbury. At the end of the meeting the zoning was upheld by only fourteen votes out of about one hundred in the hall. It was by secret ballot.

"We also learned in 1948 and 1950 that all the previous zoning regulations had no real legal teeth, anyway. The legislature had not ruled on the power of the Zoning Commission, yet. That changed in 1954. Later, when the developers came in, we realized how devious they could be, when it came to a piece of property. There was one property where, to get the required frontage, they took a two foot strip from the front of the neighboring lot, because they had plenty of frontage for that lot. We also argued that you could not put up an eyesore next to your neighbor. You really did have an obligation to him. You could lower his value by 15% or 20%, but people did not take to the argument well. They felt no matter what, it was their piece of land. Later, we had many cases that had to go to the Zoning Board of Appeals to try to overturn the rulings of the Zoning Board.

"Now we are getting into problems because more and more of the land is marginal with regard to building because of insufficient drainage. You have to get a State Building Inspector for drainage and the problem of wetlands. In the 1960s, we also had to consider larger lots.

"I was chairman of the Zoning Board when we discussed going from a two acre to a three acre lot. We knew it was going to be controversial. The new people coming in would back us up, we knew. The septic systems that we have today are really not more than forty years old. We had no idea what a long period would do to that land. Would it contaminate our soil? How would it affect our water system? Also, on sloping land the houses could line up one above the other. We kept the three acre zoning and fifty feet back from the right of way, after a good deal of controversy. We kept the rule that all land within a three quarter mile of the flagpole would remain two acre zoning. There was an "A", a "B" and a "C" area. Also a piece around the lake at Roxbury Falls that would be two acre. Those were the last regulations and amendments until the complete revision of 1982.

"Now for some of the cases. There is a rule that any member of the board shall not speak publicly before any of the other boards. I did not understand that, at first. In one case that came up, I thought because I had withdrawn from the board (for that particular meeting) because of a conflict of interest, I could speak. I went to the front of the hall - there were about 100 people there - and I began to speak. The lawyer for the other side said, "Wait a minute." I told him that I had withdrawn from the board on this issue.

"He said that I still could not speak, because it could influence the board. All I wanted to do was to remind the board that they could only define the regulations, but make sure there were no deviations whatsoever. He said, 'If you want to speak, you have to go up and resign from the board.' One of the people sitting in the front called out, 'Lewis, sit down!' I thought twice about it, and sat down.

"We have come to have more and more controversial issues that have come before the Zoning Board of Appeals. One of them is a rule that hardship cannot be financial. Another is that a decision has to be for the good of the welfare of the town. I feel that this can be in conflict with the other requirement that it can't be a hardship. We have some cases in the center of the town, where we have some nice looking places that were run down and the Zoning Board of Appeals allowed them to make alterations there, even though it was a non-conforming house. One house was non-conforming in that it was too close to the right of way. It was also too close to the side line. It also was a non-conforming lot. The zoning regulations say that you should not increase non-conformity. The house was built around 1840 or 1850. It was small. The family had no refrigerator or washer then, which we have in houses today. A family today needs more space in a house for such equipment. Practically all houses in the center do not conform by one or the other of the new requirements. I could not help but approve this application.

"It's worth a lot to the town to have all those nice old houses restored and in livable condition, even though they may be too close to the right of way or something.

"One big case in recent years was a property near Mine Hill, which also included the stores that were at Roxbury Station such as a hardware store. The name of the owner of Mine Hill was Bill Matthews. He was married to the grand niece of Charles Hodge. He was eager to look after the finances of his wife. Back in the 1940s, he said there was no one who could tell him what he was going to do with those buildings. He became really a monkey wrench in the zoning regulations as much as anybody else in town."

Controversies increased because there were more outsiders looking for homes, usually second homes. It seemed more than half of the population of Roxbury by 1987 were weekenders. Asked about this Lewis said: "The newcomers that came first also have ideas about the newcomers that come later. One family came here from New York, and they had not been here for more than a little while, and the woman came to me at our stand and said, 'I wish there would have been no more that came here.' I just had to tell her, 'You know, there were some less before you came here.' I could not help but to make that point. This party, some years after that, sub-divided their land. A lot of us who lived here - call them 'natives' - saw another great change.

"People could get together and have basically the same values. Now, it has changed and it has hurt us some. People of similar backgrounds will gather among themselves. And they want the services here that they were accustomed to in the larger urban areas. It gets to the point where you lose the values of life of a rural community. They will generally gather in their own places and pull in the people in their area of thinking, and they do not want to be bothered with the rural community aspects as much as many of us, who wish to make the community personal in all its responsibilities. That kind of passed on. We think it's a loss.

"We are not blaming the people. Nothing has broadened me more than the people I have been in touch with through boards and other contacts I have had, people who came from different parts of the world, whether they were foreign or came from as close as New York. I just feel sad that it comes with things that are objectionable about it. They are much more private than the older residents.

"We knew each other, because we had a hard time to sustain ourselves. People used to say that everybody knows everybody's business. We had a telephone service that had six party lines. When it rang everybody rushed to it to see whether it was an emergency, or to get the latest news. But if someone was sick or there was trouble. those same people were there. We sort of miss that. When the rural America that we knew disappears, we feel the country has lost something that is of great value "

Lewis was also asked about another frequently heard argument among Roxbury natives, who now say that because of the high cost of land their own children often cannot build here, anymore. A plot may cost as much as $120,000 for three acres, and only rich outsiders can afford to build on that kind of land.

Lewis said, "We had a Planning Commission chairman, whom that question was brought before. He was a man who had a business in New York, and he was pretty well off. Someone said, 'It's got to where our young people cannot live in Roxbury, unless they go out and make their way in life in a financial way and then come back.' He said, 'Well, that's their problem.' He was willing to have this town on a much higher level. Our own children could not make their lives here. They could not start out here. Very few could. Many said, 'I'm going out. And when I get older, I'm coming back to live in Roxbury.' This was heard many times. People who work for commercial airlines could live here even when they were younger. Now we have about 30 pilots, who live in Roxbury."

Of the Hurlbut's eight children, seven have moved away to work in modern activities such as computers, books, research, photography or textile design. Asked what swayed their daughter Cathy to return, Lewis said: "This girl is very much of an outdoor person. She was much closer to the farm than the others. One boy, Henry, came back for a while, but he also had other leanings, which called him. But this daughter has two children now, and one thing that was important in her life was that she wanted an environment for her children. Her life should be their life."

"But a few years ago, there was a meeting on zoning, and there was a man there, who was a developer from New York. He looked at me and said, 'You have all the regulations which you are doing very well on. But we in New York have no place to go. We can't go south to New Jersey, and we can't go to Long Island, because it's pretty well taken up. We are moving north. I know you really feel conscientious about your regula-

41

tions. But there is something that will by-pass all that.' And he rubbed his thumb against his index finger. 'That's what's going to change your regulations.' I have never forgotten that."

Lewis was then asked what he would like the town to be, despite his ambivalence about newcomers. He said: "I would like to see them also get a little horse sense about the regulations. There are things the town can do that we want to do, despite regulations, even if it sets a precedent. Some of the outsiders would like 15 acre zoning to keep others out. That's a little too greedy. We could pick an area in the town and set it aside, where young people can start out, perhaps with low income housing. We had a little apartment down by the Church, which has helped out so many young couples that were able to live there for two or three years, until they got started. We could have, say, five places for young people on low incomes. It could be done. The other thing is that we should have one place in town, where we could take care of our elderly.

"We have quite a few people in this town that have gotten older and had to leave their places, and who are being told that despite their past personal involvement with the town, they now have to leave town and go somewhere else. I think the town should bear them more responsibility than that. They owe it to these people that they are a part of this town."

As to the newcomers, or weekenders, Lewis thought, "there are a lot that have come in who have expertise that old timers cannot supply. Some have been a big help. Like Ed Barnes. He came here and really knew how to handle money. He became the Treasurer. Geddes Parsons and Leonie was another. They've been a real addition. There are others."

Finally, he was asked about some farmers in the area, who had sold their land because it had become too expensive to farm. Lewis gave his views: "When you turn that land over, you take the money out of that land. For some of us that land was left to us. We are able to operate it still. We are sort of stewards of the property that we take through our life. Like my father used to say: 'We are stewards of this property and we hand down to the next family. The family before us kept it, and they raised their family on it, and the next family did, and we are doing it now, and our obligation is to hand it down.' Not to take the whole works now and blow it on ourselves."

Lewis conceded, however, "There are not many that think that way, anymore. People are greedy. They want it all for themselves."

Growing Trees

If he'd had the chance, Lewis said, he'd have become a forester. But he felt obliged to help his father clear the family farm of its mortgage. So he never went to college. Ethel, on the other hand, graduated from Danbury Teachers' College, where she was secretary of her class. So there was a certain amount of formal schooling on hand in the Hurlbut household from which the children all benefitted. But even though they may not have had much formal education, Ethel insists, both Lewis and his father, Norman, "did a lot of reading."

Lewis also learned a lot from looking and listening. It was this way, for instance, that he learned a great deal about trees. At the Eliot Pratt Education Center in New Milford of which he was president, Lewis enjoys telling children about his first lesson on trees. "When I was a little boy," Lewis tells them, "I had a jack knife. We had mostly hard maple in front of the house. But there was a paper birch. I took my jack knife and cut a strip right off it. I peeled it off, and thought I was really great. My father took me down to the tree and I never forgot what he said to me. 'You have killed that tree.' And he took me across his knee. My interest in trees grew from that time on. I won't say that was the only reason. In later years I often worked with my father in the woods.

"We would go out in the morning and cut all day and take along some salt pork and potatoes, or sometimes homemade sausage, start a fire by one of the stumps, and noon time, we would have some fried potatoes and sausage or salt pork and that would really hold us for the rest of the day. I had a natural interest in forest work. I always listened when anything was going on about trees. There was a forester here, whose name was Pierson. He taught me more about trees and the love of the forest than anybody I ever met.

"He was a very quiet man. I must have been about 18 or 20 years old, when I first met him. He had a very soft voice when he spoke, and you had to listen very carefully. He had something about him. He would stand there and whittle on a piece of wood, but you had to listen to everything he said. He was our state forester, but eventually he went to Boston. Today, I can say that there are not many people in Roxbury, who could walk into the woods and be able to name practically every tree they passed. Not many can do that, but my father, brother Alden and I could."

He also followed the fate of Connecticut's chestnuts for more than a life time: "They started to go just about the turn of the century," he said, "There was a virus that attacked the bark, generally right down close to the ground, when the tree was about four years old. And this virus dwelt down in the cracks that normally come in the trunk of a tree when it has a little age on it.

"When it's very young the chestnut is very smooth like a black birch tree. But then, when it gets to be about four years, the bark begins to crack open. This blight started before 1900. Many of the old people used to go out in the fall and collect chestnuts. Some of the woods here were 75% chestnuts. Our chestnuts were really a northeastern tree. They reached from here out into Michigan, and it went down across the Carolinas. They grew very straight. Their average height was about 125 feet. Outland trees became enormous, about six feet in diameter at the base. People around here used them extensively for fence posts. They were really very good against the elements. They had very little rot. Not as good as redwood, but pretty close to our red cedar. They were also used for ties on the railroad.

"I know my father said that in the middle of the 1800s the first settlers had more oak. They were kind of leary about chestnuts. But I think the reason they were leary about chestnuts is because in Europe they had hardwood oaks. In a way the chestnut has a kind of coarse grain. It has a very beautiful line in it, but it is not hard. It's really a soft wood. But it will not shrink and swell."

"The chestnuts were edible. They were about half as big as the Italian chestnuts we get, but they were sweeter. You can see how they provided food for wildlife, especially wild turkeys. In the early days wild turkeys and deer fed on them, because they were all through the woods. These trees stood in the woods for many years. They were so durable. They would turn almost white. The bark peeled off after dying. Even though these trees were cut down, the virus never reached under the ground. There are trees today that have been cut seventy years, and their roots are still sending up shoots. I can show you lots of chestnuts ten feet high up here. We have some 35 feet tall, but they never get quite ready for putting in the first chestnuts. Their burs are just like the Italian chestnut. But the Italian chestnut grows just like an apple tree. At the experiment station in New Haven, they are still working on the virus. In Italy they found a virus to counteract the chestnut virus, but it does not work very well here on our chestnuts.

"The only thing is that the chestnut will grow where it's fairly wooded. But it's not very practical to treat all the trees that are coming up in the woodland. We always thought that in time these trees would develop an immune system."

"When I was a boy, I can remember we had about six of them, out-land trees, standing on our hill. We called it 'the Rocks,' where our cabin is. I helped cut those. But I can remember when I was very little, there were still some green leaves on these big chestnut trees. But they were already pretty near done. By 1915 or 1920, you'd see no more. There were still some further west and south in the Carolinas. This was one of the greatest natural catastrophes that came in the forest.

"Now we have mostly black birch, beech, walnut, hickory, not so much maple in the woods, actually. We also have ash and white wood, tulip tree, they call it. We have many varieties of oak. I can see six different oaks up here: white oak, red oak, and black, chestnut oak or rock oak, and one they call 'piss oak.'

"The chestnut would grow straight as a spear, and they split very nicely. They were also used for framing timbers. We used a lot of chestnut for rafters and braces in buildings. A building that would be cut out of oak, the braces would be chestnut. I can't see them ever putting an oak frame up, when they had chestnut, because to frame out a chestnut was so much easier, because the wood, when it was green, boy, it was nice to handle with an axe. They would get one side perfectly straight, when they were using it for rafters. They were not fussy. Today, you can tell whether it's oak or chestnut, just by putting in a jack knife. If it's oak, you won't be able to go in, but if it's chestnut, you can." Besides fence posts, Lewis said, chestnut was also used in barn siding, and the bark of the chestnut tree was very good for tanning leather. Since turkeys ate the chestnuts, there may even be a connection between their disappearance and that of the trees.

"But I think the turkey should have survived. Even though there was twice as much open land then as we have now, the hunting was probably more to blame for their disappearance. People that were hungry could get pretty good food on turkey. You'd go out and go hunting and get a sixteen pound turkey, fat on chestnuts.

"We still have a lot of old recipes that call for chestnuts. People would roast chestnuts for parties. They had wood fires. They made a great deal of chestnuts. People worked hard in those days just to provide the table. When something comes where you can go out and just pick a bunch (like bananas in Africa), you could probably tell the children to go out and pick them. They would come back with half a bushel.

"They would have to vie with the wildlife, of course. When the first frost came, the burrs would open up. You had to know when they open. Kids could not open them up before. But there were plenty. I know those outland trees up there, the ground would just be covered by them. After the burs opened, they would fall right out.

"There were also a lot of hickory nuts. I always made the mistake and called them walnuts. We had two kinds. The hickory nut grows with a nice meat in there. But they have another one in the woods that the squirrels live on now. We called them 'pig nuts.' They are very hard, and you could not crack them to save your neck. You have to smash them in order to get at the meat."

Lewis was almost struck by a chestnut tree he helped his father fell as a boy. "This one was five or six feet in diameter," he said, "We had an eight foot cross cut saw, which is heavy. We would always make an undercut on the back side so you could wedge it to go over. We did that, but the wood being dead probably had a little too much weight going the wrong way. When we put the wedges in, it broke, so the tree came the opposite way. The trunk went right across the butt of the tree. It was right on the edge of a steep hill and it slid right down that hill with the limbs cracking. It must have slid about a hundred feet going down that hill. It slid all the way to the bottom. It took my father's hat off."

So far, he said, the maple tree has not yet replaced the chestnut in the deep woods. "Hard maple is not so much of a woodland tree. Only up in Vermont they have maple groves. But we don't have an awful lot that came up in the old woods. We get it in the wet spots, what they call a swamp maple or a soft maple. The hard maple likes it a little outland. They don't like being pitched in with other trees a lot. If you want to see a beautiful hard maple, go down to Mallory Road in Roxbury Falls. It's a tree that came about six feet up and is growing into four trees. Each one part is big, and then it's a massive tree at the bottom. It's one of the greatest hard maples I've seen.

"We also had a white oak," Lewis remembered, "we called it 'King Oak,' but lightning demolished it. The white oak on the north entrance to Roxbury Center probably was there, when the men came up the Shepaug in 1673 to Good Hill to see where Woodbury was. My father was sure they sat under that oak tree to rest. I think it's three hundred years old. That is a great tree. It's the king of our forest. It is the hardiest tree. If you have a tree with a stem that goes right to the top, those trees will stay."

Lewis learned carpentry from his grandfather Henry Bronson, who had a sawmill on Jack's Brook. This helped him when the time came to expand the farm. "We took down old buildings here in town to build the chicken houses," he said, "Practically all the buildings down there my brother and I built with our own hands; all except the big barn and the main house. And we went into the chicken business, and raised turkeys. And I was able to practice my forestry, when we went into the Christmas tree business. We have probably set between 15,000 to 25,000 evergreen trees, my brother and I, first my father, and then the two of us.

"I tell young people that you can plant 800 trees on an acre. If they do it, they could cut Christmas trees from the same stumps almost for the rest of their lives. If they use Douglas Fir, they can cut them leaving the bottom swirl of branches on the stump and the next year they will turn up, and with pruning off all but one branch make another tree inside six years. They would have continual income from an acre of trees. You can figure that in ten years the original 800 trees will all be cut. The hard part for all these young people is that they want to make money quickly - to-morrow. You have to plant acres of trees and know that you can't do any-thing but take care of them for eight years. You know, people don't buy that. I tell them that for those eight years, we were still planting trees, and after those eight years, we were bringing in the money every year. I think it is the most lucrative business, even today. Just imagine, if you planted five acres, how much money it would bring."

Lewis was also able to pursue his love of trees in town as a member of the Volunteer Fire Department. "When elms were still growing," he said, "our streets in town were lined with elms on each side. But they were really beginning to go fast. We had to work with the State Highway Department, and the Garden Club wanted to plant a new tree, when one was gone. I talked very strongly against that. I wanted to plant all the trees, at once, even if there were elms there. This was in 1950. I was chairman of the Tree Committee in the Fire Department. The state people said it could not be done. They said you could not set a maple under an elm. It would not grow. I took them up and showed them two maples that were growing by my house, one of them was within two feet of an elm and was growing already three quarters up through the elm. They kind of shook their heads a little. So I said, 'Come, I'll show you another.' There was another one that was practically touching the elm and grown to the top of the elm. I said we really wanted to set that whole line at one time.

"They finally said 'yes,' and gave us the go ahead. This was our big-gest project ever. One Sunday afternoon we got a lot of people in town behind it. One fellow named Danforth Miller from New York drove the truck. He was really a wonderful sort. We had the First Selectman, who gave us the trees. He had them up in his pasture, up on Painter Hill. So we sent a crew up there taking up trees. And I had a man pruning trees. He was pretty good. I had him inspect the trees, because some had to be thrown away. The guys were not too good at knowing what to take up. We had Horace Squire down at the end of the line to make sure it was straight. We set 56 trees in one afternoon. They go from the monument along the entire Green up to my brother's and the Old Fire House.

"When we got toward the end, one of the fellows taking them up, Jerry Conway, came down and said, 'You know, damnit all, I've just been up all afternoon taking up trees. Damnit all, I'm going to set one.' So right in front of our old garage, by the Old Fire House, he set one on the corner. But I never ever told him that the next year, when we checked the trees, we had lost eight out of the fifty-six, and one of them was the one he set.

"Since that time we have been setting trees most every year. This year we are filling in the trees that have died on the Green. I've learned since that maples are not good trees sitting next to the black top. They don't like the hot weather. They don't like that hot pavement. We are going to replace them with the old American plane tree, which I like very much. It's a very unusual tree. The bark all peels off as it gets bigger. One of the signers of the Constitution had a meeting in Litchfield and he took with him 13 American plane trees, also called sycamores or Button Balls. This tree is known by all these names. He planted one for each colony. I think I know where there are two of them left. I'm just guessing. One is right next to the Church on South Street, and it is pretty near six foot in diameter. It's an enormous tree. These trees have a tendency, a little mean, about dropping off twigs in the winter. They can cuss me, when it comes to cleaning those up. They will love them long after I'm gone.

"Up on Wellers Bridge Road we set black walnuts, paper birch, and beech. From the intersection at the monument we set red maples, soft maples. But they are not a long lived tree. The ones on Wellers Bridge Road are bearing walnuts now. We may set some more maples up there.

"We set eighteen trees in 1985. A lot of them were willow trees on Wellers Bridge Road. There are twelve willows there. It's too wet. Nothing else will grow there. "

Keep the Heel Down

Sitting with some friends a few years ago, Lewis began to talk about how people went about harvesting their crops together, and how they helped each other put up barns and houses in their youth. "We had so many of the implements. Today, many people would no longer know how to use them. Even for a minister, part of his life was getting meals on the table with something other than pay for preaching to the people. We did a good deal of 'raising of wheat.' And barley. We sowed it by hand. Then we had 'cradles,' a scythe with a basket of wooden fingers behind the cutting edge, which laid out the stalks so that the heads would end up on one side and the butts on the other in rows, ready for bundling. People had to know how to use them. This 'cradle' was a rather intricate piece of equipment. My father used to say, 'Keep the heel down. You are sticking the point right into the ground.' And you had to be careful that the cradle did not fall off, when you swung it.

Bob Hodges, who participated in this interview said, "Yeah, you had to come across with the cleats up and then tip and put it into a pile, afterwards. Then you tied them up with a few straws." Lewis continued, "Then you had to leave them out to dry. You put them into what they called a 'shock,' bundles that stood together butts down and heads up. Then you took two other bundles and bent them over the top. They made a cross on top. So they shed water, when it rained, and could dry. "After they were dry, they were brought in and in the old barns you had a floor of two-inch planks. On either side were 'mows' where the loose hay was stored. You could pull the wagon by horses right into the barn. And then you could sweep the planks clean and use the floor for thrashing grain by hand. They used a flail, which was just two sticks, both of heavy oak, attached with a piece of raw hide. They looked like long Italian rolling pins. It took some experience to learn to swing and bring it down just right. The flail had to come down flat to separate the grain from the straw.

"Then you took a pitchfork. These forks were in families from one generation to the next. There was not very much change. It had three points called 'tines' to it and still does. There were also some with just two tines, about 14 inches long, used mostly for grain bundling on the field. A third tine could have split the bundle. The two-tine was just right, and the bundle would be well balanced, when you picked it up.

"Once they had the grain on the floor, they took the fork and took all the coarse straw off the top. In the very early days they would still take what you call the chaff, and they took an implement which looked like a giant dust pan with a handle on each side. That was not the most efficient piece of equipment. A lot of grain fell off the sides. We were so glad when we dropped it. The idea was that you threw the grain and the chaff up in the air, and the wind would blow the chaff away. But you were always losing grain off the edge.

"In later days they had fanning mills. That was a great improvement. You produced the wind yourself and you had shaking screens, and the grain fell through, while the wind blew a snowstorm of chaff away." Bob Hodges added that even the modern combines have not changed the system of screens too much. Then came the 'winnowing,' in which the grain was separated from the chaff.

"We also produced some flax here, because money was something they did not have much of. They had the grist mills, but then who would raise the wheat. You could take two bushels of rye there, and they would grind it into flour all ready for baking or cooking. There was not very much flat, bottom land for growing wheat. The grain was just to sustain people that lived there."

"We also had quite a few implements for building. To show you how much timber was taken out here, we had four mills on Jack's Brook and in 1850 there were ten in all of Roxbury. There was a mill on Moosehorn. There was a grist mill way down on the river in the south part of town. Then there was the mill at Roxbury Station. There were several more. In 1876 Roxbury had about the largest number.

"Even then, they were still hewing logs in the woods for framing. In the last part of the framing you went to the saw mill but the mill could only cut timber up to twenty feet, whereas some of the logs used in framing were up to forty feet, even sixty sometimes.

"Around 1900 circular saws replaced vertical saws to gain speed. When I was a kid, I still saw the up and down saw running in my grandfather Henry Bronson's mill on Jack's Brook, sawing logs. He had a plane shop for cabinet making and other work. I can very well remember seeing logs that were three and four foot in diameter. They came on a narrow rail to the saw. Then he would start the water wheel going, and the machine and the up and down saw would start in. There were dogs, or ratchets, and they would keep inching it up all the time. He would set the log and go back to the other room to work on preparing lumber for plow handles. Circular saws and band saws came later.

"After they had finished building cabins out of logs, people would still go into the woods themselves to hew timber for beams. They had an axe with a wider bit on it, and they snapped a line with blue chalk on a string. Then they would stand on top of the log and cut the chips as they went, every four inches. Then you took the carpenter's broad axe and chipped off those chips. Then you got back on the log and repeated this until you got to the snapped line. Those fellows had to have a very true eye. The axe had to run perfectly straight up and down so that, when you turned it on the next side, it would be square. It had to be by eye. There was no other way you could do it. They cut it on four sides, and when they got through, they had a square beam.

"My grandfather was a frame-builder. They would go into the woods with a cross cut saw and an axe, and boring machine, a square, and chisel and hammer, and they would 'frame out' a building. That's what they called it. They cut all the rough part of a barn or a building. It was all ready to be put together. It was the inside frame. The carpenter would come along, and then we would have an advertised house- or barn-raising. A crowd of people would get there. We would contact people by telephone on the party lines. When they got through that night, they would have the frame of the building all up. Then the carpenter could finish up the building.

"It was like a puzzle. But they did not put the rafters up right away unless they were hewn rafters. I often wondered whether they put them together in the woods first to make sure they fit. The carpenter's adze would be used to finish the tenons that would have to fit perfectly into the mortise to make a joint.

"Frame building was eventually replaced by what they called 'balloon building.' I have an old photograph from the 1850s, where they show a building frame just after it was finished. The men are standing on timber all over."

Balloon building came into full use around 1925 to 1930. "For a while, they were doing both. The advantage of balloon building was that it was stronger. You started on the ground and put in the sills, then all the uprights for the first floor. They would use two-by-fours because the walls had to be four inches wide. It was a better standard for windows and doors, too. On the corners they always used four multiple two by fours instead of hewn beams. On the second floor they would start with another set. You could go as high as you wanted. It was really a standardization, which came in with industrially cut wood."

Lewis's father, who had seen more houses framed than his son, also left a memoir on how it was done. "One of the most important get-to-gethers," he wrote, "was the day of a Raising. Both houses and barns had to be built and in those days they were substantial, you may be sure. The timbers up aloft were frequently ten or twelve inches square and made of oak. A boss carpenter would have a hard time to get men to put those timbers up there.

First of all, the owner searched his woodlands for the tall straight trees necessary. Then they were drawn to the location, where the carpenters and joiners proceeded to hew them square, bore the mortise holes and fashion the tenons, then fit the first cross work together with slightly sharpened wooden pins. The carpenters had to see to it that the holes were drawn-bored, that is the hole through the tenon must not exactly fit the hole in the post, but as the pin is driven in, must draw the two firmly together. Otherwise the frame will be loosely fitted.

"After the several cross works are all laid out and the pins and tie girts are all in readiness, the word goes out for a Raisin'. On the day appointed the whole neighborhood gathers: the husky young men at the cross works and boys ready with the pins, while the feminine part of the neighbors also get busy preparing the eats, which were always a necessary part of the ceremony. Then the main business begins. First, the end cross-work goes up with a man armed with a crow bar at the foot of each post to insure that the tenon at the bottom post enters the mortise in the sill. Then the next cross work follows the first, always taking care that the tie girts are placed in position before the post reached plumb as they cannot be placed afterward. After the last cross work the 'plate' is passed up, and if all has been rightly planned, the mortised plate will drop down on the tenons in the top of each post. Then the rafters are hoisted and placed in position, and the Raisin' is done. The boarding and covering is done by carpenters afterwards.

"Before about 1775 the frames were somewhat different. The corner posts being of greater width at the top, tapering toward the bottom, and the top having two tenons instead of one, and the plates fitted together and dropped on the posts so that one could walk clear around the building on the plate. It is very unlikely that a carpenter could be found today,who could build the frame."

Norman Hurlbut also noted that, "it is curious fact that the early frames were invariably oak. It is probable that chestnut was a new timber, and the settlers were uncertain as to its durability and they were taking no chances."

He continued, "Now, their labors done, the men adjourn to the door yard, and you may be sure they had their appetites. Those plates were frequently ten or twelve inches square, and it must have been a race of strong men, who could put them up there. Later, after about the time of the Revolution, the cross-tie plate was dropped eighteen inches and made a part of the crosswork: a simpler form of frame."

Of course, carpenters and builders have since resurrected the art of raising the old frames, especially for the barn-like structures that have become popular in this part of Connecticut of late, especially among people who like the feeling of space, living in country lofts. Nor has the light Colonial style of building ever been abandoned.

When the old whistle blew...

One of the great worries for Norman Hurlbut and other leaders of the town was that some of the finest older buildings in town had burned down. The fire company mentioned by Jeremah Decker had apparently been replaced by a bucket brigade. Lewis recalled that the town did not have a fire truck until 1935, and a real corps of volunteers was not formed again until 1948. The way he remembers it, the Grange was chiefly responsible for getting it off the ground, although there are some like Joe O'Brien, who still dispute this and say Allen Hurlburt had more to do with it. The difference of opinion may have something to do with politics. The Grange Master was a Democrat and Allen Hurlburt was a Republican. The venture needed bi-partisan support. A record of the Grange's committee preparations shows that the only thing the town then had for fire fighting was "a 1926 GMC one and a half ton truck, which was purchased several years ago, second-handed. The pump on this truck is an outmoded front end pump, which runs off the crankshaft of the truck and is not rated, or recognized as to pumping capacity per minute by the fire insurance underwriters."

At its second meeting the committee decided that "the purchasing of a fire truck would not augment completely the situation, because the Town of Roxbury had no Fire Department. We say it had no Fire Department, because the Board of Selectmen had picked approximately six or seven men outside themselves and paid them to take the engine out. If not called, they did not respond to a fire, so they were told by the First Selectman.

"We also found out by observation and experience that many of the men in the community would report without thought of financial remuneration but were unable to fight fire properly, because they had no instruction nor was there a willingness to see to it that they were organized and instructed.

"The committee then proceeded to call upon the Selectmen," the report continues, "who informed them they 'could try to organize a Volunteer Fire Department,' but as far as they were concerned, it was impossible, because they claimed to have tried it themselves, and furthermore that the town would not shoulder the burden of purchasing a new fire apparatus until they had seen a Volunteer Fire Department in action in the town for a few years."

So the losses from fire continued. Within five weeks, after the meeting between the Grange committee on the project and the Selectmen, there were four fires, which caused $55,000 worth of damage. The report states, "During this time the Grange Committee was very active discussing logically and coolly with the Brothers and the eligible men of the town." The "Brothers" were Allen and Everett Hurlburt, of course, without whose financial support the purchase of the equipment would probably not have been able to proceed as quickly as it eventually did.

A public meeting was held on February 24th, 1948, at which, according to the Committee's report, "after a lengthy discussion, thirty-six men signed their intentions to join the department. In the meantime, a group of 131 citizens petitioned the Selectmen to add to the fire-fighting facilities in the town. The Selectmen then proposed deferment in favor of the progressing Grange program."

"We, of the committee," their report says, "then knew that the Board of Selectmen by its own action had committed themselves and would have to aid us in the completion of our program." On March 3rd, 1948 the citizens of Roxbury at a town meeting voted a two-mill tax increase, knowing that the additional funds would be used to buy new fire equipment. The Roxbury Volunteer Fire Dept., Inc. was ratified by its participants a month later and started regular drills under the guidance of its elected officers.

They also proceeded to improve their equipment, including purchase of a new Dodge, 2 1/2 Ton Truck equipped with overdrive and double rear end chassis, which was to be custom-equipped by the Maxim Fire Equipment Co. of Middleboro, Mass.

The decision to purchase the truck required another town meeting, however, which was held on June 11th, 1948. The vote was unanimous. Subsequently both summer residents and year-round residents, some anonymously, made various donations to show their support. Delivery took place in February 1949 and led to a celebration at Town Hall at which the elected Fire Chief Henry C. Booth introduced his officers: R.T. Green as treasurer, Lester Coleman as secretary, Joseph O'Brien as captain, Alden Hurlbut as First Lieutenant, and Horace Miller as Second Lieutenant, while Horace Squire was named presiding officer. A group of the volunteers also posed on their new truck, including, besides the officers already mentioned, Robert Kuhn, James Acton, Lewis Hurlbut, Charles Frisbie, Stanley Finch, Norman Thompson, Carl Carlson, Leslie Thompson, Leroy Thompson, Hal Wheeler, and Frank Voytershark. Altogether there were 36 active volunteers and seven non-voting members. While waiting for their fire engine, which had cost the town $11,584, they raised another $500 and spent hundreds of hours of their time to expand the fire house, completing their work only two days before the truck arrived. But the most important thing was that Roxbury finally had its own, regular Volunteer Firemen.

Talking about the events that led up to this, Lewis recalled, "We got our first fire engine in 1935. Then, there were only about seven or eight young men whom First Selectman Allen Hurlburt had asked to be firemen. They included George Booth, Ken Conklin, Ed Felix, Joe Hartwell, Alden and myself. All of these men lived near the center of town, close to the fire house. The machine was a 1928 GMC truck bought by Allen Hurlburt second hand and taken to a fire equipment outfit to be stripped and made over into a fire engine with a front end pump and reserve 150 gallon tank of water and 150 feet of 1 1/2 inch discharge hose. Allen Hurlburt really set it up. The money that went into the fire engine was probably out of his own pocket. They had a siren on the little building that is down on Church Street now. It had only one bay in it. When the old whistle blew, we took off.

"The chief was selected by Allen Hurlburt, too. There was only one driver. We all were helpers to put out the fire, and the Chief directed us. He also drove the engine most of the time. He was a man, who worked for Allen Hurlburt in his orchard. His name was George Booth. That went on until 1948.

"One of the big fires we had in that first period was Alexander Calder's house on Painter Hill Road. He had a pond and it just so happened that the water pump was working very well. The fire was pretty well all through the inside of that building. Alexander Calder was a very sociable guy. When it was all through, he brought out the bottle. We all enjoyed going to that fire. The surprising thing is that it did not burn the building down. But it gutted it pretty badly. Since then Calder has always painted his house black.

"Another big fire was a very old place on River Road. The house belonged to a descendant of the old Smith family, Nate Smith. This was a great-great-grand daughter, who married a John Dickinson, and their house caught fire while there was deep snow on the ground. We drove down there and said, 'Just gun it.' It got stuck right next to the brook. We hooked up the fire engine and pumped. Fire was already coming out of the windows. She had some valuable papers in back of the house, which she was very anxious to get. The house had old, up-and-down planking. It got so hot that we had one person shovelling snow on our backs, and we'd take turns on the fire axe. We would take five swings and hand the axe to the next man, and then he would take another five. But we got through the wall and got the papers out. I got second degree burns on my eyes there. This happened while I was looking up at the windows, and one of the cinders came right down on my eye. It would stick to your skin. We did not think about wearing safety glasses. We had no helmets. We had nothing. We didn't even have boots. We were just there to get the fire out.

"We had another bad fire at the old Lincoln Smith house, which my father probably mentioned. He gave a description of many houses well before my time."

In his attempt at a history Norman Hurlbut had written, "It is one of the tragedies of our little town that we have lost so many old houses, many by fire, some by neglect, and others being replaced by later built homes. The worst enemy, of course, has been fire." He then proceeded to mention a few of the houses which he remembered had burnt in his own time. For instance, there was the Peter Castle house, which stood on the south side of Route 67 (Southbury Road) right after it crosses Jack's Brook.

"One noon time the men came in from the field expecting their dinner. They found their home in flames instead.

"At the top of the hill, easterly of the village, was the home of the Eastman family. It had been their home for several generations. Its owner, Dr. Josiah R. Eastman, was a well-known physician in this part of the state. His son, the honorable Herman B. Eastman, was Roxbury's Judge of Probate for more than 40 years; and Herman's son, Lyman P. Eastman, followed his father as Judge of Probate. One day, about 1910, the widow of Judge Herman Eastman, an old lady near 90 years of age, and her totally deaf daughter were alone, when in some manner the house caught fire. By the time her son and others arrived the fire was far beyond their control. This house stood about five rods easterly from the Gavel's present dwelling on the northeasterly corner of the four corners at top of Josiah's Hill.

"In 1948, a short distance from the Center Cemetery, stood the old Lincoln Smith house with its dairy barn nearby. Again a fire started. This time it was in the barn, which was destroyed while the firemen protected the house. The owner left only one man to watch the house during the night, and early the next morning the firemen were again called out. The fire had apparently smoldered through the night and now broke out with such headway that the old house was doomed."

Contemplating the loss of these houses, he wrote, "It is always a tragedy when a home burns down, but how much more, when the fire destroys a house that is a connecting link with the present and the distant past. A new house can be replaced, but the old house with its memories and the heritage of furniture and historic papers and other prized possessions are gone forever.

"One other early house stood for many years just north of the School house in the Center. Early one morning, old Mrs. Leavenworth apparently kindled too hot a fire to cook her breakfast with the result that a new house was later built on the foundation.

"On Booth Hill stood the old Ely Booth house, later the home of Hervey M. Booth. In 1910 the house was owned by Edward W. Seeley, who used it to store apples. A fire was kept in a stove to protect the fruit from frost. No person being in the house, the fire went out of control, and another house went up in smoke.

"The Gaylord Bronson foundry, plough factory and saw mill, which stood on Jack's Brook, a short distance easterly of the cemetery burned a few years after Henry Bronson sold it in 1932.

"Then, the three story factory and mill at Warner's Mill. It stood on the brook gorge on the west side of the highway. Early one morning, about 1885, a fire was discovered in the building, and again it was too late and the building was gone.

"Other houses and buildings worth mentioning include the Seward Hotel. Its foundation is still there on the westerly side of the road leading from Roxbury Station up to the old iron mine buildings. This large three story boarding house was kept by one Bill Seward, a corpulent man weighing 300 pounds. The workers at the mine and the stone cutters at the quarry kept the hotel well filled through the late 1800s. Bill had a way with him. To give evidence of his financial stability a wad of newspaper served well to wrap greenbacks around to make a bank roll big enough 'to choke a cow.' But he was also a popular man to finger a piano and call the figures for country dances.

"The Jonathan Hurlbut house stood on the bank at the foot of Woodbury Road, opposite Painter Hill Road. It was built circa 1730.

"On the south bank of the brook, just north of the foot of Ranny Hill Road and west of Painter Hill Road, one can see part of the foundation of the Bradley house, whose last resident was a negro, Caesar Broadhead."

Other houses he mentioned included the home of Roxbury's first minister, the Rev. Thomas Canfield. The house of Peace Minor, another of the early settlers, built in the shadow of the Shippauge Fort in 1730, also lasted only until the early 1900s.

There are places where the son's and the father's memories overlap. "The first fire I remember seeing," Lewis said, "was near the Warner monument. When that house burned to the ground, I was about six years old. Then, they just lined the people from the Rectory. They had buckets and stood about three feet apart. The house was then owned by a man named Bradley. It burned to the ground."

Looking back at this first group of volunteers, hand-picked by the First Selectman, Lewis said, "We were just a bunch of green, young fellows. All we did was take care of forest fires and house fires. We had no training. Later, by the time I became a warden, we had trained crews. We had State Wardens who used to come around, and they would hold an annual meeting of Litchfield County Fire Chief Associations. By then, we had a group of about six people, who could be called out. We had Indian pumps that you could put on your backs.

"We had a lot of brush fires in the spring. But there was a lot of feeling in the town that we were inadequate as house fire fighters. There was a lot of clamor here in town that we had lost houses, lost barns. We had to get modernized. We were stand-by firemen for all fires: house, barn, and also brush fires. Water holes were dug in many areas of Roxbury, especially where buildings were dense. It came to the Grange. It was quite an organization then. It was probably the strongest single organization in the town. The National Grange offered a contest and each local Grange would join in to take up a community project for the year. In 1948, we took on the project to form a Volunteer Fire Department. Joseph Dooley, the husband of Jacqueline Dooley, was the master. At the town meeting there were some die-hards, who wanted nothing to do with it."

"One fire of unique interest had occurred in 1935. A barn burned to the ground, while someone lived 150 feet from it. This was my grandmother, Mrs. Henry Bronson. She called on the phone in the morning to tell my mother that where the barn was 'is now a heap of ashes.' No one ever saw it burn, as far as we know, not even my grandmother.

"The town was very open to our recommendations. It voted to underwrite the cost of a new truck and equipment."

Some big fires were put out with the new truck, Lewis recalled: "One was about four o'clock in the morning. The Voytersharks lived out on Church Street then. But their dairy farm was up on Painter Ridge. The fire engine went before we managed to get up. There were several of us, who lived the same distance of the fire house, and always it was a contest who would get their pants and shirts on first. If you got there first, you'd be the driver. And so we were just like all young people in a fire department. We really liked to get behind that darned, old wheel. Horace Miller was right up the hill, too. Didn't take him long to get his pants on. But when I got up that time and looked out, I could see a column of black smoke up on Painter Hill Ridge. The air was a still as could be. It went straight up. It seemed like that column went up a mile. It probably didn't, but it looked that way. It was dark, dark smoke. It was the Toplands Farm barn.

"The barn was one of those curved roof barns. And the hay was all upstairs. It was a beautiful barn. I drove right up there, and got there right away. But the fire had already engulfed everything. They had pulled the cattle out. It seems to me that most of the cattle got out of it. The manager had gone there, before he called us."

"Sometimes, we would not have a fire for a month. Then, we would have two or three. The same engine took care of brush fires, too. And in the spring we were run ragged. Then, before leaves and grass starts growing, and the March winds blow - we usually have dry winds in March and April - and Buffalo grass in some areas, a fire can spread quickly.

"Once, we were down on Squire Road. Of course, when one gets to the fire, one man stays with the engine and the other jumps off and grabs that hose from the reel, and I was the one on the hose. I jumped off and it was Buffalo grass down across the old cemetery. The driver, Joe O'Brien, went right out in the field, and it was a mistake, I felt, because he drove ahead of the fire, and the fire was coming toward the fire engine, going just about as fast as a person can run, I think may be a little faster. And, of course, I went out with the hose to the fire, with the fire coming toward me. But Joe was very cool. I looked back figuring, 'Well, I'll do a little switch and run, if that water does not start.' But Joe had the engine and the water came right through on that hose, and it knocked the fire right out, just like nothing. That Buffalo grass will go right out, if you wet it down quick. But that fire had been really travelling. I did not feel at all good the way we did that. Something could have happened. Not to me. I could have run right through the fire to get to the other side. But to the engine.

"We also had a bad time in the 1950s. Some of the young people around here got the smart idea of starting fires all over town on Halloween night. We would have fires starting over on Botsford Hill, and then, pretty soon another call would come in, and there was a fire on the opposite side of town, beside the road, a brush fire on the edge of the woods, and we'd run after that one. One solution was not to put all the pumps on one truck, so we could tear off and go in different directions. But these young fellows must have had a great laugh, because they had us running all over town for these little fires. They would set them on the edge of the woods and in grasslands. We never found out who did it. We did not want to make too much of a public display of these occurrences, so that a new generation might get an idea for a kind of excitement they have not thought of themselves.

"Our own house burned down, when we were married only a year and a half, Ethel and I. At first my brother was living in that house. It was a little red house on Painter Hill Road. It had already burned when he was living there. It gutted it. That's when we still used the old engine with the front end pump. We took it down to the brook. And we put the fire out. Then the house was rebuilt. My brother moved back there with his first wife, and then they had problems. They got a divorce, and the house was empty.

"When Ethel and I moved in there, we wanted to add to it. We had one boy then and expecting another child. Ethel was in Bridgewater. I was spreading fertilizer on the hill opposite our house. I looked up and there was a column of smoke borne up there, where our house was. Of course, we called the fire department, and I went directly to the fire. The front end pump was brought up and hooked up to the brook, because there was a pretty good pool there. We figured that what had caused it was a short circuit in the electric wiring, because no one was there.

"There I was handling the hose on a ladder, and I had my head in a window upstairs. Apparently I got some gas or suffered from lack of oxygen. I went unconscious just like turning off a light bulb, and I fell off the ladder. In fact, I got some air just before hitting the ground, because I landed on my feet. And I was all right. It was just that once. It turned off just like that. It was just too much. That building had burned twice, and we never had the heart to go back there. That's when we went down and negotiated with Nate Beardsley's sister, who lived in a house on the east side of the Church. We bought the house from her. That house had no electricity and no running water, no central heating system, no telephone. There wasn't anything. But it had nine rooms. We moved in there. And we never went back to the other house. Now our nephew, Chuck Miller, has built a house there."

The house by the Church cost $4,000 in 1942, when this occurred.

The alarm system was unthinkable without party lines as was so much in Roxbury then. "At first, we just had the siren," Lewis said, "but there was a discrepancy about it. All the people that lived near could hear it. But people over the hill would not even hear it. So we worked out a telephone system whereby you could reach the whole town." Ethel explained how it worked, because as one of the housewives closest to the siren, she played a pivotal role. "I had six people to call," she said, "and each one had a list to call, and when my sister-in-law Elinor moved in across the street, she also had a button and did the calls. So I did not have to be at home all the time. Sometimes people were out, and it would take a long time before I could round up firemen. Mrs. George Booth was the first one to do this, and later Doris Richardson did it, too."

At other times it took only minutes for the first volunteer to get to the fire house. This first person would then turn off the siren, throw the door open and get behind the wheel of the truck, and the moment the second volunteer arrived, they would tear off.

Ethel said, "At the fire house was a blackboard to write down where the fire was. Now with the pagers that's, of course, much better. But the system worked pretty well for what we had."

Lewis then continued, "One of the worst fires we ever had was at Norman Shidle's house. George and Marie White were living there. It was right around Christmas or New Year's. It seems to me it was New Year's Day. It was so damned cold when we went up there, and the fire was beside the stairwell. It had gone right up, where there was an opening in the cupboard, right up to the roof. He did not call the fire department first. He just hooked up the garden hose. We went there, but I'm telling you, it was so cold that Horace Miller who, I think, was running the engine, got the worst of it. The water was running all over the house. When we got through, Miller could not get out of his jacket. It was just a coat of ice. We got the fire out, but it did burn right through the roof.

"After that, we got the new fire truck, and an old gasoline tank truck. Both were given to us. The latter was filled with 1,000 gals. of water. So we could go right to a fire. Another fire we had across the street from Nate Beardsley's house. A little white barn. That burned one morning. I know I drove one of the engines. Someone else drove the other. When I looked up, I just got started and the water froze right in the line. That's how cold it was. Usually, once you got the water started, you would be all right, because of the pressure. But you had to get started. When you have weather like that, and the water freezes just as it touches you, that's when the firemen really catch it.

Soon after they got used to the new Dodge fire engine, the volunteers discarded the hardy old 1928 GMC truck, and the Hurlbut brothers cannibalized it to use parts of it on their farm. Lewis was a little reluctant to talk about it, but apparently its pump was put to good use, while they used the stripped down carriage to haul bulky stuff. Somewhat apologetic Lewis said, "We've done worse. The minister of our church gave me a 1914 Ford with a brass radiator. We took all the cab and everything off and put a box to sit behind the wheel, and we used to tear that old thing around the farm. But that car was worth money. It was really a relic: a

1914 Ford. How were we to know that so much of the general public would resurrect so many of the throw away has-beens, which in many cases are pure junk. I will not excuse my own foolishness in some cases. Our barns are still filled with has-beens waiting for some fool to make them financially important."

Then, after a pause, he continued, "I'm going to forget those things. I am going to blame the whole Volunteer Fire Department for this. Alden and I wanted to get a hold of the engine, because he wanted some of the piping, and we thought we could have fun with it. We would strip it down. We were always stripping down cars. Alden still has the pump today. We took the tank off and used it on the farm. We did not have much money in those days, and accepted anything that could do to fulfill a purpose that was free, because we got it for nothing. The people in this town did not mind, because they considered it such an inadequate engine that they just wanted it out of their sight."

The 1948 Dodge was not kept either, once it became obsolescent. "It was sold in 1983," Lewis said, "Then we had four fire engines, including an old one. It was a 12 cylinder. Then we got a Chevrolet fire tank for just carrying water. We had a pump on that also. And we got two more fire engines since then. All of them belong to the Town. There was an early discussion of that, and it was decided that the town should own the equipment. The town also has a budget for maintaining the equipment and the needs of the Volunteer Fire Department. At one time, there were commissioners between the town and the Fire Department. Now the Finance Committee is in charge of the budget. The money the Fire Department raises through donations and the annual Roxbury Days festival goes toward paying off the mortgage on the new Fire House. Perhaps the Roxbury Days could end, once the bonds on the Fire House are paid."

Lewis then added a few more thoughts on the role he believes the Volunteer Firemen have played and will continue to play in the town. "The Roxbury Fire Department from its inception in 1935 has been a continuing example of eager participation in civic responsibility. Under the sponsorship of this organization a beautiful row of trees stands as witness of this accomplishment on Church Street and Wellers Bridge Road, along with other areas. Lastly, the Old Roxbury Days, aside from the financial accomplishment, bring together people from all walks of life in a community spirit, which is the backbone of rural America."

Hurlbut family Bicentennial Farm, owners Howard and Cathleen Bronson, and her parents — Ethel and Lewis Hurlbut — and their children (Linnea and Christopher), at Maple Bank Farm, 53 Church Street, 1988.

Courtesy New Milford Times.

Lewis Hurlbut on Maple Bank Farm's sheep shearing day, 1977.

Inge Morath

Granite quarry at Mine Hill, circa 1905.

Courtesy John West.

At Mine Hill, two charcoal kilns and a track for loading quarry stone, now all gone.

BELOW:
Visitor's Ticket to Mine Hill.

Office of the American Silver Steel Co's Works,

*Chalybes, Ct.*_____ 186

ADMIT THE BEARER to look over the Works, on condition that he or they ask no questions of the Workmen.

_____ _____*Agent.*

☞ **Good for this Day only.** ☜

ABOVE:
Mine Hill furnace, an example of fine masonry with brick arches.

BELOW:
Albert Hodge with his family. Hodge was the manager and later owner of Mine Hill and an active town leader.

Railroad stop at Roxbury Falls with creamery in background. Circa 1880. Site is now
Chase Park at Minor's Bridge Road, buildings and track are now gone.

Michael Callahan,
called "dean of
stone cutters," came
to Roxbury in the
1880's.

Courtesy of William Walker

Looking South at Roxbury Railroad Station, which is still stands south of
entrance to Mine Hill Road off Route 67. Roof overhang, tracks and
storehouse in the background are no longer there.

Hardware Store at Roxbury Station on Mine Hill Road. Charles Hodge, owner, is on the veranda. Circa 1925.

Allen Joye's store at Roxbury Station, later Ognan's Store. Now a dwelling, 6 Mine Hill Road.

Nate Beardsley, breeder of famous Devon oxen.

Percy Beardsley with a string of Devon oxen on their way to a country fair.

Roxbury Fire Department with 1926 GMC 1 1/2 ton truck. George Booth
is the driver. Joseph Hartwell is at his right, and John Matula at his left.
Standing in rear, left to right, are Ken Conklin, Ed Felix, Frank Smith and
Bill Matthews. Photo taken in spring of 1935.

Ethel Hurlbut at old Maple Bank Farm Stand, 1977

Inge Morath

A Succession of Roxbury Town Clerks, Alden, Elinor, and Peter Hurlbut. 1987 Photo.

Courtesy of Danbury News Times

Norman Hurlbut

II.

History Revisited

In Roxbury's entire history no one has served longer as a town official than Norman Hurlbut. On April 3rd, 1955, when he was 75 years old, the Waterbury Sunday Republican published a portrait of him which said in part that his 45 years as town clerk placed him second in Connecticut for length of service in that office, although his 25 years as Judge Probate and Justice of the Peace, a dozen years each on the library board, school board and cemetery association gave him more than a century of public service.

There is a fine eulogy to him by a contemporary and friend, geneologist Donald Lines Jacobus, who describes him as "throughout my youth and young manhood almost like an older brother," and revealed that Norman - just like his sons Lewis and Alden - stayed on the farm, "because his father and family needed him." He would have liked to study music, which he always loved, but his strong sense of duty prevented it.

"Tall, lean, muscular and imbued with nervous energy, he was, during most of his life, a terrific worker," Lines said. Despite his own son's disclaimer that he was never really cut out to be a farmer, the eulogist maintained that "in the days of 'small money,' with meager farm equipment and few modern conveniences, driven by the needs of a growing family, and in the scarcity of good hired labor, there were many years in which he performed, day after day, the work of two men. It was his just reward, long before he died, to see the broken down, mortgaged farm, which he had inherited, converted through his efforts and those of his two sons, into a well-organized, profitable establishment.

"If nothing more could be said of him, that in itself would have been an achievement. But Norman was a man of many attributes and many interests. There were many facets to his nature, and he would have been outstanding in any community, in any class of society, into which he might have been born. He had an inquiring mind. Everything interested him. Living close to nature, he knew the names, the seasons, of the growing things, and if he noticed an unusual stone on his land, he had to learn its name and its composition. When he could afford the time, he read widely and satisfied his curiosity about the many things which awakened his interest. He admired the qualities of the pioneers, the early settlers, and when opportunity offered, he collected the farm and household utensils which had been in use in by-gone generations: old muskets, spinning wheels, and various contraptions of doubtful application. He was never satisfied until he had learned for what purpose a tool or implement was used. He also collected, mentally, the traditions and legends of Roxbury, as told by the old-timers. Religious but not sanctimonious, he could nevertheless admire some of the traits of the swashbuckling Ethan Allen, the Roxbury native who became the hero of Ticonderoga.

"If a painter, a writer, or other person of special attainments settled or sojourned in town, he was always eager to talk to such people, ask questions, and learn how things were considered and handled in their individual fields. Some modern trends were an affront to his common sense. He could be short tempered in expressing his contempt. Yet, he always found time to do a favor for a neighbor. Loyalty to his family and friends was deeply ingrained in his character.

"He was never at a loss to express himself. He talked simply and to the point, often using homely or amusing anecdotes culled from his own experience to illustrate his meaning... With only limited opportunity for formal education, his good mind reached out in many directions, always eager to learn, while his character remained rooted in the best traditions of his New England heritage."

During Norman Hurlbut's life, Roxbury changed its appearance. Land once cleared for cultivation gradually returned to brush and forest. If one drives through the old lanes today one sees mainly trees, and here and there a small clearing with a residence hidden behind them. But the floor of the forest is lined with old stone walls, built laboriously by 18th century and 19th century farmers as they plowed their plots. Sentry Hill Road, for instance, along the 'Upper Farms' where the old Roxbury began, near Pulpit Rock, where Indian chiefs once harangued their people, and the first settlers built fortified lodges, has almost completely reverted to forest.

Sometimes, as one drives along these country roads, it seems as though a curtain had been thrown over the old Roxbury, the only openings an isolated farm or an old cemetery, where grave stones forbade the roots of trees to spread.

Norman Hurlbut decried this encroachment in vain. Driving over the same roads with the "Waterbury Sunday Republican's" reporter John DiCorpo in 1955, he said, "Isn't it too bad that all those nice meadows are going to brush. Can't see it myself. I remember when there was livestock on all the land around here, now these non-farmers are letting it go bad. Land isn't producing, that's not good for the town."

He continued, "Take back 100 years or so ago, Roxbury was a thriving town in those days. There was lots going on then in the manufacturing line." At the small brick town record hall he showed the reporter a 1845 statistical abstract that described how besides plows, hats and cast iron ware Roxbury manufactured flannel, boots, merino wool, flax, as well as livestock to support itself.

The way Norman Hurlbut explained the decline of Roxbury as a farming town was, that "people died, the young people who followed didn't take up farming. In the days of old people did not go to New York and buy their merchandise, they just got it around here, raised almost everything they needed. Even shoes. The travelling shoemaker would come around, may be once or twice a year, and make shoes for the people from hides they provided," he recounted.

"From 1875 to 1905," he said, "tobacco was one of the prime products, then beef cattle and other live stock. An acre or two of tobacco would bring $700 to $800 a year, but it was an awful lot of work keeping the crop in good shape. Tobacco is vulnerable to weather and insects. Buyers from New Milford would come and buy the crop and process it in that town to make fillers, wrappers and binders."

In 1920 one could still buy a handsome farm for $8,000, but by 1955 the price had already risen to $30,000. His own knowledge of deeds and town records was astounding. He had copied most by hand. Arthur Miller likes to recall how he came to him once looking for some records of a piece of land he wanted to buy. Norman sat in the clerk's office with shelves stacked with papers behind him on the wall. He just turned around in his seat and like an electronic arm being moved by what we now call 'random access memory' picked out a sheaf from the pile, saying, "This is probably what you're looking for." And it was.

Land was then selling for $400 an acre at most, compared to more than $20,000 in 1986 and almost twice as much again in 1987. In his nearly half a century as the town's clerk Norman Hurlbut indexed the town's land records for the past 250 years -- in long hand in five heavy, bound volumes. He also wanted to become the town's second historian, after William Cothren. 'Roxbury Remembered' is really a continuation of this effort.

First we reproduce some of the essays he wrote in which he tried to embellish both the tales of early Roxbury with new facts, while reconstructing some of the things he remembered from his youth and the days of his parents.

Shippauge

*"Shippauge, Shippauge, that doleful place,
Home of the Hurlbut crew, and the Baker race."*

The origin of that bit of doggerel is lost in the mists of the past. Whether Shippauge was a doleful place or not may be open to debate. But there can be no doubt about its loneliness.

Here the wildlife wandered at will: the wild moose fought for his mate, the bear foraged for honey and fruit, the birds built their nests and reared their young with none to disturb except an occasional red hunter.

Until a little over three hundred years ago, no white man had ever trod the soil of what is now Roxbury. The sound of the woodman's axe had never reverberated through these hills. There were no human habitations--not even an Indian's wigwam, as these hills were used only as a hunting ground. Through these hills and valleys the red hunters pursued their game with none to question their right.

Taking into account the Pootatook chiefs whose names appear on different deeds of the Indian lands, our Pootatooks (variously spelled Pootatucks, Pohtatucks) must have claimed more or less rights of ownership of the territory ranging from Bridgeport on the south to Goshen and Torrington in the north, and from Waterbury on east to the New York line on the west.

The god Manitou provided well for his red children. The forest abounded with game, the streams with fish, and the hunter needed no license to take what he needed. He did no killing for 'sport' but took of God's creatures only what was necessary for his life.

The village of the Pootatooks was on the bank of the Housatonic River about a mile southerly of the mouth of the Shepaug. The site now lies buried beneath the waters of Lake Lillinonah. There was another village at Pomperaug, now Woodbury, and the trail between these villages ran through the southerly part of Roxbury.

It is probable that the first white men to visit what is now Litchfield County were the Reverend Thomas Hooker and Captain John Marsh. They led an exploring party there about 1640 and in their report referred to the land as "ye great wilderness." Whether their party reached what is now Roxbury is not known. There were almost no cleared fields, no human habitations, no roads, everywhere lonely forests and swamps, crossed here and there by the trails of moose, bear, deer, and the other wildlife which abounded. Witness the early names which still cling in Roxbury: Moosehorn, Moosebeat, Bear Burrow, Wildcat Mountain, Painter (Panther) Hill, Hedgehog, and others.

There is no record of any serious wars between the native tribes in western Connecticut since the coming of the white man. At some earlier day the Pootatooks had been conquered by the Mohawks, whose emissaries made occasional visits to collect tribute. They came stalking through the woods like Roman legionnaires, crying "We are come, we are come to suck your blood." The terrified natives would fly for safety, even into the homes of white men. I have a collection of Mohawk war arrowheads, picked behind the plow in our fields. They are of a different shape from the Pootatook hunting arrow heads, being triangular and without the attaching to the arrow.

It is apparent that the different tribes in this part of Connecticut were but different branches of a common stock. As the white man ever encroached their domain, the Paugassetts of Derby joined with the Pootatooks, who in turn later moved in with the Wyantenucks at New Milford. Later still, all removed to the Scatacook reservation at Kent.

Perhaps we could recapture some of the scenes and experiences and appreciate the debt we owe those hardy and determined men and women, who laid the foundations for the homes and lands we enjoy. Thus, the writer has in the following pages sought to bring back to mind some of the scenes, sayings and activities, which were a part of everyday life of the men and women of an earlier day. Many of the tales and sayings are trivial, but our lives are largely made up of small things and experiences which, summed together, mold our lives and personalities into what we are. The lives our grandfathers lived were as different from ours as theirs were different from the natives whose lands they appropriated.

It has been the boast that our lands were acquired under legal purchase from the Indians. Maybe so, but how fair a deal would one consider the purchase of several square miles of land for the price of a few coats, a handful of knives, and a few yards of cloth? For instance, a purchase was recorded in 1728 of forty-eight square miles for the generous consideration of four guns, four broadcloth coats, four duffel coats, ten shirts, ten pair of stockings, four kettles, ten hatchets, forty pounds of lead, ten pounds of powder and forty knives. The simple grantors probably thought they made and excellent deal. They did not realize that they were parting with their very livelihood and that in less than one hundred and fifty years there would be left not a living representative of their people.

At the time of the settlements at Milford and Stratford, the chiefs of the Pootatooks was Pomperaug, whose name is perpetuated by the Woodbury river. Following him, about 1650, was Aquiomp, who ruled as Sachem of the tribe for many years. Towecomis and Tumasette were prominent chiefs, who later became influential with the Wyantenucks. The last chief of the Pootatooks was Mauquash, about 1740. He died in 1758. The great Wyantenuck chieftain Waramaug was also a respected figure around the council fire of the Pootatooks. The name of our river, the Shepaug, was said to be in honor of Shippauge, an early Bantam chieftain.

On September 23rd, 1675, during King Philip's War, the Pootatooks had signed a treaty with the colonists near them to continue "friendly with the white settlers and to be enemies to their enemies and discover them timely and destroy them," a treaty which they respected. A considerable agitation was aroused in 1720 by the knowledge that a black wampum belt had been received by the Connecticut Indians."

The General Assembly inquired into the matter and directed that it be sent back. It ordered that in future no such presents should be received without notice of the magistrates. They were taking no chances.

The Housatonic River was called the Pootatook or Ousatonic. In the first days of the white settlers it was generally referred to as 'Ye Great River,' and in one instance, in October 1728, the General Court called it the "House of Tunnack River" and again the "Owassatunnuck River." The Shepaug was also known as the Rocky River

In 1723 to 1724, during the trouble with the Indians far to the north, there were a few raids and the garrison of six men at the Shippauge Fort was kept on the alert for trouble. In 1724, Lt. Ebenezer Warner was commissioned to raise a company for scout duty. He paid his men for their services, including their services on the Sabbath Day, which was disallowed. Lt. Warner was compelled to appeal to the General Court for relief-with what result we do not know. At this time the Indians were forbidden to hunt north of the path from Woodbury to Wyantenuck (New Milford) but by October they were allowed to move more freely again in the country, provided they wore something white on their heads.

Chief Tumassettee was long remembered for his fine apple orchard, near the Pootatook village. It was mentioned in a deed of 1753, where it was referred to as Tumassettee's "Old Orchard," and in 1853 some thirteen of his old trees were still living.

If the party of Rev. Thomas Hooker did not reach Roxbury, then it is likely that the first white settlers were the band from Stratford in 1673, who had been instructed to travel up the Housatonic, until they came to a level plain with a river flowing in from the east, meaning the Pomperaug. On reaching that stream they reasoned that it was too small to be called a river, so they continued on until they reached the Shepaug, then went up that river until they came about to Mine Hill. Then, deciding that the country there did not meet the description they had received of the land of their destination, either, they left the river and laid their course over the hills to the east. On reaching the hill overlooking Woodbury valley, they realized that their Promised Land was in sight. It is recorded that the leader of the party, Deacon John Minor, and others fell on their knees and gave thanks for the safe journey. So to this day is called Good Hill. Considering the lay of the land, it is fairly certain that their path from Mine Hill to Good Hill followed very closely the route of the present highway. About midway on this trail, still stands an ancient white oak, the only ancient tree in the entire five miles. It is very probable that the weary travelers may have stopped for a rest under its branches.

Soon after 1700, a few courageous pioneers had established their homes within what is now Roxbury and soon a fort was built at Shippauge. This stockade or fort stood a short distance northeasterly from the bend in the road that leads from the village to Roxbury Station as it turns down river. The fort served for many years in the defense of the settlement at Shippauge. At the west from the fort and easterly of the river is the high hill still known as Sentry Hill. Here sentries were posted to warn of enemy approach. After the building of the fort land was rapidly taken up.

The first settlement in Roxbury was made by one Joseph Hurlbut who built a fort at what was then known as Shippauge. However, it is pretty certain that Joseph was aided by his four stalwart sons: Cornelius, Joseph Jr., John, and Jonathan, and by his son-in-law John Baker, who most certainly helped him to lug those logs. The Hurlbut sawmill at Moosehorn, about two miles northerly of the fort, had been in operation since about 1700 and plenty of lumber was now available.

There is no trace of the first Baker house, but it stood near two large boulders that still lie a few rods south of the old road. This old house was standing as late as 1860. Here John moved his little family from Good Hill in 1715 and made their home here until about 1730, when the Baker family, apparently having prospered, built what must have been for those days a very sumptuous mansion at the corner made by the road to the fort and the road that turned down river from the fort. This house is still standing staunch and strong and is likely good for another hundred years.

(The Baker house is now the oldest house in Roxbury, and was more recently described by town historian Elmer Worthington, when it was in the hands of Dr. Leon Root. Worthington writes: "It is located at the junction of Route 67 and Sentry Hill Road, once known as Tamarack Swamp Road. Built in 1733 it was occupied by the Baker family until 1796, for many years being known as the Remember Baker house. This ancient dwelling is still in excellent condition. It is of wooden construction, two stories high, with a gambrel roof and small overhang. It was built about a central chimney which contained three fireplaces. The small windows, 12 panes over 12, with some of the original glass, remain, as do the original floors and old panelling. Some of the doors are of the early batten construction, two planks think, and the early hardware is still in place. In the attic are an early smoke house and a loom.)

The level land adjoining the river near the fort became known as the Upper Farms, while the plains above Roxbury Falls were called the Lower Farms. By this time homes were being located on the westerly side of Good Hill, where David Hurd had built a stout house also used as a fort. This stood about a quarter mile southerly of the present Good Hill Road. The lands easterly of Painter Hill were settled by the family of Leavenworths and are still known as the Leavenworth district. Even before Shippauge Fort was built, there was a lively settlement at Moosehorn

Hollow, where Cornelius Hurlbut and his brothers had erected a saw mill. This was before, or very soon after, 1700, and was unquestionably the first business venture in Roxbury. The old dam and raceway are plainly in evidence today. There were a few houses near the old mill, now all gone back to wilderness.

About 1730 the center of the town or settlement was agreed upon at about a mile and a half southeast of the present village. Here was built a small Presbyterian (Congregational) meeting house, a cemetery established nearby, and still later, an Episcopal Church was erected. Here the inhabitants gathered for worship until 1795 when, owing to the difficulty of getting water, it was decided to remove to the present location.

The Indian name of Shippauge clung to this part of old Woodbury until after many appeals to the General Court. The General Assembly in 1743 ordered that part of Woodbury known as Shippauge, to be set off and to be known as the parish of Roxbury. Here it is interesting to note the number of -burys in this part of the state: Waterbury, Woodbury, Roxbury, Danbury, Middlebury, Southbury, as well as earlier, Northbury (Plymouth), Westbury (Watertown), Newbury (Brookfield), and Farmingbury (Wolcott). The suffix 'bury, meaning dwelling place, and the reason for the different names may be well understood.

In early days Roxbury was frequently spelled as Roksbury, and anyone who has helped clear a field hereabouts needs no instruction on the origin of the name. The story is told of one farmer, showing his field to a friend, assures him of the splendid value of his, "good, strong land." The friend retorts, "Huh. Got to be to hold up all these stones."

That sturdy race of men has long since passed and their names near forgotten, but evidence of their labors still abounds. Take a walk in our back fields and woodlots and view the innumerable stone walls, built by strong muscles and the help of the ever present oxen. The labor was heavy and the hours long. One story tells of a farmer who hired a crew to help him build a wall, but made them come so early in the morning that it was still too dark to lay stone. Another one tells of Levi Squire, a wall builder then, who was engaged to build a considerable wall for a well-to-do man, who exerted himself to treat the men to the best food, beef steak and so on. After a time, Levi came to his employer and said, "Now, laying stone is hard work, and my men are beginning to complain of the feed." The man was taken aback. "Why, Mister Squire, I thought I was giving them of the best. What do they want?"

"They've got to have some salt pork." They got it. Those men knew what stood by them in those long hours.

As previously told, Roxbury was set free from Woodbury as a separate Ecclesiastical Parish in 1743, but in civil affairs remained a part of Woodbury. In 1796, through the efforts of Ephraim Hinman, Elihu Canfield, Samuel Weller, and others, acting as agents for the town, the General Assembly allowed Roxbury to be incorporated as a township.

Demise of the Pootatooks

Many of the Indians accepted the teaching of the ministers and one, Atchetoset (Hatchet Tousey) in May 1741 addressed a petition to the General Assembly that his family might attend school and receive Christian teachings. The petition was also signed by certain of our Roxbury men: Teley Blakesley, Henry Cassell, Eleasor Warner and Adam Hurd. His petition was granted, and twenty pounds were deposited with Reverend Stoddard and Colonel Preston for the instruction of the family. In May 1742 the Pootatooks with thirty Wyantenucks followed suit, viz;

"To the Honourable General Assembly, sitting at Hartford, May, Anno Dom. 1742. "The humble memorial of Mowehu, Cheery and others, hereunto subscribing, Being Indian Natives of the Land Humbly showeth that there at New Milford and Pootatuck the Places where they dwell, about seventy souls of us poor natives, who are now awakened, many of us to some curiosity of Being Taught the word of God and the gospel of Jesus Christ in order to obtain Eternal Life through Him. And now humbly crave the care of this Assembly that we and our children may be Taught to read the English tongue and have some minister appointed to preach the Gospel of Jesus Christ unto us, and to Instruct us in the Principals of the Christian Religion, and we also Humbly ask as a Deed of the Highest Charity to us that the Government will Bestow something on us to support some person or persons in Teaching us, and preaching to us, that our souls may not perish for want of Vision in this Land of Light, and it may be the means of saving any soul of us, the gospel which you are favored with assures you that you shall not loose your Reward, and your Petitioners hath hereunto put our mark."
Hartford, Mat 13th, 1742

It was signed by Mehewu, Job, Sam, Feeney, John Cocksure, Pukin, John Sherman, Cheery, and Simon. One of the signers, Mohewu, was a prominent Pequot, who had joined the Pootatooks. The General Assembly granted their petition and twenty-five pounds were allotted to the

Indians of Woodbury. The money was placed in the hands of Rev. Anthony Stoddard and the minister at Newtown. They were requested to take them under their care and aid them in attending school and religious worship in Woodbury or Newtown.

In May, 1750, the Pootatooks, through one Tom Sherman, sold their last acre of ground, including the site of their village on the Housatonic and removed to the reservation at Scatacook. Many years later one lone squaw revisited the old home of her people and gazing at the familiar scenes, and with tears rolling down her cheeks, moaned, "There lies Pootatook."

So has passed a native race and an alien people have taken possession of the domain where the red man once roamed in proud and independent freedom.

> From my well-beloved cabin the sunlight is gone;
> The day long has since closed in the far distant west;
> And Womoqui now in this wide world is alone,
> Composes himself for his deep silent rest.
>
> His braves are all scattered like leaves in the wind;
> Departed the valor that inspired them of yore;
> While he still is left, in his sadness behind;
> And earnestly looks for the spirit-lands shore.
>
> The graves of my people encompass me round;
> My brothers long gone, lie slumbering near;
> Scarce a trace of the red man is now to be found;
> And a few of my race are still lingering here.
>
> Farewell, my tired spirit now pants to be free;
> Farewell, ye who stay on the earth's sullen shore;
> Farewell, for your faces no longer I see,
> Farewell, faithful friends, I'm with you no more.
>
> The chief has ceased, and his spirit fled;
> The chief of the hoary hair,
> A grave near the falls his people made
> And they buried the chieftain there.

This poem was written by Woodbury's sole historian William Cothren about 1876. By then Roxbury had long been a white man's land. The old order had passed. The child of the forest had parted with his ancestral lands forever, and the last member of the tribe had departed.

Men of Renown

There were giants on the earth in those days,
The same became mighty men which were of
old, men of renown.

Genesis 6, Verse 4

The author of the ancient book of Genesis did not have Roxbury in mind, but the words of the quotation could be well applied as the list of "men of renown," who were born in Roxbury, or spent their early days here is one of which Roxbury of today may well be proud.

The list includes one Connecticut Secretary of State, United States Senators, Judges, Physicians, State Senators, Clergymen, Teachers and others. Our little town certainly did raise 'men of renown.'

Perhaps the family of Richard Smith should hold a high place in the list, having two United States Senators, one member of Congress, and later a grand-daughter married a third Senator, making three Senators and a member of Congress in his more or less immediate family. Richard Smith in 1754 purchased from one Thomas Smith a dwelling house which formerly stood on the westerly side of the Roxbury-Woodbury Road, about some ten rods southerly of Tophet Road. This old house has been gone these many years, but fifty years ago, there still remained several of the large black cherry trees that were so common in the door yards of our fathers. Some writers give Nathaniel's birthplace as Washington, Judea Society, but Cothren's History tells us that Richard removed to Roxbury after the birth of his first child. Now, his first child was Daniel, then his second, Phineas, while Nathaniel was the third child, and further it is curious that Richard should be living in Washington in 1762, the date of Nathaniel's birth, when he had purchased a home in Roxbury in 1754. At any rate, Roxbury was Nathaniel's home during his early youth, and here he attended the little one-room school house, where was laid the foundation for one of the most brilliant minds of our state.

Nathaniel was born January 6th, 1762, and the circumstances attending his decision to study law is told here. Nathaniel, in company with his younger brother, Nathan, was engaged as what would now be called travelling salesmen. On one occasion they were to meet in Rutland, Vermont. Nathaniel, arriving at the rendezvous before Nathan, entered the court house and listened to the lawyers conducting the case. He was so impressed with the lack of legal talent shown by the lawyers that on Nathan's appearance he told him that if it didn't take any more ability than was shown by those lawyers, he was going to study law. On his return to Connecticut he applied to Judge Reeves at the Reeves Law School in Litchfield for admission. After an examination, Judge Reeves, learning of Nathaniel's very limited education, tried to dissuade him from his ambition, but on Nathaniel's insistence and determination Judge Reeves told him, "Take this book home and read it, and come back in a week and we will see." On Nathaniel's next visit Judge Reeves was so convinced of his ability that he made no further objection, and Nathaniel entered the school, where his natural ability carned him admittance to the bar in 1787, and thereafter he removed to Woodbury, where he practiced law until his death in 1822.

In 1789, at the early age of 27, he was elected a member of the General Assembly and re-elected in 1795, when he was elected as a member of Congress, which office he served until he was elected in 1799 to the Connecticut Senate, and in 1806 appointed Judge of the Superior Court. Here he served with distinction as one of Connecticut's great judges until his health failed in 1819. Judge Smith was one of Connecticut's seven delegates to the Hartford Convention of December 14th, 1814, where his wisdom was of supreme credit to the deliberations of that body. In 1797, Yale conferred on Nathaniel the degree of Master of Arts, and later he was elected Fellow of Connecticut Academy of Arts and Sciences.

Judge Smith was above medium height and of a fine appearance, his face showing marks of high intelligence and solid judgment, his voice both pleasing and powerful when speaking. The judge held his listeners with profound respect and attention. Connecticut lost one of its great judges at his death, March 9th, 1822, at the age of sixty. At the time of his death a Connecticut governor said of him that the state had never produced a greater intellect. Judge Reeves said, "I will not say that Judge Smith has not left his equal. But I will say that he has left no superior living." In a few words, "As a man of mind, of exalted capabilities and pure aspirations, few of his generation might be compared to him."

The story of Judge Smith's life, showing to what heights from a lowly beginning a boy can climb, when he possesses the ability and determination to make use of his talents, can be an inspiration to many a young man of our generation.

The law also became the road to renown and political influence for two of Nathaniel's brothers. Nathan, who was born in Roxbury in 1770, followed Nathaniel to the Judge Reeves School in Litchfield and, after serving as U.S. District Attorney in Connecticut, went on to the Senate, after having (unsuccessfully) challenged Oliver Wolcott for governor in 1825.

Phineas, born in 1759 as the second son of Richard Smith, built a fine house opposite his father's on the westerly corner of Southbury Road in Roxbury village, after he became the town's first representative at Hartford in 1797. His first born son, Truman, also joined the bar after graduating from Yale college, and served in the Connecticut legislature from 1831 to 1834, in the U.S. Congress from 1840 and finally in the Senate 1849. He declined President Zachary Taylor's appointment to become his Secretary of the Interior, but accepted President Abraham Lincoln's to serve as one of the first judges of a court in New York set up by treaty with Britain to combat the slave trade.

There is only one man to whom Roxbury has erected a monument on the town green. His name is Seth Warner. He was descended from John Warner of Farmington, whose grandson Ebenezer Warner first settled in Woodbury and about 1715 joined the early settlers at Shippauge Fort. He built his home on the easterly side of the river, about a half mile southerly of Wellers Bridge. Ebenezer was a physician of some note and to secure his services the town granted him sixty acres of land, "for the Incurigement to practice phissick in ye town and to attend the sick in ye town rather than strangers."

Dr. Warner was the progenitor of nine physicians: Dr. Ebenezer, II, Dr. Ebenezer, III, Dr. Ebenezer, IV, Dr. Benjamin, Dr. Benjamin Jr., Dr. Reuben, who died in the west, Dr. Abner, who also died in the west, and Dr. Ephraim. His son Dr. Benjamin was the father of Colonel Seth Warner, and a daughter, Tamar, married Remember Baker and became the mother of Capt. Remember Baker, who served in the Green Mountain Boys with Seth and Ethan Allen.

Dr. Ebenezer Warner soon after his arrival was a leader of the young community and appointed lieutenant of the North Company train band, as well as a deputy to the General Assembly.

These doctors were not necessarily college-educated, but were skilled in the use of herbs, roots, and other medicines, even if it is said that some used "the gall from rattlesnakes." Even in later years, doctors still knew of the value of some of nature's remedies. There was a large slippery elm tree near our house for many years from which Dr. Myron Downes, for instance, stripped bark to use on his patients with throat ailments. The offspring of this tree stands today behind the Maple Bank Farm stand.

The Mountain Boys

Norman Hurlbut also wrote his own portrait of Roxbury's revolutionary heroes Ethan Allen, Seth Warner, and their cousin and companion in arms, Remember Baker even though their stories had been well told elsewhere. Perhaps he felt he had to write about them, because they were related. All of them intermarried with members of the Hurlbut crew.

Remember Baker was the oldest. He was born in 1737, and according to Norman Hurlbut, "was one of the greatest frontiersmen Roxbury ever sent out into the world. He was a tough, redheaded, freckle-faced young giant, a man with whom it was best not to tangle, if it could be avoided. Sheriff John Munro learned his lesson in March in 1772, when he and his gang thought they could take Remember to Albany and collect the reward that had been placed on his head. They never reached Albany.

(Town Historian Elmer Worthington wrote: "Remember was descended from John Baker, who married Sarah Hurlbut, a daughter of Joseph Hurlbut, reputedly the first man to finish a house near Shippauge Fort, and who gave him a plot of land on Good Hill in 1704. They were probably the first young couple to make their home here. Mary, the future mother of Ethan Allen, was one of their daughters, born in 1708.

"Mary Baker, daughter of John, was baptized in March, 1709, and married Joseph Allen, March 11, 1736 or 1737. Shortly after Remember's birth, his father, Remember Baker, Sr., was killed in a hunting accident in Roxbury by a Hurlbut, but his son married Desire Hurlbut. Shortly after his marriage he joined his cousins Seth Warner and Ethan Allen in Vermont.

"His own son Remember Baker III moved to Stafford, New York. He served as an officer and friend of General Winfield Scott during the war of 1812. His son, General Lafayette Baker, was born in Stafford in 1826. General Lafayette Baker became Chief of the National Detective Service under President Lincoln. He also wrote, in 1867, the "History of the United States Secret Service."

"Lafayette's grandson Newton D. Baker, was Secretary of War in President Wilson's Cabinet from 1913 to 1921."

According to Norman Hurlbut, the Baker house was undoubtedly the scene of Mary's wedding to Joseph Allen in 1736, and here Remember brought his bride, Tamar Warner, the sister of Col. Seth's father, and also here was brought his body that June 1st, 1737, after the fatal hunting accident on Mine Hill.

The fatherless boy grew up in his grandfather's home and with the companionship of cousin Ethan and the soldiers at the fort, until September 11th, 1755, when at the age of eighteen, he enlisted in the Northern army and served through most of the French and Indian War.

In 1758, Remember, now a non-commissioned officer was serving under General Israel Putnam, when Putnam's forces met a detachment of French at Ticonderoga. With Putnam was Lord Howe, a young English officer much beloved by the men. During the action a stray bullet struck Howe. When the men saw their idol fall, they went wild and, fighting like tigers, tore diagonally through the French lines and then, receiving reinforcements, turned and attacked from the rear, killing some three hundred men and taking one hundred and forty-eight prisoners. A heavy price the enemy paid for a stray shot.

Here it is interesting to note that Roxbury was represented in that encounter, as witness the copy of an affidavit made by General Hinman in 1810: "I, Israel Minor of Roxbury, in Litchfield County, in the State of Connecticut, of lawful age, testify to say that I was formerly well acquainted with Solomon Squire, formerly of this town, that I knew him to be a soldier in the French War in the years 1755, 1756, and 1758 as I was with him in the years 1756, and 1758, that he served under the late Col. Benjamin Hinman in his several grades from Capt. to Lt. Col. That in the year 1758, he served as one of Rogers Rangers, and I knew him to be a gallant soldier and much respected by his superior officers. I also testify that I have been well acquainted with Reuben Castle formerly of this town but now residing in Woodbury, in this County, from early life; and I knew him to be a drummer in the said war under the above-mentioned Lt. Col. Hinman as I saw him in said service at Ticonderoga at the time Lord Howe was killed. But as I did not belong to the same regiment cannot recollect how many seasons the said Castle served in said army.

And further the deponent saith not.

Israel Minor

N.B. My meaning is that I did not serve under the said Benjamin Hinman all the time I was in said service, the last year I belonged to Col. Wooster's Regiment."

After the insertion of this document, Norman Hurlbut continued his history: Solomon Squire was a brother of my great-great grandmother, Olive Squire Hurlbut, and after the Revolution emigrated to Tennessee, where he took up a large tract of land, and where he died. Col. Hinman was a native of Southbury and a well-known officer in the Revolution.

Col. Wooster, later Gen. Wooster, was killed at Danbury, May 2nd, 1777. He was at this time the senior Brigadier General in the Continental Army. Jonathan Stoughton, another of those present, signed the following proof for Reuben Castle:

"I, Jonathan Stoughton of Woodbury, in Litchfield County, in Connecticut State, of lawful age, testify and say that I am well acquainted with Reuben Castle of said Woodbury, and I further testify that said Castle was a soldier in the late French War in the year 1758, that he served as a drummer under Lieut-Col. Benjmanin Hinman of Ticonderoga. That I was clerk of the same Company in the service of the now United States, and that in the month of November in said year we were discharged from said service."

These affidavits are among others that belonged to General Ephraim Hinman of Roxbury, under whom my grandfather's brother served, 1810-1815 and have remained in my family, sealed for more than 125 years, until I unsealed them a few years ago. There were others from Roxbury active in the campaigns in the French War whose names cannot be ascertained at this late date, and one of whom did not return. Lovewell Hurd was killed in the 1758 campaign.

After the war, whether Remember returned to his home in Roxbury or lingered on in the north country is not known, but he was here in 1760 as in that year he married his cousin, Desire Hurlbut, the daughter of Consider Hurlbut. In fact, all three boys came back to Roxbury for their brides. Remember for Desire Hurlbut, Seth Warner for Esther Hurd, also a distant cousin, and Ethan Allen for Mary, the daughter of Cornelius Brownson, the miller of Southbury. Must be Roxbury girls were as pretty then as now.

It is not known where the young folks made their homes for the first years, but in 1764, Remember brought his little family, wife, and son Ozi, along a rude road to Arlington, Vermont, which town at Proprietors Meeting had offered to grant 50 acres of land to anyone who would build a grist mill to be in operation by November 1765. Remember accepted the challenge and built the first grist and saw mill in Arlington. Now, Remember had to settle down, what with tending his mill, building the home for his family, and hunting meat, he was a busy man. Soon, he was joined by the Warner family and several of his wife's relations, and still later, Ethan Allen arrived on the scene in time to join in the 'scraps' with the 'Yorkers.' Ethan's brother soon arrived also and became engaged in land surveying.

Not long after Seth Warner's arrival, he had a message from Remember. He had seen New York surveyors going up country and he was worried. The settlers held their titles under grants from Bennington Wentworth, Governor of New Hampshire, and now the New York authorities claimed their titles invalid and they must repurchase under Gov. Tryon of New York. "I tell you Seth, we've got to drive 'em out or we'll lose our homes, and if we do, they'll have us in their courts." Not long after, Committees of Safety were being formed in the various towns through the Grants, as they were called, and a meeting was called at the old Catamount Tavern kept by one Stephen Fay, who had mounted a stuffed wildcat atop a pole before his tavern.

Here gathered a motley number of the younger men of the hills, hardened hunters and rangers of the mountains, who were not disposed to submit tamely to injustice. The organization to be known as 'The Green Mountain Boys' was here begun with Ethan Allen as Col. Commander, and Seth Warner, Remember Baker, Robert Cochran, and Peleg Sunderland appointed as Captains. Remember and others now made up a 'Judgment Seat,' a court for sitting in judgement on the usurpers from New York, and Ethan, Seth, Remember, and Cochran were named as judges. It was a court which some of the worst offenders later had excellent cause to respect.

Finally, the situation grew so serious that on December 9, 1772, Governor Tryon placed a reward of twenty pounds on the heads of Seth, Ethan, and Remember. Ethan immediately offered a reward of fifteen pounds for certain New York officials, to be delivered at Fay's tavern. Said he, "They ain't worth as much as we be"

One night in March, the New York Sheriff John Munro gathered a posse and -- coming to Remember's home -- broke in the door with axes. On their entry they were met by a fighting fury of a man armed with only a cudgel and a woman and child just roused from their bed. The fight raged for a time until the beset and outnumbered man sprang up the ladder to the loft and leaped out into the snow, where he was soon overpowered and, without dressing his wounded hand, the start was made for Albany. Remember asked leave to see his injured wife and child, but only gained the brutal reply: "She can see you at the jail." This brought from Remember, "If she's hurt bad, Munro, I'll kill you." He was told, "In the Albany jail, where you'll be, you won't kill anybody for quite some spell."

But Remember didn't get to the Albany jail, for his captors failed to realize the size of the hornet's nest they had aroused. For hardly had they struck the road than the cry rang through the night, "It's Remember, they got Remember." Soon grim-faced men were riding in from all directions, and the pursuit was on. Taking a different road the pursuers raced ahead and came out on the Albany Road before Munro and his men who, when they saw them, scattered in the woods like frightened rabbits. Remember was carried back and his wounds dressed and his wife and son cared for.

The next day Seth rode out to Munro's place and demanded Remember's gun. "What gun," replied Munro. "The gun you stole the night you tried to murder him," Seth said. With visions of that reward in his mind Munro seized the bridle of Seth's horse and called on his men to make the arrest. Rising in his stirrups Seth brought the flat of his sword down on Munro's head, felling him to the ground, where he forgot all about making any arrest. A few days later, the town of Poultney, Vermont, voted Seth a hundred acres of land, "for his valor in cracking the head of the hated Yorker."

Some time afterwards, when an opponent demanded his authority for this action, Remember, holding up his mutilated thumb, declared, "There's my warrant good in any court in the Green Mountains." By May, 1773, Ira Allen and Remember, as the Allen and Baker Land Co., owned some 45,000 acres of virgin land along the Onion River, near Burlington. That year there were no roads north of Castleton, and Baker and Allen cut a road through the forest for seventy miles so that supplies could be brought in from Lake Champlain and in the summer they settled on their land and built a stout log house across the river from Burlington, later called Fort Frederick. His brother Ira, being unmarried, lived with Remember. Soon came the outbreak with England, and forgetting their troubles with New York, they joined forces against the common enemy.

The day after the capture of Ticonderoga, Remember, at the Onion River was asked by Seth to join him in the occupation of Crown Point. He started at once and on the way intercepted two boats sent by the British to warn St. Johnsbury of the fall of the fort. They did not deliver their message as Remember kindly took them along with him while he met with Seth. Remember was now in frequent demand for scout duty. In August he was sent by General Schuyler to gain information on the condition of the British forces in Canada, and on his return was immediately sent back for more details. On August 19, 1775, he left Crown Point with four or five men, and on August 20, was on the schooner "Liberty" at the foot of Champlain, and next morning started down the Sorel River. Leaving a man named Griffin and an Indian of the west side of the river, he pushed on further. This is the last Griffin saw of Remember.

Hiding his canoe in the bushes, Remember crept up a little further, but on his return found that a party of Indians had discovered his canoe and were making off with it. He demanded they return it, and on their refusal opened fire, killing one of them. Then, his flint needing some adjustment, he leaned against a tree, when a shot struck him in the forehead and killed him instantly. The Indians returned, cut off his head and right hand with the mutilated thumb, and carried them to Canada to collect the bounty. So died one of Vermont's great pre-revolutionary men.

At the time he was killed, one of the Indians took possession of Remember's powder horn, and he kept it. But a day or two later, when the Indian was also killed, the horn came back to Remember's friends, who sent it to his son, Ozi. Later, it disappeared and was not found until 1928, when it was discovered behind a rafter in an old house. Now it is a treasured relic in the Vermont museum in Montpelier. On it is inscribed, cut into the horn: "Remember Baker, Bennington., Vt. Ye Sept. 9, 1774." In Roxbury still stands the old house by the cross-roads, but the family that lived there in those days are entirely forgotten. The level land that stretched northward from the Episcopal church for three-fourths of a mile used to be known as the Baker Plains. The lone white oak still stands by the road as an ancient landmark.

Of the three mountain boys from Roxbury, the poorest was Seth Warner. Among the papers kept by Norman Hurlbut is a copy of an interview with Seth Warner Jr., the younger son of Colonel Seth Warner, in which he recalls how George Washington visited his home in person, after the War of Independence, and paid off the mortgage on it. Seth Warner Jr., then 75, and living in Lower Canada had come to the capital of Vermont to petition the legislature for compensation for some lands formerly granted to Col. Warner's heirs. "It was there and then that the writer of this reminiscence was introduced to him," Norman's paper states, "and held several interesting conversations."

He recorded the following statement, "It was in the month of September 1789, the fall that General Washington made his tour through the eastern states. We had kept ourselves tolerably well posted about the progress of this tour and heard that he was to be in New Haven or Hartford somewhere near the time at which the event I am going to relate took place. But as either of those places was quite a number of miles from Woodbury, where we lived, we had not more idea of seeing him than the man in the moon. My elder brother, Israel Putnam Warner, then a grown man, and myself a lad of twelve or thirteen, were both living with our mother at the time. And at that particular time of day I refer to, Israel was in the yard grooming father's old war horse, which he had been compelled to go with father through all his campaigns to take charge of, for the fiery and proud old fellow would never let anybody but his master, the Colonel, and his son Israel mount or come near him, though he had now tamed down by old age that he would behave quite meekly with me or anybody. I was in the house with mother, who happened to be unusually downcast that day and was brooding over the family embarrassments. She had just been saying, 'No, no, Seth, I can never pay, nor with our means hardly begin to pay this dreadful mortgage. And now I hear it is about to be foreclosed. Soon we must be driven from our pleasant home, where we have lived so long and, until your father's death, so happily. My husband, the Colonel, fought as well as the bravest of them and did all he could and more than his part for the good cause, they all are willing to allow. And I know very well that he wore himself out in the service and was thus brought to a premature grave. And yet here is his family almost on the verge of beggary.' Tears here started in mother's eyes, which so touched me that I rose and went and looked out of the window, when to my surprise, I saw entering into the yard two well-mounted stranger gentlemen, whom from something about their general appearance, I took to be old military officers of pretty high rank, or at least one of them, who was large and had a very commanding look.

"Having significantly beckoned mother to my side, who eagerly gazed out at the newcomers in silence a moment, when she suddenly gave a start and with an excited air exclaimed, 'Seth, just take notice of the noble looking one. Why he looks ever so much like the picture I once saw of but no, that surely couldn't be!' I said, 'Well, at any rate, mother, he must be a man of some consequence, for see brother Israel, who acts as if he knew him, is swinging his hat from his head clear away at arm's length and bowing lower than he would to a king. Israel is quite too stiff-necked to do that for any common man. But they are beginning to talk. I will just open the door here a little mite and perhaps we can hear what they are saying.' I did so, and the first words I distinguished were those of the personage, who had so attracted our attention and who was addressing my brother, and pointing to the horse by the side of which he was standing, asked, 'Is not that the horse Colonel Warner used to ride in the war?' 'Ah, yes, I thought so,' resumed the former, turning to his companion or attache, and pointing to the old war steed with that interest with which he was known ever to regard fine horses. 'I thought it could be no other. Just glance at his leading points, finely shaped head, arched neck, deep chest, haunches and limbs. I have seen Colonel Warner riding him on parade, when I noted him as a rare animal and thought that the horse and rider, taken together, for Warner, a model of a figure and several inches taller than I am, made a military appearance second to none in the Continental Army. But my business is with your mother, my young friend, and I will now, if you will take charge of my horse a few minutes, go in and see her at once.'

"Hearing this announcement, mother and I hastily retreated to our former seats, and with the curiosity and excitement, which what we had witnessed naturally raised in us, silently awaited the entry of the expected visitor. We had been thus seated, but two or three minutes before he came in, and bowing graciously to my mother said, 'I take this to be Mistress Warner, the widow of my most esteemed friend, the late Colonel Warner of the Continental Army?' 'It is, Sir,' she replied tremulously. 'Will you permit me to introduce myself to you, madam?" he resumed with that winning air of dignity I had noticed in him from the first. 'I am General Washington, and after I arrived in this section of the country a few days ago, I hope you will pardon the liberty I took with your private affairs. I made some inquiries about you and the situation of your family when learning, to my deep regret, that your late husband, in consequence of his long, continued absence from his home and business, while in the service of his country, and his subsequent shattered health, resulting from the hardships of war, left you laboring under pecuniary embarrassments, I was prompted to come and see you.' She replied, 'I had little dreamed of such an honor and such a kindness, General,' nearly overpowered by her emotions and the imposing presence of her august visitor. 'There is a mortgage,' he rejoined, without responding in any way to her last remarks, 'a rather heavy mortgage on your homestead?' 'I am sorry,' she replied sadly, 'very sorry to be compelled to say there is, General, a much heavier one than I can ever pay.' 'So I had ascertained,' he proceeded, 'and I have also, before coming here, been at the pains of ascertaining the exact amount now due, and required to cancel this, to you doubtless, a ruinous encumbrance, and I propose now to leave with you the sum of money you will need for effecting that desirable object.' 'Does the money come from the government, Sir?' she asked doubtfully, and with a look that seemed to say, if it does, then all right.

"Washington looked at her, hesitated a little at first, but soon, while taking up the valise he had brought in with him, slowly responded, 'In one sense it does, I may say, madam, if you have delicacies on the subject. I am in receipt of a liberal salary from the government, from which it is discretionary with me to impart sometimes to deserving objectives, and I certainly know of none so than one which will relieve the family of so meritorious an officer as your late self-sacrificing husband.' Without waiting for any rejoinder to these remarks, he opened his valise and took from a bag of silver money, and deliberately proceeded to draw out and count from it, till he had reached the sum of nine hundred and some odd dollars, which afterwards proved to be precisely the sum demanded in principal, interest, and fees for the discharge of the mortgage on our place.

"He then, after returning the money to the bags and setting it aside for the purpose he had designated, and taking the hand of my mother, who seemed inclined to remonstrate but could not force the words from her quivering lips, tenderly but with an air that seemed to forbid any attempt at refusal, said to her, 'Accept it. Don't hesitate to accept it. Take it and get the mortgage discharged at once, and then all your immediately pressing anxieties will be relieved and soon you will find those brighter days the God of the widow has kept in store for you. And now, as my time is quite limited, it only remains for me to say, Heaven bless you, dear madam, heaven bless you. Farewell.'

'I was present during the whole interview between General Washington and my mother, heard every word they both said and saw all the money counted down on the table and feel very confident that I have neither taken from nor added to anything that there took place. On leaving the house, Washington immediately mounted his horse and rode away, leaving us quite unable, for a while, to realize this unexpected visit and the still more unexpected benefaction."

This reminiscence is widely believed, although it sounds too good to be true. Elmer Worthington, for one, disputes the son's account. "Washington never came anywhere near here," he says, "Stratford is the nearest place he came, after he became president." But he also admits that, "Washington and Warner were friends. I believe that Washington sent Connecticut's delegate to the Continental Congress William Samuel Johnson. I imagine probably a trooper came along with Johnson, and the kid, twelve years old, thought 'Gee, this is Washington,' because he had a uniform on."

Seth Warner Jr. may have embellished on the story to substantiate his and his family's petition for further compensation. It was not the first. Petitions on behalf of his family had been filed with Congress by friends of the family as well as with William Samuel Johnson, Connecticut's delegate, personally. Norman Hurlbut searched the journal of the Continental Congress for the years 1786 and 1789 a century and a half later, as well as William Samuel Johnson's papers, but, "could find no reference to any action being taken on the petitions." He died wondering how Congress could have ignored a petition signed by such prominent men as Vermont's governor Thomas Chittenden, and Warner's comrade in arms Ethan Allen, the most famous of the Green Mountain Boys.

In 1858, about 75 years after he had been buried in one of Roxbury's cemeteries, public interest was once more aroused about his role in the War of Independence, and the General Assembly voted $750 toward the construction of a monument on the condition that Roxbury raise $250 toward the same end. In the autumn of 1858 his remains were brought to the Green in the center of town, and by the Spring of 1859 an obelisk of Quincy granite was erected. Col. Warner's daughter Abigail, who had been nine years old when he died, then 84, was present at the reburial. The monument looks like a smaller version of the Washington monument and has since served as the spot where the town's Memorial Service is held each year.

Worthington says the Warner's house stood on River Road, but except for descendants on the distaff side, Roxbury saw the last of the 'Baker clan' in 1790. The differences of opinion between him and the Hurlbuts, as we shall see in another chapter, are not limited to whether Washington visited the Warner home, either.

Ethan Allen

Few of Roxbury's famous men have so captured the imagination of their contemporaries as Brigadier General Ethan Allen. There are probably few American school boys who could not quote his famous summons to the commander of Fort Ticonderoga: "Surrender in the name of the great Jehovah and the Continental Congress."

Ethan Allen was one of the most daring, and popular soldiers of early American history. Gifted by nature with the frame of a giant, he added to nature's gift by developing a most excellent opinion of himself and a confidence in his ability to handle any problem that confronted him.

Seth Warner was nearly six feet, three inches, and it was said that when walking together, Ethan towered far above Seth, so it is likely that Ethan was six feet, six inches tall. A demonstration of his strength and agility was shown at the time of his surrender at Montreal, when he grasped an English officer and by whirling him about, used him as a shield until some attacking Indians were driven off. It is easy to understand his self-confidence. However, this same trait most certainly contributed to his defeat in the election at Dorset, when Seth Warner was chosen to command the Green Mountain Boys in place of Ethan.

Ethan's father, Joseph Allen, was born October 14th, 1708, the son of Samuel Allen and his wife, Mercy Wright, and grandson of Nehemiah Allen, who moved from Windsor, Connecticut, with his mother, Ann Allen, widow of Samuel, to North Hampton, Massachusetts.

Mercy Wright was born in 1669, the second child of Judah Wright and Mercy Burt. Samuel and Mercy moved from place to place and finally to Coventry, Connecticut, where apparently Samuel died. About 1720 his widow moved to Litchfield, where she died, in 1728. Her son Daniel was named executor of the estate, while another son, Joseph was allotted one third of his mother's estate. In 1732 he gave deed to his sister Lydia and in March 1733 a deed to one Paul Pack, Jr. These deeds were for a hundred acres each and by these Joseph conveyed all the real estate he had received from his mother except right to certain "wild lands" which he retained until 1742, when he sold to one Harrison.

Some time after 1733, when he had parted with the homestead and other real estate in Litchfield, he moved to Woodbury to the neighborhood of Shippauge Fort, where he became acquainted with Mary, the daughter of John Baker, a prominent resident of the new settlement. Joseph and Mary were married on March 11, 1736 by the Rev. Anthony Stoddard, the second minister of Woodbury.

About 1715 John Baker had moved from his cabin on Good Hill to Shippauge and built his small house near the fort, where he lived for fifteen years. Then in 1730 he built the larger house that still survives. Joseph and Mary then made their home in the vacant house until about 1740, when they moved to Cornwall, Connecticut. Ethan was born in Roxbury on January 10th, 1737.

Norman put all of these dates so succinctly because of an argument with Litchfield historians, who claim that Ethan was born there. The evidence, Norman says, is based on entries on the first page of Volume One of the Litchfield Records, where it says: "Daniel Allen was married to Mary Grant, April 28, 1736 by ye Rev. Mr. Timothy Collen, Minister of the Gospel.

"Joseph Allen and Mary Baker were joined in marriage by ye reverend Anthony Stoddard of Woodbury, March 11, 1736.

"Ethan Allen, ye son of Joseph Allen and Mary, his wife, was born January 10th, 1737.

"Elihu Allen, son of Daniel Allen and Mary, his wife, was born May 4, 1739.

"Mercy Allen, ye daughter of Daniel Allen and Mary, his wife, was born January 24th, 1737."

The following pages carry entries dating back to 1723 and on to 1750: Rev. Stoddard's records in Woodbury contain the entry: "Joseph Allen and Mary Baker were joined together in marriage by ye Anthony Stoddard, March ye 11th, 1736."

You will note that none of the entries mentioned where the event took place. In the record of Litchfield it shows only the date, his name, his parent's names and the fact that they were legally married; and the same regarding the records of his brother Daniel. Apparently, these records were all entered the same day and covered a space of three years. Furthermore, the marriage record of Joseph and Mary is there. Now, if we are to assume that because the marriage is on the records of Litchfield, it is proof that it occurred there, then we are asked to believe that Mary, accompanied by her minister, and with her family and friends, journeyed on horseback some twenty miles through an almost unbroken wilderness to a frontier town for her wedding. Somewhat hard to believe. Far more likely is that the wedding took place in her father's new house. If the record of the marriage is not proof of the place, then why does not the same course of reasoning apply to the birth of Ethan?

One can find the same kind of entries in the early records of Roxbury. A father would bring in the Registrar's office the record of his family: John, born on such a date, Samuel on such a date, and so on. Nothing was said as to the place where the birth occurred, apparently they didn't think it was important. In one instance an entire page is given to the record of one family. Do these records prove that all the events mentioned took place in Roxbury? By no means. Some of them may have happened before the family moved here. In one case of a family moving from Stratford to Woodbury the birth of the child is recorded in both Stratford and Woodbury. It is easy to understand the father's action. Not knowing whether the births had been recorded in his place of former residence, he had them recorded wherever he was making his new home. But note the coincidence that Joseph and Mary were married in March, while Daniel and Mary were married in April. Both brides were named Mary. Joseph's son Ethan was born on January 10th, Daniel's daughter Mercy was born on January 24th. It is more than possible that the families wanted these coincidences a matter of record, regardless of where they took place.

Furthermore, Dr. William Allen, a noted author, historian and biographer, president of Bowdoin College from 1820 to 1839, and a member of the American Antiquarian Society, wrote in his American Biographical and Historical Dictionary: 'Brigadier General Ethan Allen was born at Woodbury (Roxbury was then part of Woodbury) January 10th, 1737.' Dr. Allen himself was born in 1784 and was five years old at the time of Ethan Allen's death. Ethan was the fourth generation from Samuel Allen of Windsor and Northhampton, and Dr. Allen the fifth. It is more than probable that he knew from his own family where Ethan was born. In any event, a statement made by a historian of the prestige of Dr. Allen is not to be lightly thrust aside.

On September 25th, 1775, Ethan, in an unfortunate attempt to capture Montreal, was taken prisoner by the British and carried to England. After his release in 1778, he published a booklet giving an account of his experience as a prisoner of war. A reprint of the little volume is in my possession. The preface, not written by Ethan, states the following: "Ethan Allen, the author and subject of the following narrative was certainly one of the most noted and notable men of his time. Bold, ardent and unyielding, he possessed an unusual degree of vigor both of body and of mind, and an unlimited confidence in his own abilities. He was born in Roxbury, Litchfield County, Connecticut, on the 10th of January 1737. He married in Connecticut and migrated to Vermont about the year 1769, where he spent most of his later life."

Also, the History of Ancient Litchfield County, published in 1881 by the J.W. Lewis and Co., Philadelphia, gives Roxbury as the place of his birth, as well as a publication called The Family Magazine in 1837. William Cothren in his History of Ancient Woodbury devotes a considerable space in support of his conviction that Roxbury was the place of Ethan's birth. Can the statements in various publications be cast aside as of no moment? It is hardly possible. However, I believe that Ethan's spirit, in whatsoever shades it may be wandering, would likely chuckle over the controversy over where he first entered this vale of sorrow, when all his life he was much more concerned as to where, when, and how he might have to leave it.

Joseph, soon after the birth of Ethan, removed to Cornwall, where his several children were born and where he died on April 14, 1755. Ethan spent much of his youth at his grandfather's home in Roxbury, which was also the home of his cousin, Remember Baker, and not far away was the home of Remember's cousin, Seth Warner. The three boys grew up on tales of military affairs. Grandfather Baker and Seth's father and grandfather Warner were prominent officers in the "train band," somewhat similar to our militia of later days. Grandfather Baker's home was but a stone's throw from the fort on Sentry Hill. No doubt the boys spent many an hour listening to the soldiers. With the training from early boyhood in matters military, they were being fitted for the roles they were to play in the stirring times before and during the Revolution.

Remember, enlisting in the Northern Army at the age of eighteen, brought back tales of adventure and danger that helped to fan the imagination of Ethan and Seth. Remember was just half a dozen years older than Ethan and Seth. Ethan had settled in Cornwall, and in 1762, started in the iron business in Salisbury. In the same year he was married to Mary, the daughter of Cornelius Brownson, the miller. He was married by the Rev. Daniel Brinsmade, paying him four shillings.

In 1764, while a resident of Salisbury, he purchased a one-sixteenth interest in the mining rights of Mine Hill in Roxbury, but more exciting fields were calling. About 1772, leaving the scenes of his boyhood, he joined Remember and Seth in the new lands in the Green Mountains. Almost immediately he became, with Remember and Seth, an acknowledged leader of the settlers in their resistance to the New York authorities over land titles and they offered 50 pounds for his apprehension.

On one occasion, accepting a dare from his friends, Ethan mounted his horse and, riding to Albany, entered a tavern and called for a bowl of punch. After attending to the punch he placed his hands on his hips and announced to the company, "My name's Allen, now who wants that reward?" Faced with such a giant the bystanders apparently decided discretion was the better part of valor and let him return to the hills of Vermont.

Soon after the outbreak of the Revolution pushed the differences with New York into the background, the plans for the capture of Ticonderoga were under way. About four o'clock on the morning of May 10, 1775, Col. Ethan Allen was delivering his famous order to Commander de la Place to surrender. Allen continued in the lead in the activities of the war until the 24th of September, 1775, when he and thirty-eight of his men were captured in an ill-advised attack on Montreal. Ethan, in his narrative, tells of the incidents of his surrender. It seems that the plan agreed upon was that Major Brown was to lead a force around the rear of the town, and when they reached their position to give three loud huzzas, which were to be answered by Allen's men, so serving notice that the attack was to begin. Through some mistake Brown's men failed to give the signal and Allen's men were forced to withstand the attack of the entire English garrison as their retreat was cut off by the river. Allen's men numbered only about one hundred and ten, while the English forces were as high as five hundred. Meanwhile, Allen had ordered two detachments to guard his flanks. Both grasped the opportunity to make good their own escape, leaving Allen with about forty men to cope with five hundred. Faced with such odds Allen at last agreed to surrender, "Provided I could be treated with honor." How this promise was kept Allen tells later.

A half minute after he had given his sword, a naked, painted savage came running and at a dozen feet or so drew his firelock at him. Immediately, Allen grasped the officer to whom he had delivered his sword and, whirling him about, kept him as a shield, until a second savage joined in the attack, forcing Allen's shield to move so swiftly as almost to leave the ground. At this stage of the game, an Irishman came to Allen's defense with a fixed bayonet and swearing, "By Jesus, I will kill the Devil."

Allen was treated with decent courtesy until he came before General Prescott, who enquired if he was the Allen who took Ticonderoga. Allen replied that he was the very man, at which General Prescott flew into a rage, shaking his cane over Allen's head and calling him hard names. Allen warned him not to cane him and shaking his huge fists in Prescott's face, assured him, if he made the attempt, it would be his last act.

Prescott then ordered Allen taken on board a schooner of war lying before Montreal and had both his wrists and legs shackled with chains. The handcuffs were of usual size, but Allen says that the leg irons would weigh thirty pounds. They were fastened to an iron bar eight feet long in such a way that he could lie down only on his back. He was placed in the lowest part of the vessel and given a wooden chest to sit on and use for bed at night.

In this manner he was confined under chains and insults on board this boat for six weeks. In one instance, after being goaded to fury by the insults, he twisted a nail out of his handcuffs with his teeth and heard one of his guards say, 'Why, damn him. Does he eat iron?' After that they fastened the cuffs with a small padlock. To help cheer his spirits he was frequently taunted with the remark that the sole purpose of being carried to England was that he might, "grace a halter at Tyburn." Allen and his men to the number of thirty-four were forced into a small room lined with white oak plank and measuring possibly twenty by twenty-two feet. Later, two more were added, and in this filthy enclosure they were confined for forty days, until the boat landed at Falmouth.

The populace had heard of the rebel who had dared to attack the King's fortress was coming, and they gathered in such numbers that the guards were obliged to force their way through the mob with drawn swords. Ethan says the housetops and rising ground were lined with people as the prisoners were marched to Pendennis Castle for, 'to see a gentleman in England regularly dressed and well behaved would be no sight at all, but such a rebel, as they were pleased to call me, it is probable, was never before seen in England.' It must have been a sensation for those Britishers to glimpse this giant from the forests of America, dressed in a fawn-skin jacket with underdress and breeches of sagatha (a woolen material similar to broadcloth), worsted stocking and worsted cap.

During his confinement at the Castle he was visited by many of the curious, some gentlemen saying they had come fifty miles to see him. Most of the visitors expressed their opinion that he was to be hanged sooner or later which, of course, did not add to his peace of mind. About the first of January, contrary to the expectations of his captors, Allen and his men were placed on board ship for the return to America as prisoners of war, and on the third of May cast anchor in the harbor of Cape Fear, in North Carolina. Soon after, the prisoners were transferred to the frigate Mercury, and on May 2th, set sail for Halifax. The frigate came to anchor on the Hook of New York, where she remained for three days. Here the boat was visited by Gov. Tryon and Mr. Kemp, the Tories from Albany, Allen's old enemies. They held no conversation with Allen, but he noticed that after his visitors departed their treatment by the officers was more severe. The boat again took off for Halifax, where they arrived about the middle of June. Not long after, the prisoners were again transferred to New York, arriving there late in October. Here Allen was placed on parole and allowed the limits of New York City. His constitution, which had been almost worn out by his barbarous treatment during his long confinement, now began to mend, and in six months, he nearly regained his usual health.

During his parole in New York, he was called to the residence of an English officer and told that his faithfulness, though in a wrong cause, had recommended him to General Howe, who had promised him a prominent position in the English army in return for his allegiance and when the war was over, large grants of land to be confiscated from the Rebels. 'I replied that if by faithfulness I had recommended myself to General Howe, I should be loth by unfaithfulness to lose the General's good opinion. Besides, I viewed the offer of land not unlike that of the devil to Jesus Christ, to give him all the kingdoms of the world, if he would fall down and worship him, when all the time the old devil didn't own a foot of ground on earth.' This ended the conversation and he was sent back to the post as incorrigible.

Ethan was finally exchanged on May 3, 1778, for a Col. Campbell, after having been confined to the provost-jail in New York since the 26th of August. He was taken out under guard and conducted to the quarters of General Campbell, "where I was admitted to eat and drink with the General and several other British officers and treated in a polite manner." The next day, Col. Campbell arrived, conducted by Elias Boudinot, (later president of the Continental Congress). "Col. Campbell saluted me in a handsome manner saying he was never more glad to see a gentleman in his life. I gave him to understand that I was equally glad to see him." One can well understand Allen's pleasure at meeting his exchange, after three years of insult and abuse.

"At Valley Forge I was courteously received by Gen. Washington and was introduced to most of the generals, who treated me with respect. I took my leave of his Excellency and set out with General Gates and his suite for Fishkill, where we arrived the latter end of May. I then bid farewell to my noble general and set out for Bennington, where I arrived to their great surprise, for I was to them as one arose from the dead." Cannon were fired and friends gathered round with every expression of joy. Their idol was back. Next day, Colonel Herrick ordered fourteen discharges of cannon, thirteen for the United States and one for young Vermont.

As soon as his exchange had been effected, Congress appointed Allen a Colonel in the Continental Army, although it is not certain he ever entered into actual service. Shortly after his return to Vermont, he was appointed a General and Commander of the militia of the state. At the next election he was chosen as a Representative in the Assembly.

On his retirement from military affairs he engaged in frontier farming and in writing his conclusions on various religious subjects. His "Conclusions" in these subjects scandalized the strict orthodox clergy of his day, some of whom referred to him as that "awful infidel." But in my study of Allen, I believe he was not so much an infidel, but an agnostic, a searcher after truth, and one who could not accept the dogmatic teaching of the clergy of his time.

The year 1789 had been very unfavorable for farm operations. Late in the winter, Ethan's supply of hay became nearly exhausted. His brother offered him a load, and he, with a negro driver, came across the river with his oxcart and was to spend the night. By evening the news that Ethan was come had been noised about, and old cronies began to arrive at the Allen home. Stories of old days and memories of the war were told and retold with, of course, the rounds of drinks to quicken their memories. Late that night the old warriors withdrew and quiet reigned for a time, but in the morning Ethan was astir and he and his driver started for home. Not far on their journey, the driver noticed that Ethan was in a bad way. He whipped up his team, but it was late in the afternoon when they reached home. Late that night, February 12, 1789, Ethan Allen's stormy life came to its end.

The one thing prominent in the life of Ethan Allen was his almost unlimited confidence in his ability to cope with whatever difficulty confronted him. Little can be added to the eulogy written by the historian, Jared Sparks, an early president of Harvard College: "There is much to admire in the character of Ethan Allen. He was brave, generous and frank, true to his country, consistent and unyielding in his purpose, seeking at all times to promote the best good of mankind, a lover of social harmony, and a determined foe to the artifices of injustice and the encroachments of power. Few have suffered more in the cause of freedom. Few have borne their sufferings with a firmer constancy or a loftier spirit. His enemies never had cause to question his magnanimity, or his friends regret confidence or expectations disappointed. He was kind, benevolent, and placable."

In short here was a man, whom Roxbury may well be proud to say: "He was born here."

Ethan could never be browbeaten. On one occasion, when as a prisoner of war, he was walking the deck, and officer accosted him, "Sir, don't you know that this deck is for gentlemen only?" His reply: "By God, I do, Sir. That's why I'm here." One of the earlier stories is to the effect that certain of his friends thought to throw a scare, and donning white sheets, hid under a bridge, waiting for Ethan to pass by. On their appearance Ethan halts and accosts the ghosts, "Well, if you're angels of light, I'm happy to meet you, and if devils, come home with me, I married your sister."

In the Historical Museum at Montpelier, Vermont, there is a brick from the roof of the cell, where he was confined as a prisoner of war by the British, his wooden canteen, snuff box, and his gun. In memory of him there is a park at Burlington, Vermont, a military post, and also the Ethan Allen Highway."

But Norman Hurlbut was not averse to searching for deeper truths in history, and concluded his chapter on the Green Mountain Boys and Ethan Allen with the following reflection: "Before we take leave of Ethan, let us ponder a moment the vagaries of fate. Earlier in the chapter, I referred to the ill-advised attack on Montreal, but just a moment. Carel-tone, believing he was threatened by a considerable force, was on the point of abandoning the town, when word reached him of the weakness of the enemy, and he prepared for battle. Now, had Major Brown fulfilled his part of the strategy, it is quite likely that their combined forces would have taken the town. Then they could have heard the plaudits winging through the colonies: 'The great Ethan Allen, the hero of Ticonderoga, has added to his laurels by the capture of the stronghold of Montreal.' What a hero he would have become. But fate was looking the other way, and Ethan was a prisoner of war and his participation in the war was over.

"Again let us suppose that on that May morning at Ticonderoga, Commander de la Place had been warned of Allen's approach and had prepared a reception for him. As Allen and Arnold came through that sally-port, instead of being challenged by a single sentry, they would have faced the guns of an alert garrison, and the first volley would have killed both Allen and Arnold as well as many of the men while the survivors would never have been able to escape by the boats. Allen would have been branded as a hare-brained enthusiast, who thought he could with a few men at his back take possession of the King's fortress of Ticonderoga. But this time fortune or fate, whichever one wishes to call it, smiled, and Ethan Allen became one of America's heroes."

III.
A Day on the Farm

In order to have people recall how their parents toiled in the days of his parents and his own youth, Norman Hurlbut started a chapter for his history in which he wanted to put down in simple words the cycle of one day's work. He wrote that:

There was no place on the farm in those days for a lazy man nor for a woman either. Work was the order of the day, and with mother work did not cease at the close of day, either. It is one of the mysteries of those days. How did mothers get the work done, which they were required to accomplish?

As for the men, it is told of one hired man who, on being called by the boss before daylight, inquired what they were to do this day, and received the answer, "We're sowing oats."

"Are they wild oats?"

"No."

"Then why do we sneak up on them in the dark?"

If plowing was the order of the day, Buck and Bill, the patient oxen, are yoked and hitched to the drogue. Now it becomes a stone boat. The plow is put aboard and the start is made for the field. They did not plow them level as they did later. Two furrows were lapped together and the corn planted in the line between the two, and when the corn became high enough for the hoe, the ground was stirred again by the plow or a rude kind of cultivator, and the rest was done by hoes in the hands of dad and the boys and the hired man, if one was around.

Hired help was cheap. Fifty cents per day was good pay. This job with the hoe was not like the operation of my day in the fields, made light and loose with modern machinery. In some cases the fields were so filled with rocks and stones that it is hard to believe they were ever used for cultivation. One hired man put stone around one hill of corn, claiming he could not get enough dirt between the stone for hoeing. Corn was planted by hand. No automatic planters in those days.

Haying time. The summer really began. No mowing machines, but early in the morning the old grindstone began to turn under a scythe held down by a good strong man and with a boy at the crank, turning until dad would straighten up and feel the edge, then bend over and bear on harder than before, until the boy was ready to drop. At last the edge seemed satisfactory to dad, and he and the boy started for the meadow, where the scythe laid the fresh grass in windrows which it was the task of the boy to scatter for drying--that last half hour before dinner was the most trying of the day. Then, after dinner, the hand rakes came into use. No horse rakes. Hay must be raked into windrows by hand and heaped. Then the oxen again. It took an experienced man on the cart to arrange the hay. If too much were placed forward, the weight bore down too hard on the yoke, and if too much rearward, you might have the oxen walk on their hind legs. Also, it took experience to load on these side hills, for when the load apparently was evenly divided as to weight--when you reached level ground, or turned a side hill, you might find your calculations were all wrong, and part of your load might leave you and return to the ground.

One afternoon many years ago, on a large meadow, a gang of men were putting in the hay. A part of the men were loading their cart at the top of the hill and were thinking of having a little fun. One of the men mischievously shouted to those lower down that word so feared by hay makers: "Shower, shower." "There," says the owner, "hurry, mustn't get this hay wet." Those at the top whipped up their oxen, the wheel hit a stone, turning the load over. "Never mind that," shouts the owner, "come and get this." So after the men finished, they had to go and pitch that load back up, and the joke sort of back-fired.

The same owner cared little for bumble bees, which were plentiful in those days, and when a nest was disturbed, he would run for a hay heap and bury his head to protect his face and call for his men to defend him. One day, one of his men had a pin and the owner was stung rather badly.

Later came the grain harvest. No machinery there, either, but the cradles were brought out and again the grindstone was put in operation. While the cradle scythe was much heavier and larger, it did not get so dull, and the turning was not quite so laborious. The swing of a cradle is entirely different from the swing of a scythe, and unless one had the experience and kept the heel down, one would find the point of the scythe sticking in the ground. After a day or two, the rye would be ready for binding, and one raked the grain into bundles, while the second man put the bands of grain straws around them. It was the boast that an expert, having a band ready, could toss one bundle in the air and bind the next one, before the first hit the ground.

Potato growing was also different. Potato bugs were unknown and potato rot did not appear here until 1850, or later. The farmer could put his oxcart into a field and fill it with thirty bushels without moving it.

Another farm tool that few men can use today was the flail. When the rye was ready, two men placed the straw on the barn floor in a double row with the heads touching. Then the men took their places facing each other about six feet apart and started the flails swinging. It was always best to have a man opposite, who knew his flail, otherwise a rap on the head would not do so well.

Norman Hurlbut then goes on to describe winnowing much the way Lewis has already described it, but added, that fanning mills started to be used as early as 1800, because winnowing "was hard work for any but a strong man." It required half a bushel of grain to be thrown in the air at a time. In winter the principal work was to keep the supply of wood coming from the wood lot. Again it was mostly muscle that handled the job. Good axes were, of course, available but the saw left much to be desired. One can get more wood today in an hour than a man could in a day.

Meanwhile, what was mother doing indoors? First, in the morning, after tending to the needs of the generally present young ones of the family, she must plan a good substantial breakfast for the head of the house and the growing family. No electric stove then. No wood fire stove, either. But the always present fireplace with the crane hung with hooks and a trammel iron, an ingenious contrivance of a hook hung on an iron with graduated holes, allowing the tea kettle or any other receptacle to be hung near the fire or higher for less heat. Incidentally, the young folks had a stock conundrum based on this contraption: "What is it that is full of holes, yet holds water?" Mother must manage to cook that breakfast on this source of heat, and one can imagine that our fathers ate plenty of ashes. Oh well, a little is probably good for you.

If it's a Monday, it means wash day. The big brass kettle must be filled from the well or spring and hung over the fire. The wash bench -- a six-foot bench made of a slab or plank of wood with four legs -- on which the wooden tubs (having previously been kept in the cellar or other damp place to prevent their becoming dry and leaky) are put. Then the wash is placed in the water. Mother had never heard of a "detergent." She went to the tub of soft soap in the cellar and got a dipperful. With the help of the soap suds and plenty of elbow grease on the wash board she finally got the wash out on the line. The next day, or may be that night, the fine clothes must be gone over with the iron. Here again, no electric iron, no sad iron (this iron was well named), but mother brings out an iron fitted to contain a small amount of charcoal with a smokestack about four inches in height, which she filled with live coal from the fireplace.

The next day, mother is at the never ending job of providing clothing for her family. There was no store for her to buy ready-made clothes nor cloth to make them at home, and the wool and flax with spinning wheel, loom, and other parts of the weaving process had to be operated for long tedious hours. Then the fashioning had to be done by hand.

When it came to baking, probably on a Saturday, the men folk, usually the boys, kindled the fire in the brick oven. When hot enough, the ashes were swept out clean, and mother was at work preparing the bread, pies, biscuits and other things that she knew so well how to make taste good. And it was no meager supply, either. The rear of my grandmother's oven cannot be reached with a yard stick. And when baking day was over, the supply had to last until the next one; if it didn't, that was your hard luck.

Besides the regular routine labors of grandmother, there were the incidental things that had to be attended to: making the soft soap was of no little concern. First, there was a large flat stone with a groove cut around the edge on which was placed a barrel of wood ashes, and water being poured occasionally, the seepage carried the lye from the ashes, which mother carefully gathered, and when ready for soap making, the fat, lye and other ingredients were cooked and laid in the tub in the cellar.

Another of the tasks in the fall was the making of "boiled cider apple butter," usually made with sweet apples, cooked in the big brass kettle, with boiled-down sweet cider, and this was also placed in a tub in the cellar. And any time grandma needed some sauce to brighten up the dinner, she could go to the cellar and get a bowl full.

So that mother would not have too much leisure, it was usually her job to raise what few poultry were on the farm, and maybe she could have a little time to care for a few flowers.

On the Sabbath day work as such could be laid aside, but that did not necessarily mean rest. Our fathers took their religion seriously. The Sabbath began at sundown on Saturday, and Sabbath morning attendance at church must be observed, or better have an excuse. In the beginning, for people in Roxbury this meant a six mile or seven mile trip on horseback or on foot, no easy car or wagon. Remember, it was 1732, before Roxbury had a separate church service, and then only for a few weeks in the winter season. And with that long journey over the hills in all kinds of weather, and then having to listen to hours of service, morning and afternoon, in the cold church and return home, many times wet and cold, it is small wonder that our old cemeteries are dotted with grave stones in memory of S.-- relict of J.-- aged 25, 30, or 35 years of age. Church trials were not unusual for delinquent church members. However, church-going was almost the only occasion that mother could get away from the scenes of home with its almost continual labors and in many cases just household drudgery.

Another of grandmother's chores was cheese and butter making. The name for the room adjoining the kitchen in earlier days was "pantry," derived from the manner of "setting" the milk in pans to allow the cream to rise. When a substantial amount had accumulated, the old-time churn was brought out, and whoever might be available was set to the task of bringing the butter. There have been many types of churns from the early piston churn to the different types of paddle to a more rare barrel churn. This was a small iron-bound barrel set in a standard with a lid that was fastened by a clamp, which must be set securely. Then the crank handle turned the barrel over and over, until a small round glass in the lid came clear, showing that the butter had 'come.' I have seen the operator neglect to fasten the cover properly when, on turning the churn, it dropped, and the entire contents were deposited on the floor. Another name for the pantry, which frequently was used in our family, was "butry."

The housewife took particular pride in the quality of her cheese. One housewife, having sold a cheese to a neighbor, and on meeting him later, might ask how he found her cheese. "Well, it was pretty good, except for one thing."

"What was that?"

"Well, it wasn't very durable," which reply made things all right.

Another food that is entirely forgotten was "samp," which was made by taking corn before it was dry enough to take to the grist mill and putting a small amount of the half-dry corn in a certain hollowed out log, about two feet height, then with a wooden pestle, about eighteen inches long, with a handle two feet long, one pounded the corn into a coarse kind of meal which, when cooked, was both appetizing and nourishing. Altogether Grandma and mother were kept busy most of the time, and some of their handiwork left us beautiful blankets and table spreads.

Norman Hurlbut never got to finish his account of a day on the farm, so Lewis thought of adding a description of at least one of the chores in which men participated in a big way, at home. This was butchering.

"In the spring time," he says, "whether they were farmers or not, even the minister, would have one or two pigs. They fed them during the summer from the scraps of their tables and gardens. Usually they had them right outdoors in a pen. Pigs did not mind whether it was wet or not. They liked the cool water when it was hot. A pig suffers a great deal from very hot weather. But when it come cold weather in the fall, a group of farmers, when it was getting along towards Thanksgivings and

Christmas time, when the fall work was over, they would get together. They had these big wooden 'hog's heads' that they would have the water in. They would have big boiling cauldrons, which they would jack up on stones, and get the water hot. Then they would pour the water into these big tubs. A group of farmers would get together and bring their pigs there. The equipment they had would be what they called gambrels. They were sticks that had some curve in them. Usually they would use oak or hickory. They would smooth them down. Then there would be a block and tackle. They drew it up on a limb of a tree. They would go under some good size trees. They would throw the chain up over the limb, and then take the tackle block and get under the pig and draw it up.

"Let me go back and explain some of the other equipment. Of course, they would have to have sharp butcher knives. They also had hooks with handles on them. It gets into the pig's mouth, hooks under the bone, where it could handle a pig. The 'hog's heads' were very large, like half barrels. They were also used in cider making a lot. The temperature would have to be brought up to 145 degrees or 150 degrees. We know that now. The old farmers would just pour hot water into the tub, and then they would take cold water. They could tell by putting their hand into the water what the right temperature was. If they had the water too hot, it would set the hair, and they would have a heck of a hard time getting the hair off. If it's the right temperature, and the pigs soak long enough, they would be able to get it off.

"Of course, the pig is dead by the time it gets put into the water. Two or three husky farmers grab a hold of the pig and slide it over on its side. They have a sticking knife that's very sharp on both sides. They would stick that into the throat to bleed them. They would only do one or two so that they would not let them stand too long. Some of these hogs weighed 500 or 600 pounds. Then they took the dead animal and put it into the 'hog's head' filled with hot water. When the hair was loosened enough, they would pull it back out. Then they had a tool called a 'candlestick,' because like old candlesticks it had a very strong iron round bottom. These had an edge to them. They would use these to scrape the hair off. Once they got the hair pretty well off the pig, they would wash it down good with hot and cold water.

"Then they cut the tendons in the hind legs, and slid the curved gambrels right in through both legs, and put a tackle on the middle of it. They then hauled the pig up into the tree, head down. They would then proceed to open the pig, starting on the top. They would cut right down from between the legs to the throat. When they took the guts out, they were always very careful to save the fat around the stomach. That fat, or leaf lard, they used to call it, was used for cooking doughnuts. It's the nicest fat on the pig. The other grades of fat would be used for storing the sausage. There might be six or eight pigs all hung up next to each other. They did not go to one place all the time. One farmer might have most of the equipment. That's where they went. Generally, they left the pigs hang overnight to let them cool down. This would be November or early December. Each farmer would then take care of cutting up his pig. They would take the outside part of the pig, along the back. Those strips would be taken off and that would become their home salt pork. Then they would trim off the hams and shoulder the same way Then they would take the ridge of the back, which would be all the chops and roasts, and all the belly would become bacon.

"They'd have all this salted down. Each farmer had his buckets for that. Usually he cut it at home. They cut it into quarters first. Each farmer also had his own way of curing the pork. Many smoked it. They would put it into brine for a period of time. There was salt and saltpeter in it to make it firm. The mixture had to float an egg-sized potato. The women-folk had their job. They had the fat, and they would know which fat to use for different purposes. They would put the leaf lard into one jar, and it would be marked. And another part of the fat would be used for when they cooked up the sausage. Many cooked the sausage and put it into crocks and then poured in the hot fat over it, so when they went to use it in the wintertime, they would just dig in and get the sausage out of the fat. If the pig was big, the salt pork from the back might be two inches thick. That would be cut in pieces and packed in jars with salt between the layers. There would be a lid over it, but the liquid had to be all the way to the top, or the pork would spoil. The people really relied on salt pork in the wintertime a great deal.

"Many farmers prided themselves that their wives had a secret way of making sausage. They would not give anyone the recipe. It used to be really nice tasting pork, too. Most of the farmers also did their own smoking. The best ones had a little smokehouse where they would hang up all the meat. They would have a fire out away from it, and the smoke would come up through a pipe cold into the bottom of the smokehouse. And that smoke would permeate all the inside of the building. They would leave it there, until it got smoked the way they liked it. The smoked bacon would stay a certain length of time. And the ham and shoulders which were heavier, they would stay longer. The chops and roast would just be kept in brine.

"They also boiled the head meat for one or two meals. We used to call it 'souse.' It was terribly fat, but it was awfully good. Then they took the rest of the cooked meat and cut it all up fine, skin and fat, cheeks, everything. They packed that up and it formed gelatin. They put that into dishes, and you could slice it off. That was delicious meat. Pig's feet and hocks, the upper part of the foot, would be smoked and used for cooking, and in making beans. The day after butchering we would always have the liver for breakfast, pan-fried. One of the best parts of the pig for me was the sweetbreads (Pancreas), a very small piece but the most delectable tasting part. The kidneys were stewed with rice and onions.

"Mutton was also raised quite a lot and dressed. They would hang that in a cold spot down in the cellar. It could get so it was even covered in mold. You just scraped it off, and that meat was really beautiful tasting. In the high priced hotels they would do that with their beef: hang it. You can't do it with pork. Pork will really spoil. There was little venison. The deer were much more scarce than they are today. Probably in the 18th century, there were many more shot. There were no turkeys, either. Even raccoons were a very scarce animal. Everybody had chicken. They used to hatch the chickens. The roast chicken was used most special Sundays. The pig was used in the fall for fresh pork and the stored meat was for the winter. Turkey was had--when they could get turkey--at Thanksgiving. There was always goose at Christmas. And a small roast pig, really a piglet, for New Years. They'd roast the whole pig. That was a great New England dinner: roast pig.

"They also stored turnips and potatoes in bins. They kept bins full of apples. Eggs were kept in waterglass in a crock." Ethel Hurlbut interjected, "I remember how cold and gooey it was to reach in." She said the women also canned beans, and canned corn in glass jars. "We also canned peaches and pears."

Some people raised many more apples than others did. One of the poorest apples grown was the Ben Davis, but it would keep no matter how hot the weather got. They were packed in barrels and shipped by freight to Florida. It had only half the water the others had. "A good many people raised more apples and made money on them," Lewis said. "Making apple butter was also one of the great fall operations." They would cook the apples with the cider, and put in spices, and keep stirring it until it had the right thickness, and then they would pack it in jars. People also often made their own cider. "It was stored in the cellar," Ethel said, "A lot of it became vinegar, but a lot of it was drinking cider. You can't store soft cider. It gets hard." Lewis added that again, "people had all sorts of ways of storing cider. Some made cider brandy," but Ethel quickly reminded him that "my family were teetotalers, so we made vinegar." But "the biggest portion of people did have apple cider in their cellars." And it was hard.

"Of course, they also had cabbage stored. It was stored fresh in leaves outside, packed in leaves so they would not freeze. Hubbard squashes would be packed upstairs under the bed. They would have to be dry and not too cold. We also dried stuff, especially apples.

"Before the railroad came through," Lewis said, "you kept the extra milk you had in a spring, or the well. Milk was very local, it did not travel to sell much. They also had it in their pantry shelves. They used to know just what pans were the oldest milk. When they milked the cow, they would cool the milk down in the pantry. As soon as it was the right age for making butter, they would skim off the cream, and if there was a lot of extra milk, it just went to the pigs or they would make cheese. Or you could take a pound of butter and some eggs down to the store and get some groceries in exchange."

In the winter the farmers also cut and stored ice. "Most farmers had a little ice house," Lewis recalled, "It might be ten by ten or by twelve. They would be square buildings. They would cut the ice on ponds or down by the river. They'd clear the snow off. Lee's pond down on South Street was one. A lot of ice was cut there. They would wait until January, until the ice got ten or twelve inches, sometimes two feet thick. They had an ice plow and you could go across the ice with a horse and put corks on the shoes of the horse so it would not slip. They made one mark across the ice. Then they threw the gauge over on the other side and make another mark. In the end it would look like a checker board, and each block would be about two feet square. I think it was about 20 inches by 18 inches.

"Then, when they got it all marked, they would keep going along the same lines, until they got about four inches deep. Then they would bring out the saws, which had very large teeth. They took an axe and cut out one corner. Then the saw could get in. They would saw two sides, and then take an iron chisel and break them off. They had tongs and hooks. They pushed the chunks up to one end of the pond, and took the tongs to draw them out. They used horse teams with a sled to drag the ice to their ice houses.

"Because there were saw mills, they always had plenty of saw dust. They would put that down first inside the building at about three or four or five inches. All smooth. Then they would put the ice cakes on, close together. They would leave maybe eight to ten inches between the out-side block and the wall of the building. After laying the first tier of blocks they would fill everything with sawdust around the outside, as well as about two inches on top of the ice. Then you could start the next layer and do the same thing, until you had eight or ten layers.

"When it came to the summertime, you had a chisel and started out on one corner and on the weakest spot, because those blocks of ice would grow together. In August you could still be taking ice out. That sawdust really kept it. In the fall, they shovelled it out, and then put new sawdust in. This ice was also used to make ice cream in the summer."

So a day on the farm was different from season to season, filled with as many pleasures as it was with strain.

Hoeing
tobacco
behind the
Town Hall,
circa 1900.

Another farmer gives up farming -- John Coyle's herd leaving home at
199 Tophet Road.

Inga Morath

IV.
What Clayton Squire Remembered

Clayton Squire was 96 years old when Lewis Hurlbut interviewed him in 1975, and then the oldest living person in Roxbury. A former farmer and carpenter, after whose family Squire Road had been renamed (from Castle Road), he could remember as far back as 1885, when he was six years old. Roxbury was doing quite well as a town then, and absorbing new people, who came with the Shepaug Iron Company and the railroad. But farming and small mills were still the main industries. Brooks were full of fish, and Squire was known in his day as one of the town's most avid anglers. He did not like to miss any opportunity to be out on the water, or when the shad were running upstream. He was also an expert fox hunter. He cured the pelts himself in the open air, before selling them.

The renaming of Castle Road caused a good deal of controversy. Many townspeople wanted the name Castle preserved. They had been one of its oldest families. But the Squire name won out. Squire said the reason was that no one by the name of Castle lived there, anymore. He shared the Yankee trait of never saying anything unkind or controversial and shied away from discussing the matter even 50 years later. He had learned to keep his real opinions to himself. In a small town that was probably just as well. He said his father, after whom the road had been renamed, also lived a long time. He was 97 years old, when he died. Clayton's son, Horace, when he was 70 years old, surprised the staff of a hospital in Florida, when he told them he would stay with his father for a while, after his release. His wife had died earlier, and he had no other place to go.

In a 1923 newspaper clipping, which Norman Hurlbut kept, there is the last will and testament of a Celia A. Castle, showing that there actually was still someone by that family name living then. The way she bequeathed her wealth dollar by dollar and listed her belongings down to the last bit of tableware gives a glimpse of what an established member of this farming community could leave to her heirs then. So we decided to reproduce the will at this place:

"Be it known to all persons that I, Celia A. Castle of the Town of Roxbury, in the County of Litchfield, and the State of Connecticut, being of lawful age and of sound disposing mind, memory and judgment, do hereby make, publish and declare this to be my last Will and Testament, hereby revoking all previous wills and codicils by me made.

"1st. I will and direct that all my just debts and my funeral expenses be paid by my executor hereinafter named.

"2d. I will and direct that a suitable monument be erected to Leverett S. Castle, and to Celia A. Castle, his wife, one monument for both not to exceed Three hundred and Fifty Dollars in cost if said monument shall not have been already erected at the time of my decease.

"3d. I give and bequeath to Christ Episcopal Church in Roxbury, Connecticut, Five hundred Dollars, the same to be held in trust as a fund and the interest to be used annually toward the payment of the Apportionment Fund required of said Church..

"4th. I give and bequeath to the Missionary Society of the Diocese of Connecticut, for the support of the poor and feeble Protestant Episcopal Churches in the Diocese of Connecticut, as shall be designated and apportioned by the person who shall be Bishop, Three hundred Dollars.

"5th. I give and bequeath to Christ Episcopal Church in said Roxbury, for services or for repairs on property belonging to said Church, One Thousand Dollars.

"6th. I give and bequeath to my husband, Leverett S. Castle, if he survives me, One Thousand Dollars.

"7th. I give and bequeath to my niece, Elizabeth Richards, now of Glastonbury, Conn., my silver teaspoons marked D.B., and E.R., and table spoons (2) marked C.A.R., and also my tall silver candlesticks (2), my brilliant pin, my gold ring marked M.H.R., and Five-Hundred Dollars, to her and her heirs forever.

"9th. I give and bequeath to Katie Collins, wife of Frank Collins Sr., of said Roxbury, my wearing apparel of every description, the remainder of my jewelry and Five-Hundred Dollars, to her and her heirs forever.

"10th. I give and bequeath to Mary Jane Baldwin, sister of my husband, Leverett S. Castle, if she survives me, One Hundred and Fifty Dollars.

"11th. I give and bequeath to Albert H. Buckingham, son of George Buckingham of Roxbury, Conn., if he survives me, One Hundred Dollars.

"12th. I give and bequeath to my husband, Leverett S. Castle, if he survives me, the use and income from the remainder of my property both real and personal during his life time and at his decease, I will and direct that said remainder shall be disposed of as follows:

"13th. I give and bequeath to Mrs. Walter Downes Humphrey, wife of Rev. Walter Downes Humphrey, of said Roxbury, my house with such window curtains and carpets as may remain at the decease of my husband aforesaid, my buildings and lands situated in Roxbury Center, Conn. and One Thousand Dollars to her and her heirs forever.

"14th. I give and bequeath to Christ Episcopal Church of Roxbury, Conn., for the use in the Rectory, belonging to said Church, two (2) black walnut, marble-topped, bedroom sets, consisting of sixteen in all; one marble-topped parlor table, and one mahogany hall table.

"15th. I give and bequeath to Christ Episcopal Church of Roxbury, Conn., whatever interest I may have in two horse sheds situated in the rear of said Church.

"16th. I give and bequeath to Elizabeth Richards, my niece, now of Glastonbury, Conn., one large oil painting in a gilt frame, portraits of my father, mother and brother, Charles, in a large gilt frame, a portrait of my sister, Ophelia, in an oak frame, and my own portrait in a smaller gilt frame, and One Thousand Dollars to her and her heirs forever.

"17th. I give and bequeath to Katie Collins, wife of Frank Collins Sr., of said Roxbury, my piano and the remainder of my household furnishings of every description, including table linen, silverware, bric-a-brac, beds, bedding, pictures, and books and One Thousand Dollars to her and her heirs forever.

"18th. I give and bequeath to the Roxbury Cemetery Association of said Roxbury, in trust, the sum of One Hundred and Fifty Dollars, to invest the same and use the interest to take proper care of the Randall lot in the cemetery, which care shall include the painting of the railings when necessary, and the keeping of the monuments and headstones clean and free from moss.

"19th. I give and bequeath to Rev. Francis Barnett Sr., now of Newtown, Conn., One Thousand Dollars to him and his heirs forever.

"20th. I will and direct that the remainder of my property be divided as follows:

"21st. I give and bequeath one third part thereof to the Domestic Missionary Society of the Protestant Episcopal Church of the United States of America.

"22d. I give and bequeath a one third part thereof to the Foreign Missionary Society of the Protestant Episcopal Church.

"23d. I give and bequeath one sixth part thereof to the Missionary Society of the Protestant Church of the Diocese of Connecticut, as a fund, in trust, the interest to be used for the support of the poor and feeble Churches of the Diocese, as shall be designed and apportioned by the person who shall be Bishop and his successors.

"24th. I give and bequeath the remaining one sixth part thereof to Christ Episcopal Church of Roxbury, Conn., to be invested as a fund of said Church, the interest to be used for repairs or for building on property of said Church or for services as required by said Church.

"25th. I appoint my husband, Leverett S. Castle, the Executor of this my last Will and Trustee of the property left in his hands thereby, and direct that no bonds be required of him for said office, he to have the power to make investments as he in his judgment thinks best,

"In Witness Whereof, I have hereunto set my hand and seal at said Roxbury on the 12th day of October 1912, A.D. Celia S. Castle (L.S.)

"Signed, Sealed, Published, and Declared by the said Celia A Castle, as and for the last Will and Testament in presence of us who at her request in her presence and in the presence of each other have hereunto subscribed our names as Witnesses on the 12th day of October 1912, A.D.

> Sarah E. Hurlburt,
> George W. Hurlburt,
> Mary E. Crofut,
> Witnesses"

The will was probated by Norman H. Hurlburt (sic), Judge, in the District Court of Roxbury, as a true copy of said Will on file in this Court, on May 16th, 1923.

It proved difficult for Clayton Squire to remember some things, and frequently Lewis had to entice his memory with small anecdotes. For instance, he started by asking him about a famous boarding house mentioned in The Roxbury Cookbook which tells of a Bridget Berry, its legendary proprietor. The Boarding House was in Paradise Valley, as the Shepaug Valley near Minor's Bridge was then called. Clayton said he had never heard of her. What he did remember was that, "Down in the woods is where Jim Berry lived. If you go up to Bill Dickinson's place and take that left hand road. His (Berry's) son lived there and raised a family."

Lewis tried to remind him that the story about Bridget Berry went back to the days of the silica and garnet quarries in Roxbury. Speaking of silica, Squire remembered: "You see, Hen Bronson and I built a storage house. I was working for Henry, learning my trade. We built the storage next to the railroad track. Then we had a platform the whole length, where the car could load and unload right in this building. The stuff (silica) was ground over in the factory. We had an endless belt that brought the bags to the store house. There were different grades of it. Some of it was fine enough to make paint. Some of it was for sandpaper. It could be loaded through the slits in there." The belt came into the building through slits and then went out on the other side. The name of the foreman at the silica factory was George Northrop.

Farmers used to haul pieces of silica rock, which they found on their land, usually while plowing, to the factory for a few dollars, even a few cents. It was one of their few sources of cash. They knew there was money in an outcropping, if they found one on their land. Some holes were ten to twelve feet deep, others only six feet. The stone is as white as marble, hence easy to identify.

Returning to his tale, Clayton continued, "I think George Northrop came from Newtown. And, you know, when he gave the contract (to build the storage house) to Bronson, there was nothing said about an opening. That building was built without a window or a door. And when we nailed the last corner board on - which I did - it was a solid building. No opening. Just a big box. Then, they had to have doors. They had to have one on the side of the tracks to get the material out. And they had to have one on the other side to get the material in. That was extra. Bronson made damn good on that."

The Bronson to whom Clayton Squire kept referring as the builder was Lewis Hurlbut's grandfather on his mother's side, and there is a good account of the Bronson mill on Squire (then still Castle) Road in another newspaper clipping. It was written by George A. Beers, born in 1859, who was a nephew of Gaylord Bronson, the first owner of the Bronson mill on Jack's Brook and Henry Bronson's father. Beers played in it as a boy, later worked in it for a year, and shortly after it burned down in 1955 he wrote down some of his memories of it in a letter to the "Waterbury Republican." It said in part:

"I well remember when there were three saw mills of the old fashioned variety with the up and down saw on Jack's Brook. First the mill about which this is being written, half a mile up stream on the Baldwin property another, and a quarter of a mile further up, another mill on the Castle property."

All three mills are clearly marked on the 1874 map of Roxbury, which also shows the homes of M.P. (Merritt Platt) Beers, the writer's father, and D.G. Bronson, the writer's uncle. Alden Beers and his wife Clara Platt Beers originally owned the land on which the Bronson mill stood. She deeded it to Daniel Gaylord (D.G.) Bronson and his wife Eliza, her daughter, after they were married. When it burned down, a house remained, which stood near the mill and then served as the summer home of the widow of William Bronson and her children. William was Gaylord's older son. His second son, Henry, was only five months older than George Beers and one of his boyhood playmates around the mill. *(See family chart on page 140.)*

Beers says the mill had planing machines unlike anything he had ever seen. "There was a lathe for turning iron and steel, also for turning wood, a boring machine and various other contrivances for doing certain kinds of work. Overhead there was a perfect maze of belts and pulleys used to drive the machinery. All of the machinery was contrived by Gaylord Bronson and constructed by him with certain parts that had to be bought.

"Downstairs were the water wheels, the big undershot wheel that drove the up and down saw in the other mill, where also was located a cut-off saw to cut the slabs from logs into stove lengths, and a band saw used for sawing out circular pieces of lumber to be used for various purposes.

The circular saw was 24 inches in diameter and used for sawing out shingles. Practically all shingles used on buildings in those days were of chestnut and most of Roxbury's roof shingles were sawed in Bronson's shop. Another saw frame with a saw 12 inches in diameter was used for splitting board and plank "not too thick."

On the lower floor of the mill, Beers wrote, "was located a blacksmith shop, and Gaylord Bronson was visited sooner or later by nearly every farmer in Roxbury who had broken a tool or implement used on his farm or about the premises. It is not too much to say that Gaylord Bronson would find a way to fix and repair anything that was brought to him. On this floor was located at one time a cider mill and also a blower for the furnace that was built well within the memory of the writer.

"The furnace or foundry, as might be a better name for it, was used only for a short time in the fall when the castings were made for all parts of plows, also for road scrapers used in repairing roads and in excavating for cellars. The writer has watched the molten iron being drawn from the melting pot and poured into the molds, prepared the molds for many hours during the days of his youth. While the castings for plows and scrapers were made during the fall months, the woodwork on them was done in the main shop during the winter and thus was created an industry that lasted most of the year and which, while not a big one, was profitable."

"Henry Bronson was the one who visited hardware stores in Connecticut in the late winter and took the orders for delivery in the spring."

George Beers then states that he "believes Gaylord Bronson was a mechanical genius, and that had he been placed under different circumstances, he might not have become a Henry Ford or Thomas Edison, but he would have measured up high as an inventor." Gaylord Bronson apparently also grew a good crop of apples on his land: Rhode Island Greening, Russet, and Baldwins, "and in those days it was not necessary to spray trees," Beers said.

He also confirmed Clayton Squire's impression that the brooks around Roxbury carried more water then than they did later. "In the olden days there was always plenty of snow," he claims, "and when it melted in the spring for many weeks Jack's Brook was a stream carrying a large body of water."

Bronson's workshop, he says, "was a meeting place for the neighborhood on a cold wintry afternoon," when Gaylord entertained his friends and neighbors with "tall stories," and heard others told by Harry Seymour, who had enlisted in the Union Army early in the Civil War, "and was reported missing, but after a time returned to his home in Roxbury, a brick mason by trade but who could do anything required on a farm and was a splendid worker in every capacity." Lewis adds that, "One day he drove with his horse to Watertown and the horse was later found in a shed. He was never seen again."

Lewis asked Clayton whether most of the silica ground at the mill was brought by individual farmers, or whether it came from the quarry.

"It was everywhere," Clayton said. "There was some in Rocky Mountain. There was a quarry up by Em (Emma) Beers that belonged to Wellington (probably Wellington Ford). There is a big hole in the ground there now. Most of it came from Flag Swamp down by Ralph Seymour. They drilled it and blasted it; drilled it by hand."

Only a few years after they had built it, the storage house burnt to the ground, and was never rebuilt.

Squire also remembered the first garnet mine in Roxbury, "which my dad sold. It was on 180 acres, which my dad owned. We used to raise cattle for butchering there. Bronson built the building." Asked whether there was any 'refuse' from that mine, like there was from Lyman Green's mine, which was used for a long time to repair the town's dirt roads, Clayton explained, "Lyman Green's and ours were two separate projects."

The buildings, after the mine was closed down, had been moved all the way to Nova Scotia, "because the stone there was softer that held the garnets and it cost much less to cut it and get it out." He did not know

121

what happened to the buildings on Lyman Green's, but did know that there were two completely different companies working the two mines. The one on his father's land was called Armour Co., "I don't know when father sold that land. And it run only for about three years. The stone was too hard. It cost too much to get a ton of the garnet."

Lewis then asked him to tell how his father, Charles Squire, was wounded in the Civil War. "He was wounded in the Battle of Winchester," Clayton said, "in Virginia." And that is all he remembered.

Next he was asked, "Clayton, do you remember the blizzard of 1888,"

"Sure, I remember it. At our house the drifts were from the horse barn across the road to the top row of windows. I remember getting my high chair to look out the top of the windows. My dad, and grandfather, and Sam Baldwin - there were three families of Baldwins on Squire Road back in those days - Tully Thomas' wife was having a baby. They got hold of old lady Whittlesey. They put her into a piano box, chained the box on a wood sled, and had three pair of oxen."

Oxen were much better in snow than horses. Often they were used to 'break open' roads after a snowfall by going over roads pulling heavily weighted sleds. This time, "they went into lots everywhere, because the drifts were too high on the roads, over to the Thomas'. That's how Millie Thomas was born. She married Everett Davenport." Clayton's father tunneled his way through the snow, "from the kitchen door, across to the horse barn. He tunneled under there to water the horses. We went in and out the upstairs windows for a long time."

The blizzard was probably the worst ever to have swept across this part of Connecticut.

Another man with an even better memory of the blizzard of 1888 was Phineas Clark of New Milford who, in 1953, when he was 88 years old, told this story about it:

He was 22 years old and still living with his parents on Bull Mountain, about three miles out of New Milford on the Litchfield Road. "On the morning when the blizzard started, I left the farm at 7:OO a.m. to take six cans of milk to New Milford to the creamery, which stood at S.D. Green's, where the wooden horse still (i.e. in 1953) stands, and all the harness and stuff, for sale. I drove up to the door and shouted: 'You boys will have to help me; these horses can't stand the hail. It's biting right into them.' Sure enough, two men came out and carried the milk, while I held the horses; they were sure enough beat. 'You might let me have six other cans,' I told them. 'And then I won't have to wait.' But they didn't have a can in the place and I had to go home and pour 165 quarts of milk on the manure heap for 14 days. But that's getting ahead of my story.

"I drove to the store to get some groceries for my mother. This time, I got two men to hold the horses. I wasn't in there very long, when I heard them shouting to me to come back quick, the horses couldn't stand it.

"I went out, without the groceries. It didn't matter. We had potatoes and plenty of corned beef and pork. It was the horses that mattered. And the sleet cut my face something terrible. I took the blankets off the horses, put them on the sleigh, and lay down on top of them, with my head toward the horses, and drove that way. As I drove out Park Lane, it got worse. I couldn't see a thing. The horses were wonderful. We went up Gunn Hill where Perry Walker lived. He was a stone mason and helped build the town hall in New Milford.

"Well, by Perry's house, the horses fell, picking up balls of wet snow under the heavy coating of frozen sleet. I got out of the sleigh. The snow by then was above my waist. I was sorry for the horses because I had broken them myself, from colts, and they would do anything I told them. So, I talked to them, kindly-like and unfastened the sleigh from them, leaving it in the middle of the road. We kept on, along the road, I driving the horses ahead of me, and suddenly, there in front of me was Tom Richmond's barn, collapsed, flat in the middle of the road. I couldn't get by. I looked off to the east and noticed a ridge, with a stone wall, and I knew that I could follow that wall to our barn if I could get through the wire fence. So, I cut the fence and made my way up through the field, barely making the top of the ridge. As I went by the Richmond barn, I noticed a dead cow lying beside her dead newborn calf.

"There were several chicken, frozen by the roadside. I picked one up by the legs, and it was so cold that the legs snapped off. Tom Richmond had left his house that morning, I learned later, and gone to Lon Fuller's, just under the brow of the hill, because the wind had raised up Tom's house from its foundation, and he thought, 'I better get right out of here.'

"Well, I kept going, following the stone wall. I managed to get through the wire fence up there and went through the swamp, which was frozen solid. Once the wind stopped for a short time, and I found myself heading in the exact opposite direction from my father's house. Then, I saw the wall again, our wall, and followed it smack to the side of our barn. I hammered on the door. Paul, our hired man, let me in. 'Take these horses,' I said, 'and rub 'em down good, until they are dry, and then give them some water, not too much or too cold.' It was sort of warm in the barn on account of 30 head of cattle, and I was wore out. I dropped to the floor to take a rest. 'These horses will have to wait,' said Paul, "till I get the word to your Ma that you are all right. She's plumb crazy from worry.'

"Pretty soon Paul and my Pa came out and kind of eased me into the house. It was like getting into glory; it was so warm and nice. Ma was satisfied. 'How are the horses?' asked Pa. 'All right,' I said."

The Clarks were housebound by the snow for two weeks. "You know the state did not dig us out, the way they do now," Phineas Clark said, "We found 300 feet of snow on the road, and we cut out hunks and passed them up to a man who was higher up, and in that way we dug out. On the driveway into our yard I was walking along our best cherry tree, and I cut a notch in the trunk. Next spring, as I was picking cherries I measured that notch from the ground, and it was 25 feet. In July, four months after the blizzard, I went on a tour of inspection of the Northrop Farm, the one I bought later, and I came upon a pasture lot which was in a sort of depression with a brook running through it. And there, right in the bed of the brook, was two feet of solid ice. That summer, maybe on account of the storm, we had the best crops we ever had."

Clayton was asked to tell what he remembered of George W. Hurlburt's business at Roxbury Center, the first trade between the town and New Haven. The Hurlburts sold pork and other farm produce from Roxbury farms and imported dry goods and staples not produced on local farms.

"George Hurlburt used to draw produce down to New Haven and draw his groceries back. He had three horses. He had a pair of sorrel, whitefaced mare on the lead, and hooked onto the end of the pole tongue. He told the story of having barrels of sugar and barrels of crackers, over a ton, and somewhere on the road the bolt broke on the whipple-tree. And this horse drew that whole load over the water butts.

"These butts, or gullies, were also known as 'Thank You Mums.' Horses drawing a wagon or carriage would stop in front of them, which allowed a young man out with his girlfriend in a buggy to plant a kiss on her mouth."

His brother owned a wholesale store in New Haven. Squire said, "they bought the farmers' eggs, their butter, and they bought their fat calves and sold them in New Haven."

Through his hat shop business and other activities, George W. Hurlburt's father, the Colonel George Hurlbut became one of the richer men in town, but not the most popular. "I pitched hay for him once and broke his fork," Squire remembered, "It was an old fork. It wasn't good for anything. Of course, being a young squirt, I bore onto it a little more than I should, and George Hurlbut had to get a new fork. He was some coot."

He laughed, as if embarrassed about the incident 80 years later. At the Colonel's funeral, he recalled, someone in the town said, when his hearse was going by, "there goes the meanest man in town." Squire thought, "That about covers it."

Asked to say something about Allen Hurlburt, the grandson of Col. George Hurlbut, and for many years the town's First Selectman. Squire's only comment on the man they also called "The Czar" was, "There was none better."

We will see in the next chapter that Allen, unlike his father, dedicated what wealth he had to the town and eased it into the 20th century.

Lewis also asked him about the steeple of the Episcopal Church, which was removed in the 1930s or 1940s. He said he had nothing to do with its removal, but remembered that, "it was not safe. The last time I painted that steeple it was pretty blame shaky. I did not dare go up it, if there was any wind, at all. But I do not know who did take it down."

Asked whether he knew anything about a foundry on South Street, of which Lewis had heard talk, Squire remembered another shop, "They made razors there. They made them out of old rasps. I've got one or two at the house." The shop was right across from his barn. A man named Cogswell ran it. But the store burnt down in his father's day.

Lewis then asked him about Henry Bronson, and the mill on Squire Road and whether it was built by Gaylord Bronson. Squire said, "Yes, so far as I know," confirming the account by George Beers above. But Squire said in his day the Bronsons were also making plows, a business they had taken over from the Wakely Co. of Southbury. "I made plow handles day after day," Squire said, "Also, I used to mold plowshares, when I worked for Henry, but Bill (his older brother) made the mold boards, the big pieces. Henry couldn't do it. For what reason we never knew. You see, we used molding sand. Everything had to be done by hand. They had irons to tamp them in. They were different shapes. And for the plowshares: why, I would mold plowshares just as fast as Henry could, after a little. But then there was old Oliver Johnson. He and I made most of the plowshares." Lewis asked him whether some of the metal came from scrap, and Squire said, "they also had some new." He had no idea where it came from. It could conceivably have come from the Roxbury mine. He also confirmed that there was still an up and down saw, driven by the water wheel.

But there was another mill, a saw mill, on the upper northeast corner of the present Land Trust Property, known as the Tierney Preserve, of which Squire said, "I think it was still running when I was a young boy." He also remembered a third mill, down by Mumford's place, of which he said, "That was a grist mill, and cider mill. Bates ran it. They also made soap there," Squire said, "and they used to make files, the Bagland files. They were known all over the world. I walked in that waterwheel when I went to the district school. It was a big overshot wheel."

Lewis reminded him that most of the mills in Roxbury were run off Jack's Brook in that area. It was called Big Jack's Brook, and there was yet another mill, Wetmore's. Squire ignored the question, and said, "You know, there was more than twice the water in those brooks then. The brooks never got below the banks much of the summer." The biggest mill, he recalled, was the one at Roxbury Station on the Shepaug. And most mills were still operating when Squire was a young boy, but they stopped by the time he had grown into manhood.

There were also a lot of hatshops. Lewis remembered two: one on Wellers Bridge Road, and the other on South Street, just before Squire Road. Squire said, "There were two more in Roxbury Station. They were very small businesses. They did a little bit in each one. Why they did not put up a big building and consolidate them; but they did not do those things in those days. They would rather work for themselves."

And did he remember the Callahan baseball team? "There was a family of nine boys that played ball. And one girl. She was the umpire. I know when they went to New Milford and got beat. They were hard to beat down here on their own field. I went to school with several of them." Lewis reminded him that in one year, just when they were going to go on a barnstorming tour of the United States, one of the boys died. Squire said that one of the boys, the one named Jack, worked on the railroad as a conductor, "but he used to get days off to play ball. He was more of a man than any of them. Some of them weren't much."

And what about the Leatherman? He was another well-known character, who always wore a thick coat made of old leather patches, and who regularly toured the region, accepting hand-outs and food, but slept like a hermit in caves. He eventually died in a cave in New York state. Once, Henry Hurlbut, Lewis' grandfather, saw him standing by a spring on his land. He had taken off his leather coat. And he noticed that underneath it he wore a regular suit. But all his visible clothes were made of leather. It was said that he could stop at three houses and eat three full meals in one afternoon.

To Clayton Squire's parents and other people in Connecticut the Leatherman remained a mystery, although a rich lore had grown around him. No one shed much light on the mystery until 1984, when Sarah and Leroy W. Foote, a couple from Middlebury, who had retraced his itinerary and revisited the places where he stopped and slept, organized a memorial exhibition. They discovered that he spent more than 30 years walking a 365 mile circuit between the Connecticut and Hudson rivers, which took him 34 days to complete. He walked through Danbury, Meriden, Middletown, Saybrook, Stratford and Greenwich and through Armonk, Pound Ridge, and Brewster in New York. His pattern was so regular that housewives along the route knew exactly when to expect him, and had food ready. He was apparently compulsive about his clockwise route and rarely missed a stop. Only once was he late -- during the blizzard of 1888.

"When people saw him coming in the spring, they'd say, "Time to plow." When they saw him in the fall, they'd say, 'Time to shake the carpets,'" Sara Foote, then 81 years old herself, told Stephanie Della Cagna of the "The Hartford Courant" in August 1984. Sarah and Leroy Foote were exploring caves in the region, when they first heard of the Leatherman.

His real name was probably Jules Bourglay, and according to legend, he came from Lyons, France, where he fell in love with a young woman named Marguerite Laron, the daughter of a successful leather merchant. Although Marguerite returned his affection, the father considered him unsuitable as a son-in-law. Bourglay was the son of a woodcarver, several stations below the merchant in social standing. Young Bourglay, however, managed to convince him to let him work at his firm and if he did well to allow him to become a partner and then let him have the hand of his daughter. In a short time, he was doing very well, buying and selling leather. But just when things seemed to working out, the leather market crashed. Bourglay lacked the experience to handle the volatile market and wound up having bought too much leather, and forced his prospective father-in-law into bankruptcy.

The shock and deep disappointment forced him into a mental institution for several years, before he emigrated clandestinely to America. He made his appearance, clad in a patchwork of leather, in Connecticut, at about the time of the Civil War. At first women were afraid of him. They scooped up their children whenever he appeared, ran inside and bolted their doors. But the Leatherman would simply walk up and point his finger to his mouth. Gradually they grew used to him and his regular appearances every 34 days. If a meal was not set out for him at the proper time, he would leave that house and never return to it.

One man, Chauncey Hotchkiss of Forestville, once followed him in his horse carriage to learn more about his route. About two thirds of his circuit, 240 miles, was in Connecticut; another 120 miles was in New York. At the end of every ten-mile daily trek, the Leatherman would start a fire in one of the 34 caves he had fashioned into shelters, and light one of his homemade pipes. His tobacco came from cigar butts. A group of rowdies once tried to get him drunk to get him to talk. The incident served Dick Gackenbach as the story of a boy's book, The Leatherman, Seabury Press 1977. He reacted with neither anger nor pleasure to the frequent jeers and cruel pranks he had to suffer. "He had a wandering, innocent and at the same time intelligent look," A.B. Stewart wrote of him in a pamphlet for the Globe Museum, "He furtively watched every move as if afraid of something."

Around 1887 a raw sore on the Leatherman's lip appeared and gradually spread. He began to crumble his bread and soaked it in coffee. He placed a small piece of leather over the sore before he drank. Some people viewed the sore with alarm. In 1888 they had him arrested and taken to a hospital in Hartford, but he did not want to stay. Authorities apparently realized that they had no legal right to detain him, and he was released. He later showed up in North Haven. He was a pitiful sight as he hobbled down the road. His leather suit became even heavier as death drew near. Sometime around the middle of March in 1889 he walked into the woods near Dell farm in Briarcliff, New York, and he was found dead by two young lovers on an afternoon stroll through the woods on March 24th, 1889.

George Sutton, the coroner wrote, "Leather Man's lower jaw eaten away by cancer supposed to be cause of death. His emaciated body was dressed in a burial gown and he was buried in Sparta Cemetery, near Ossining, New York. The leather coat was promptly put on display in John L. Birdsall's cigar shop in Ossining. Afterwards it was exhibited in museums in New York City, and then, as mysteriously as the Leather Man himself, it disappeared." On May 16th, 1953 a plaque dedicated to the Leatherman was put up on the cemetery, which reads: "The Final Resting Place of JULES BOURGLAY of Lyons, France, "The Leather Man." Who regularly walked a 365 mile route through Westchester and Connecticut from the Connecticut River to the Hudson living in caves in the years 1858-1889."

Another old clip kept by the Hurlbuts sheds even more light on the mystery of the Leatherman's lonely life. James F. Rodgers, writing the

"New Haven Register" sometime after 1885, wrote that he too followed the Leatherman and even got him to talk a little:

"I waited until he was a few rods further on, then started out after him. Soon he left the dusty highway for the shady protection of some adjacent maples, and shortly afterwards turned into a gateway leading up to the porch of a great white farmhouse. Here he paused a moment; then gently tapping the door with his staff, seated himself on a bench to wait the result.

"Soon a quiet, motherly looking lady, who has attended to his summons for a quarter of a century, opened the door and looked pityingly on the wanderer as he placed his great rough hand upon his lips and muttered the words, 'Eat, eat, eat.!' Then disappearing, she returned laden with dishes which had been thoughtfully laid aside for him. In silence he ate his meal; then placing the remainder in his bag and taking up his staff, he was again ready for the road.

"Summoning up my courage, I stepped out with him, and accompanied him up the street. For nearly a mile I walked beside him, but he continued silent as the stones in his pathway. At times he looked inquiringly at me, but in no other way deigned to acknowledge my presence. Finally, as we reached the summit of Plant's hill, I ventured to speak, and looking him full in the face said, 'Leathery, this is a hard life of yours.'

"He gradually lifted his eyes until they met mine, then in a faint, sad voice answered, 'Yes, yes.'

"'But,' I continued, 'will you not tell me why you lead such a life?' He stood still a moment, and looked absently at me, then slowly shook his head and went on. I saw it was useless to question further, and stood watching him until he disappeared beyond the hilltop.

"He is about the average height, though very compactly built. His thick dark hair straggles from under the great leather cap in tangled confusion. His face is swarthy and nearly obscured by a short, coarse beard and overhanging eyebrows, in whose shadows lurk his keen, grey eyes with a piercing glitter. His nose and mouth are well shaped, though the other parts of the face somewhat destroy their symmetry. His leather garments, from which he takes the name of the Leather Man, are made up wholly of boot tops, which have been from time to time patched and mended until scarcely a vestige of the original texture remains visible. His shoes are not unlike those worn by the peasants of Norway and Sweden, though far more cumbersome; over his shoulder he carries a large leather bag, and in his hand a hickory staff surmounted by a wooden ball. Such is a faulty picture of this unknown man, who for nearly thirty years, has excited the curiosity of all, and who is now more than ever encircled in mystery.

"On April 2, 1885 I saw him toiling up the road, bent under his burden, and hurried to the farm-house with a firm resolution to try and entice him into conversation with me. 'Leathery,' I said, 'will you please tell me your name?' 'Yes,' he answered, 'it is E-zek.' I then asked him if he was tired, and again came that melancholy, 'Yes.' 'Do you wish to go back to France?' I asked. He shuddered perceptibly and answered, 'No! No! No!'

"I knew from the little I had seen that it was an easy matter to arouse his suspicious nature by questioning, and decided not to trouble him by other queries until he had known me better, and as I turned to leave him at the gate, he extended me his brawny hand, which I shook heartily, and felt at last that old Leathery had taken me into his confidence.

"I awaited the next arrival with anxious anticipation, and just thirty-two days afterward, I saw him trudging up the road. I went out to him and was pleased to see he had not forgotten me, for he came forward with outstretched hand. and smiled when I took it. 'Come Leathery, and have something to eat with me,' I said, and pointed to my house. He shifted his bag to his other shoulder and directed his cumbersome bulk toward the gate as I led the way. I could not get him to enter the house, so telling him to sit down on the porch, went and brought him some food. He ate for a few minutes, but upon the appearance of two or three more on the scene, manifested signs of uneasiness, and taking me by the arm pointed toward the great farm-house. I went with him and waited until he had eaten, then started up the road, walking beside him. He willingly answered the few questions which my limited knowledge of French would allow me to put to him. I asked him where he was going, and he told me that 'in a little time to his cave.' Again he extended his hand, as at Plant's bridge he turned to leave the road, and said, 'Adieu! I will see you again.'

"I hurried home, and after putting up a little lunch, and arousing the dormant ambition of my friend 'Jock,' we started for the Leatherman's cave. He had gone by way of the railroad, and I knew it was customary for him to sit down and rest for some time. I reached the cave in early afternoon, and he had not arrived. It was now nearing 3 o'clock, and every moment I expected to hear the crackle of the underbrush foretell the coming of the old man, and soon I heard the long wished for crackling. Yes; without a doubt, the Leatherman was coming, and if he possessed any nature, he would show it. I lay still as dead and told Jock to do the same, and ere many moments had elapsed, I saw through my screen of boughs the well-known features of old Leathery. He came direct to the cave, carrying in his hand a black tin pail. When he reached the entrance he listened for what seemed to be twenty minutes, then threw down his sack and put the pail inside.

"He drew a long breath as he seated himself on a rock and looked about him; and I confess I felt rather uncomfortable when I saw him put his hand around under his coat and, taking therefrom an axe, deliberately put his hand on the other side and bring forth the handle. This he fitted into it, and after two or three raps upon a stone, proceeded to chop a prostrate tree trunk into short pieces for his fire. 'Now Jock,' I said, 'keep close to me,' and slipped out from under my ambuscade. The old man heard the first crackle, which betrayed our presence, and in all my life I never beheld a person more surprised. He looked at Jock, then looked at my crutches and myself in utter astonishment, until I shouted, 'Hello, Leathery!' Then, coming forward, he shook my hand heartily. I bade Jock take the axe, which the old man rather reluctantly gave him, and proceed with the chopping.

"'Now Leathery,' I said, as he placed a great flat stone for me to sit on, 'will you sit still?' He answered, 'Yes,' and seated himself beside me; and as I endeavored to transfer his rugged picture to my paper, I asked him these questions:

"'How long have you been tramping?'

"'Twenty-seven years,' he answered in his broken English.

"'How old are you?' I went on.

"He muttered in a low voice, 'Sixty-Eight.'

"'And are you not tired?'

"'No. I am sorry.' As he dwelt upon the words I saw every limb tremble.

"'Sorry for what?' I queried. 'What should you be sorry for?'

'For much. For much.' He sighed and bent his head upon his hand.

'Will you tell me why you wear this leather suit?'

"He slowly raised his head and mournfully repeated the words, 'I don't know, but I am sorry.'

"'Did you make it?'

"'Yes, a long time ago.'

"'But,' I reasoned, 'why do you not throw it off, and live among your fellow men?'

"'No, no; never.'

"The old man raised his voice and every nerve seemed strained to pronounce the words. I did not break the silence that followed, but worked steadily until the gathering dusk closed in about us. He arose after awhile and bending over my shoulder looked down on the rude sketch I was making.

"'Ah, from France,' he said as his wary eye caught sight of the crayon pencil in my hand upon which was stamped with some Parisian advertisement. 'Yes,' I answered, though my conscience smote me for so doing, as I am confident the pencil was no more made in Paris than the rock I sat on. It had grown chilly, and I told Jock to light the fire; but the old man heard my request and hastened to comply. The Leatherman seated himself on a stone near me, and, as Jock filled the great pipe for him, I ventured to break the monotony.

"'Leathery are you not going to tell me something more?' I asked, and placed my hand upon his shoulder. He reached his hand into a crevice and drew therefrom a leather wallet, and, untying the fastening, drew out a large paper and handed it to me. I unfolded it, and by the aid of the firelight, saw it was completely covered with curious characters, written in pencil and red chalk, and with scrupulous regularity. 'What are these?' I asked with surprise.

"He waved his hand in a circle about his head, by which I concluded he meant his route; and these strange characters were indeed records of his journeys, for he took from the wallet sheet after sheet written in the same manner. I asked him for the one I held, and he said, 'Yes, keep it.' He then took out another, though smaller wallet, which contained a pair of scissors, some thread, a bone comb, and a piece of cloth. He took the latter in his hand and slowly unwinding it disclosed a worn old French prayer-book, and a rosary with a small crucifix attached, before which he reverentially bowed his head.

"The thought flashed upon me that he was a religious monomaniac living a life of terrible penance. I became very eager to question him farther, and I am afraid he perceived my excitement, for when I asked him to tell me about his life, he sorrowfully shook his head and whispered. 'Not tonight-not tonight; but when you come again.' Then, taking off his cap and kneeling down, he placed the crucifix in the crevice before him, and opening his prayerbook, bent over the firelight.

"I did not want to excite his ill will, and knew that he now wished to be left alone, so, taking his hand, I bade him goodnight. Coming out into the darkness, we groped our way down the hillside and through the hemlocks, pausing only when we reached the open lot at the head of the lake.

"Poor, lonely wanderer! No companion, no home; naught but the sighing pines and silent stars of heaven. Years have come and gone and he has shared their sorrow for with him pleasure is unknown. Let no taunting tongue molest him, for the Leatherman will soon be known only in memories of the past and possibilities of the future. Should any of my readers visit his lonely hovel, let no sacrilegious hand be raised to hurry the crumbling pile to its destruction, for I look hopefully forward toward the coming night, when under its scanty shelter I shall see his dark features tinted by the fitful firelight, and hear him repeat in his low sad voice The Leather Man's Story."

Squire talked briefly about his marriage to a woman from New Haven in 1904, a close friend of Lewis' mother Clara. Together with several other women of the same age, they founded what they called the 'Shepaug Club' of Roxbury, a floating gathering of young women at each others' homes. Squire's wife's maiden name was Bertha Platt. She died very early in life, and Squire married again, but much later.

They also recalled the Sunday Picnics that used to be held in the summer at Roxbury Falls. Squire recounted, "Yes, I sold the ice cream, bananas, peanuts, and candy at every picnic, after I was big enough to make ice cream." He stored it in barrels packed with ice in milk cans, and said, "We done a good business there." People came to these picnics from all over. There were a few hundred people each time, "and they always had to have their candy and ice cream." Squire used to stay up all night making it. "Charley Crofut, George Crofut's son, and I did all the work. We built the stands and had a tent."

He then asked Lewis whether he ever knew that the Harrison's had a boat with treads on it. "They used to take passengers in the dam for ten cents. That was Oakie and Grover Harrison's father." Grover worked for Squire as a carpenter later, for twenty years. "He was working for me when I fixed your house. The last job he ever did, he was working for your brother. One morning he did not come to work. I went down there and the door was locked." Grover was dead.

Squire also remembered Ben Preston's store - one of the two mentioned in Jeremah Decker's essay - in the old toll house on Oxford Turnpike, now Route 67, on the southern exit of town. "Ben Preston had it before Ed Preston had it," he said, but seemed to remember little more.

Lewis also wanted to know about the fishing - whether it was true that shad still ran all the way to Roxbury Falls in his youth. Squire said, "Tom Tyrell and my grandfather went down there in what was called the 'dipping hole.' It's the same hole where we fish today. They got shad before they built the dam at Shelton. They used to take an ox cart down there and get a half a barrel full in two or three hauls." They used nets. "The shad came up to spawn just as they do in Avon," he said, "we passed them around town," which means they sold them.

Lewis' father once wrote, "in my father's day shad were plentiful in the Shepaug and so cheap that if the frugal housewife was cooking one for her family and a neighbor appeared in sight, the shad took an ignominious flip over the backlog, and something more in keeping with their station in life was forthcoming." Today they are considered something of a delicacy, especially when fried with bacon on a board propped up next to a fire of maple wood.

Lewis also wanted to know about the location of the former Baptist Church, which was supposed to have stood on North Road near Moose Horn Brook, just past Wilbur Smith's house. "I do not remember that," Squire said. The church was torn down in the early 19th century, before our story begins. Town records were interrupted around 1800, a lifetime before Squire's time.

Next they talked about a house on Mallory Road which had the date 1712 on the fire place. The owners had put it over the door later, even though the town's historian William Cothren said the first houses in Roxbury were built in 1713.

Squire did remember that Roxbury at one time had three post offices: one was in the Center at the Hurlburt store, another at Roxbury Station, and a third at Roxbury Falls. There were also three creameries. "I worked at one as a carpenter," Squire said, "I remember those well. I worked for Mitchell. I was old enough to do carpentry work. The one at Roxbury Station was the biggest. It was run by someone named Helmut, whom we nicknamed Helluva Man."

Lewis then asked him where they went, if they could not get something in Roxbury. "New Milford," Squire said, without pausing, and if New Milford did not have it, they went to Danbury. A lot of new families had come to Roxbury before 1949. But then the railroad stopped running. "We had quite a population when the silica mill was operating," he remembered, "and the three garnet, and the quarry at Mine Hill. You see, Mine Hill alone employed about 145 people. And there were about 140 down here at the silica mill." The people working the Silica mine, "were entirely Polish, except the foreman." They went into farming afterwards. The Dooleys were also of Irish descent. But they had come to Roxbury several generations before most of the others. They were one of the older families in Roxbury. As elsewhere it took a little time for the other Irish to breach the social barrier Yankees of English descent erected against them.

"When this railroad come through in 1872, a lot of people moved here at that time. They were working on the road. The Bewes family, and the Collins Family, they were English," he said. Lewis recalled that the Collinses were excellent metal workers, and did all the metal work in the interior of the Episcopal church.

When he wanted to know how the older families had reacted to the newcomers, especially with regard to their religion and the town business, Squire dodged the question again. "Way back," he said, "we had no Catholic church." For a while, "The Catholics went to Washington to go to church." (But Roxbury's Roman Catholic Church was built before Washington's.)

And how did the countryside look in those days? "Right down on Route 67, on the left hand side, where the trees in the woods are this large," - he showed 16 inches with his hands - "they used to mow that land." The same was true of the left hand side of Painter Hill Road from Toplands farm to Good Hill Road. It was all pasture, and "all over town it was the same way."

The Shepaug Railroad

A few people in Roxbury may still recall the Shepaug Railroad mentioned by Clayton Squire. One man, Ralph Mumford, who worked on the track as a young man, took a ride on it shortly before it was closed down for good. Forty years later he could still recite the stops and sights from Hawleyville all the way to Washington Depot. Here's how he remembered it:

"We start from Hawleyville. My wife and I are there. We're waiting for the engineer. They've got to slow down and get off to throw the switch to get off the main line. When the train goes by the switch I ask the conductor; 'Is there a chance of getting a ride up to Litchfield?' He says, 'Well, you look like a railroad guy.' I had my railroad jacket and hat on. I snuck in quick and off we went.

"First, it's just up and through the back woods. There was not too much to see until we got to the Housatonic River. There the train slowed down to get across a real big bridge. It was pretty high and pretty long, and the train made quite a lot of noise going across. Then, on the other side of the bridge, we started to pick up a little grade as we got nearer to Roxbury Falls. Then you could hear it puffing a little bit. We did not have too much of a freight train on there. I guess we probably had about ten or twelve cars, which was a pretty good load for that line. We did have a couple of coal cars on it. They made a little bit of weight, and some lumber. The engine was always more or less a back line engine.

"When we got near Roxbury Falls, you could really hear her lay it on a little bit. The speed limit, I remember, was 15 MPH to 20 MPH. You couldn't go more than that. The tracks were not in very good shape, either. About one out of six ties were good. One out of four was fair. And the rest you could take your foot and kick 'em, see. The bolts and the plates were all loose. Between the slack, the bearings and the engine and the slack in the track, we were going like this all the time. And if you're back in the caboose - all the way to the back - it was one on top of that. Center pin was gone. Of course, all these guys are on the retiring line with only two or three more years to go: the engineer, the fireman and the brakeman.

"At that time Roxbury Falls was still pretty quaint. It had all dirt roads and the old bridges were still there. Part of the old wooden dam for the factory was there. The foundations of that were still there. The smokery and creamery were still there. In fact, the old boiler was still inside. They still had ice stored in the creamery. And they still had the old pond out back. You had a real dirt crossing at Roxbury Falls. In Roxbury Falls we slowed down to about five miles an hour, and blew the whistle like a son of a gun.

"A lot of the guys that go through don't look, you know. They only ran that train every other day, and that did not include Saturdays and Sundays. It did not include holidays, and if something happened, if the weather was real bad, we wouldn't bother for a few days.

"The next interesting thing out of Roxbury Falls, the track follows the river. In those days they did not do everything with poured concrete like we do now. So they had these huge big, granite slabs, about four or five feet thick, and ten or twelve feet long. They were all laid up and made a terrific wall right next to the river. They slowed down for that, too, because if you went down that wall you'd go down about 60 feet. He told us to put a few extra ties in at this spot. But that part of the line was interesting, because we went up past old Pop Ognan's farm, which we played in when I was a kid. (It is now Craigmyles'). You could always distinguish his place by the little hill with the green pines on it. The next place was the Erbacher's Farm. He was a big dairy man, just like old man Ognan. He had a couple of grate crossings, and there was also a place where they used to cross with the farm wagons, a shallow place in the river where the banks sloped down.

"After you got by his place, the track followed the river real close again and slowed down for that, because there is a good roll down into the river. Not too far behind that we came up on the Dickinson's farm, and you got a nice view of the fields. Then you start to come into Roxbury Station. And he would blow the whistle for Route 67. There is a nice, rounded arch stone bridge just before you get to 67, and that is still there.

"Then of course, when you come into Roxbury Station it's a little scenic. Maude Ognan and her husband had a grocery store there. And they came out for the train. He made a switch of a few cars, so we were there several minutes.

"But as soon as we got out of Roxbury Station, we followed the river a little bit, and followed Mine Hill. You could make out the smelter. Years before there were sidings in there and you could bring out the iron ore. That was a big thing for the railroad. Then, there was the big quarry just above that. You went real close to the quarry. You could hear the engines echo back into the quarry. That would bounce back and we could pick it up right again in the caboose. Even though it was low there it was still pulling a little bit. He did not have the ten cars. He left off a couple in Roxbury Station. At the same time we left off two longer ones. We left off a couple of empties. Evidently, it was easy for him to switch them there. Some of the stone that built some of the bridges came out of there.

"After that it was Judds Bridge Farm. That was a quaint spot in those times, because the railroad came in right through the middle of the farm. You had a grate crossing, and you had the little Judds Bridge. That old bridge is still there. We blew the whistle pretty good for that point. Almost everywhere we went there was somebody out waving. I guess they knew it was pretty near the end for the steam engines. They knew this railroad was not going to be there much longer. You went right through the middle of the barns. The smoke bounced right off the houses. The farm tenants' house used to be so close. You were still on the west side of the river.

"The first crossing came after Judds Bridge Farm at the big bridge. It wasn't as big as the one across the Housatonic, but it is a pretty good size bridge. (A one-time train station at Judds Bridge is still there as a residence.) But that station was one of the first to go. After crossing the bridge you went only a very short distance and you were into the tunnel. You'd really hear the engine bellow through that. The tunnel is longer than most people realize. It's got a bend in it even.

"My wife was following us in the car. She would toot the horn at every crossing. The guy in the caboose would say, 'Hey, good looking little red head.'

"'That's my wife.'

"'Pretty young. You look pretty young yourself. How old are you?'

"'Twenty-one.'

"'Well, I guess she's going to follow us all the way.' Once you got out of the tunnel, it was pretty wild country all along the river.

"Then we got into Washington Depot. Just outside was the prettiest railroad crossing anywhere in the state of Connecticut at that time. It was a little wooden bridge there, and you had an old fashioned iron sign on a wooden post. You could hear the river gushing past below. In Washington Depot they stopped and put on water. This engine leaked more water than it used to. We were going so slow going around all the corners, you could hear the squeaking in the flanges coming up through there. It followed every bend in the river. They just gouged out a little piece between the river and the mountain to get by. So they had real sharp turns, and you got worn flanges, and you got worn axles, and you got bad bushings, and you got tracks that are a mile out. They look like an inch-worm. Some looked like spaghetti. The wheels are bouncing and ricocheting off that. They whole train is whipping in all directions all the time, one car this way, and another that way.

"A bunch of kids might be standing near the track. So he would open up the valve mechanism on the pistons that would allow the steam to blow out. We just clobbered those kids with steam. They thought it was great, but it scared the heck out of them. And then somebody rang the fire engine bell.

"There wasn't too much in Washington, except there was the old Washington Supply, which still had its coal silos up there. In fact, we left off a couple of hoppers full of coal for them. Washington Supply was also stocking up on the lumber while the railroad was still there. They were still getting better freight rates, and there was a lot of talk that the railroad would be abandoned the next year.

"Then we headed into Morris. We had a big, long swamp to go through, so you could not see too much. The next big thing was pulling into Litchfield. You did not realize you were in Litchfield until you were there. The interesting part of Litchfield was the turn-table. We came into the yard. They'd pull down, back-switched off and got rid of the cars. They left off three or four full cars of coal, couple of cars of lumber. And he had four or five empty cars to come back. He'd switch the engine around on the turn-table. I helped him hand-turn it. There were rollers in the center and rollers all around it. It was so well balanced that you did not need any gears. He let me turn the engine all by myself. Once you started it you could keep it going. It was just like pushing barges."

Mumford's memories of seeing the train go by when he was still a boy are just as vivid. "When I was a kid it was real quaint," he said, "They did not yet have spray to kill the weeds on the railroad bed. It was all hand cut. They had it all hand-trenched so the water would drain out and the track would not get washed out. In the winter they had a plow car they put in front of the engine.

"What I used to do every time I heard the whistle at the Roxbury Falls creamery crossing, I used to run up the hill. Erbacher's Hill we called it. It is the highest point on his property. On top of the hill there was a 75 foot pine tree. It must have been about two and a half feet in diameter on the bottom. It was just like a ladder all the way up. I used to go up that thing. I bet it did not take me more than two minutes. My father, when he was a young kid, had cut the top off. He had a little platform. You could sit there and watch that train come up, and you could hear it huffing and puffing out of Roxbury Falls. There was a straightaway right behind Erbacher's. Most of the time he had the head lights on. And then you could stay there and hear him blow the whistle again before he pulled into Roxbury Station. Once in a great while, when the wind was right, you could hear him blowing from Judds Bridge. That impressed me more than anything else, when I was a kid. I don't know what it was. My whole life ambition was someday to drive a steam engine to Litchfield and back. The nearest thing I got to it was a ride up in the caboose."

From a tape by Peter Frisbee and Wayne Piskura

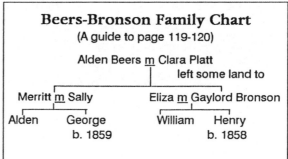

Beers-Bronson Family Chart
(A guide to page 119-120)

Alden Beers m Clara Platt
left some land to

Merritt m Sally   Eliza m Gaylord Bronson

Alden   George   William   Henry
b. 1859   b. 1858

LEFT:
Clayton Squire, who once built a store-house without any windows or doors.

Clayton as a boy in foreground. Stepmother and father in front of house still standing on South Street opposite Squire Road, now home of Charles M. Squire.

Courtesy Charles M. Squire

V.
The Czar

The most influential man of the past 50 years in Roxbury was Allen S. Hurlburt, the town's First Selectman from 1926 to 1955. Like Norman Hurlbut he was proud of its Yankee heritage, and gave much of himself to the town. He left no written record of his tenure, but it still bears his imprint.

Normally Roxbury changed its First Selectmen as often as it did Congregational ministers. He was the exception. Allen S. Hurlburt was born in 1876, the year of the Centennial, as the second son of George W. Hurlburt, who had the largest dry goods store in town. Allen died of old age in 1964. Like Norman Hurlbut, the town clerk for more than 45 years, Allen was usually nominated by both parties, although Allen was a Republican and Norman a Democrat.

Long before his death Allen Hurlburt had become known as "Mr. Roxbury" and to some outsiders as The Czar. For 29 years, little happened that he had not initiated and nothing without his approval. He brought the sleepy, farming town into the 20th century. He introduced zoning, before the state government began to enforce it, paved Roxbury's roads, persuaded people to accept electrification of their homes, revived a volunteer fire department, expanded the Booth Free School, and helped the town library by an astute investment of its small endowment.

In 1942, when the library had only $3,900 in liquid assets, he persuaded the board to invest it in stock of the Connecticut General Life Insurance Co., saying his brother Everett knew the officers and they "were good men and hard workers." One hundred and fifty shares were bought for $26 a share. Seven years later, the company declared a 100% stock dividend. Four years later the 300 shares were worth $105 a share, and the library sold half of them for $15,750, about four times what it had invested, and still had 150 shares left, worth again as much.

His greatest effort, perhaps, went into surfacing the town's roads. According to his obituary in the "Waterbury Republican," it was said that "When he became First Selectman, the town owned one horse-drawn road scraper and had no town road surfaced. At the time of his retirement, the town had few dirt roads remaining and thousands of dollars worth of highway equipment." In 1986 his daughter, Sarah Houck, recalled, "He would have breakfast at about 6 o'clock in the morning and go -- when the men came to the town barn at 7 o'clock -- check on what they were going to do for the day. Then, at about 11 o'clock or 2 o'clock in the afternoon, go again to see what was doing. They had like two or three workers. Of course, they were getting some money from the state, but he had to make sure it was well spent, that people were not leaning on shovels and goofing off. But in a kindly way."

Allen and his older brother Everett both went to Yale University, after preparing at the Hopkins Grammar School in New Haven, but had their early schooling in Roxbury's Center School one-room and its Select School. Allen was a member of Yale's wrestling team. He had studied chemistry at Sheffield Scientific School, and during World War I he served as a captain in the chemical warfare department of the U.S. Army. Later, after some years with the General Chemical Co., he joined Everett at the J.B. Williams Company, a Glastonbury soap manufacturer, where he specialized in developing scents and perfumes. The company was very successful with the Aqua Velva after shave lotion Everett had invented. Everett eventually became the chief executive, but Allen left in 1923, then 49 years old, and stayed in Roxbury.

Sarah Houck was the fourth generation Hurlburt to live in the large house on the corner of South and Main Streets with her husband Seth. When they retired in 1986 they sold it, along with eight acres of land, to the town for $600,000. Before they left the town, she told us: "My father came back to Roxbury in 1923, when my grandfather was in his last illness, to help his mother and thought he would stay a year. He spent the rest of his life here. At first he worked for General Chemical, I think in Brooklyn. At J.B. Williams, after the war, he had his own laboratory. He sold his laboratory in East Hartford, where I was born, and we came out here to be with my grand-mother.

"Three years after we came out, they asked him to be First Selectman. He stayed because he loved the town so much. Saturday afternoons we always went for walks. According to the regulations the Selectman should walk (the town's) lines every five years. This had been ignored for many years. My father did it with joy. He would ask the other Selectmen from neighboring towns such as Bridgewater, 'wouldn't you like to walk the lines with me.' Also those from Southbury, Woodbury, and Washington. It was pretty rough in those days, up hill, down dale."

Lewis mentioned that they do have markers on them, "but the new officers do not have one idea, where those markers are," she said. "He was concerned about the line. He was also concerned about fire protection. He would put a bucket of water out and say the first fellow who could get the water flowing and turn over the bucket had won the prize, which in those days was five dollars. He was concerned about land use, and that is how they got into zoning. His brother came out from Glastonbury, saying they had zoning there, and they discussed it and got legal advice. It went in 1932."

"And did he ever continue farming. My mother would be out with some of her flossy friends and Grace Butler would say to him, 'Get along. Don't speak to us.' He had the eight acres around the house, where he had some apple trees planted, and asparagus, and hay for the horses. On the hill (up Ranny Hill Road) there are 63 or 64 acres. This is where he had the apple orchard. There was also some land there that was not useful for growing anything, so he put red pines in. That was fine until the root disease came. He even had a stand to sell his apples at the foot of the hill. Also pears. He would get up like three o'clock in the morning to pick his apples and get them to Seymour to sell them. That was the closest place for wholesaling.

"During prohibition my father was not entirely dry. He did not like buying the bootleg, so he planted his own grapes and made his own wine. The orchard had grapes, peaches, cherries, he tried everything. He hired people to help him. He used a horse drawn sprayer." Lewis estimated that he probably harvested 10,000 bushels of apples a year.

"A childhood memory I have," Sarah Houck said, "was the fragrance of those apples in our basement. He built racks for them. We would eat Macs as long as they would last, and then go into others." It was never a profitable enterprise, however. "In his later days, he would say, 'you know, my one regret is that I could not make the hill pay.'"

Lewis recalled that when he finally gave it up, because he was too old, Allen let him have his sprayer and said, "you give it a try. You may make a go of it, I know I couldn't." Lewis also recalled seeing him up there late at night on an old International tractor, "it was one of the very first ones out. It had a platform on it with a steering wheel. He'd stand up behind the steering wheel with no hat on and he'd be going up and down those rows with the dust flying. I never saw him sitting down by the wheel on that tractor. He was always standing up."

Sarah Houck agreed that it was in the early 1930s that people started to come in from New York, and buy weekend houses in Roxbury. Asked how he responded to them, she said, "He welcomed them. He would say to my mother, 'there are new people in somebody's house and we should go and see them.' I never heard my father say, 'let's stop these people coming.' I think he felt there was strength coming from these people. For instance, George DeVoe, who was up at the Judds Bridge Dairy, was interested in the town's development. He was interested in the Republican town committee. He gave of his talents to the town. John Gerald gave of his talents. So were some of these people who did indeed give to the town." She said this in response to a remark by Lewis, who complained that few of the newcomers did any volunteer work and left it to the natives to keep the town in its rural character. But he agreed, "I probably broadened my view of things more from those people than any other way."

One of Allen Hurlburt's ideas the outsiders certainly supported was the zoning. "They wanted three acres and not have ticky-tacky houses," she said. "He was aware of what we are all aware of, which is that the land will not support many houses close together. He wanted to see it developed in an orderly manner. There were some who resisted the zoning and thought that my father was very unfair to push it and press it upon them." The state did not have any teeth in the law yet until 1954, Lewis remarked. "We had that town hall full one night in the 1940s. We had some of the darndest arguments. We won by 14 votes on whether we would have zoning or not. The point was that the way Al Hurlburt did it was the only way you could do it. He would ask people, who were actually building something, 'you just sign here to show that you are starting a garage.' Some people would respond, 'Damn it, I own this land and you're not going to tell me what I'm going to do with it. People said that these two brothers got together over a Zinfandel wine..." and hatched zoning.

"But there was another thing that Daddy did even before the zoning and maybe even before he became Selectman," Sarah Houck said, "When electricity came through, he had to sell people on the idea of having their house wired. Remember that, Lewis?"

"He and John Butler were working on that one."

"When we first came out here, my mother hated cleaning kerosene lamps. And there were hand pumps in the kitchen. There were so many things that came in my father's time."

They talked of his wife, Julia. "She was a southern lady," her daughter said. Allen Hurlburt had met his wife, the former Julia Barnard, in Ashville, North Carolina, when he was in that town on business, and they were married there in 1916. Pointing to some well-polished brass fenders at the fire place in the parlor, her daughter said, "Stonewall Jackson sat and warmed his feet at that fender. And there was a picture of Sherman's march to the sea in this house, and my mother said she would not come up until that was down." Lewis said, "She gave it to my father."

He also said, "She brought some of the customs of the south. At New Years's every year they would have open house, and it was kind of like the old south."

Allen Hurlburt once told a newspaper reporter that he got the job of First Selectman, "because it's a job not too many people want." It paid only $100 a year, when he first took it, and $1,000 a year in 1955, when he retired.

He became a fixture in it, in part, because he could afford it. He was also known to have helped many people in town financially, providing them with private loans, when they could not raise mortgages from a bank.

Allen's older brother, who outlived him by many years, continued in such eleemosynary acts, after he returned. He was 96 years old when he died. On his 95th birthday the town thanked him officially for his "many contributions," which included, "the community tennis courts, an addition to the Hodge Memorial Library, a sixteen acre parcel of land in the Rocky Mountain-Apple Lane district for future town needs, gifts of trees for the Booth Free School, and an ambulance for the Roxbury Ambulance Association." Everett and the Rev. Walter Downes Humphrey together had started Roxbury's first public library in the back of the town hall in 1896.

Lewis recalled that while his son Gaylord, one of his eight children, was attending Union College, they sometimes found that his tuition had been paid by someone.

While they lived the two brothers were often accused of 'hatching things' between them. Their proposals for improvements were sometimes vociferously opposed. Perhaps people found them a little too patronizing. Everett often had the ideas, but it was Allen's personality and way with people, which allowed them to put them across, Sarah Houck recalled. "He gave of himself, his time and his goods to the town. The town meant as much to him as his family."

Burton Hodge and his son Philo took over his father's store and the Post Office soon after Allen Hurlburt returned. The old building next to his house was removed, and a new store was built at the present location. Burton Hodge had a share in the old store, and even later, Sarah Houck recalled, "They would deliver groceries by sled in the winter and use my father's horses." The store had been in the family 86 years, having been opened in 1850 by Col. George Hurlburt, who still called himself Hurlbut then. After it was removed, a builder named Ralph Woodruff used the old beams to build a new home with it in neighboring Washington, but he kept the original shingle over its door which stated "1850 - Hurlbut's Store." An old newspaper account said that Burton Hodge had worked in the store from the time he was 16 years old until he was 82 years old. He acquired a half interest in the store in 1900 and bought the remainder from Allen Hurlburt in 1923. The store was not moved until 1936. The house into which it was transformed was called "Sundown." It still stands on Route 109 in Washington.

Sarah and Lewis, as they reminisced in her living room about their fathers, also buried an old hatchet between their families. To distinguish himself from the other Hurlbuts, who were still farmers, her grandmother, the wife of George W. Hurlburt, had inserted an 'r' at the end of the name. The family gravestones gave Col. George Hurlbut's name without the 'r' and his son with it, and she had apparently insisted on their two sons using the extra 'r.' This led to a certain amount of ill feeling, although clearly both were descended from common ancestors.

Philo Hodge delivering groceries for Allen Hurlburt's store.

Courtesy of Emeline Hodge

Allen Hurlburt

Everett Hurlburt

VI.
One-Room Schools

Like other New England towns Roxbury had a lot of one-room schoolhouses of which few remain (see map). In his historical essay Norman Hurlbut said that "In any conversation on the subject of education in these modern days, the 'Little Red School-House' seems to be disparaged. But a study of the quality of men who began their education in those little buildings," he insisted, "must convince the searcher that they did turn out men in those days."

When Roxbury's first school-houses were built, or which one was the earliest, he writes, "is hard now to decide. In most cases the land was bought by individuals in the district and the building built later. However, it is likely that the one located in the Center and the one at Weller's Bridge were the first to gather the children to learn their ABC's. The town soon listed their school districts as Center, Weller, Warner's Mill, Burritt, North, Painter Hill and Good Hill. The business of governing the schools was in the hands of a District Committee of one elected person, whose task it was to hire the teachers, attend to the needs of the buildings and to provide the supply of wood to try to have the drafty building made as comfortable as possible.

"The Center School stood on the southerly side of the highway nearly opposite the Warner monument and my father told me that it was moved across the road to its location (now the Episcopal Parish house) while the school was in session. I doubt that much attention was paid to their studies by the scholars.

"The school for Weller District formerly stood just westerly of the River bridge. In those days the road, after crossing the bridge, parted; one branch turned northerly and one southerly forming a triangle, and on this triangle stood the early school house.

"A word picture given to our Roxbury librarian some years ago by an old man, who in his youth was a 'scholar' at the Burritt school, is an interesting description of what our early schools were like: In its early days the building was probably unpainted but later was beautified by a coat of bright yellow paint. Inside the slab benches extended around the walls for the use of the scholars with smaller ones for the little ones and a single desk for the use of those writing lessons. Textbooks were few and with readers and spelling books, geography, and history books the getting of knowledge was a slow and tedious task. However, if a student showed ability in some subject he was not bound to the class but would go ahead on his own with the teacher's help.

"Generally for the winter term the committee looked for a male teacher as a female might not be able to cope with the men-grown boys that could be spared from the farm to attend school in the winter months. In those days the adage, 'Spare the rod and spoil the child' was vigorously observed. Schoolmaster Canfield, it is said, made it a practice to chastise the entire school every Saturday on the presumption that each child had undoubtedly transgressed in some undetected manner and deserved punishment.

"The schools were visited yearly by a man elected by the town and styled 'School Visitor.' The day the School Visitor came was a trying day for the teacher, unless the children were on their good behavior.

"The cash the teacher received would look small in this day of high wages. Sometimes it was not more than three or four dollars a week. Even at the turn of this century, six dollars a week was the usual wage, and when a teacher paid three dollars for board, what was left did not go far toward providing for a trousseau. At first the teacher was expected to board around, perhaps a week at each family for each pupil sent to school.

"About 1850 Reverend Foote, the Episcopal clergyman, taught what was called a Select School. At first, his class assembled in the basement of the Episcopal Rectory. There students who desired could take studies further advanced than what could be had in the common schools.

"The scholars of those days, on their way to school, were not burdened with a lot of books. I have a textbook of the time of my great-grandfather. It is about five inches by three and can be held between the thumb and finger. In it are all the subjects the pupil needed: arithmetic, geography, history, and so on. Another is entitled Elements of Useful Knowledge."

This is where Norman Hurlbut ended his reminiscence. We managed to take it a little further by interviewing one of the last women to teach at a one-room school in Roxbury. Her name is Mary Pokrywka and the interview took place at her home on New Milford Road near Sentry Hill Road in the spring of 1985.

First we asked what was taught at these schools and she replied: "They had a curriculum. It was a printed curriculum, which we more or less followed. The standard first, second and third grades were like city schools in teaching and learning of reading, writing and arithmetic. After the fourth or fifth grade we would double the fifth and sixth and seventh and eighth as far as the Social Studies curriculum, which would be

History and Geography. One year we followed the sixth grade curriculum, and then that group would follow the seventh grade next. So every two years you changed. That way you had fewer classes in the day.

"And you had about 15 to 20 minutes of individual class instruction on each subject, and the children would work alone or in groups together. Sometimes the older children would help the younger ones, which was very helpful."

Did the children do their homework in school? "Right. And what was also very good about that was that if the youngster had been out sick for several weeks and might have missed a certain amount of arithmetic, the following year, the teacher, knowing what he had missed, would be able to get him back into the fold. Or if a student had not got the full knowledge that he should have, even in Reading, they could bring him or her in and work with the group below them or the group above them."

How many students did you have in a School? "I always taught at the same one: Warner's Mill, down on the southern end of town. I taught there for two years. I taught for many more years in Bloomfield, and later in the regular big school up here, the Booth School. And then I taught in New Milford in the last seven years. The stint in the one-room school was my first. It was in 1931 to 1934. I was then 19 years old. I had come from Brooklyn. I went to Danbury Normal School, which was a two-year course for teachers. They had closed the Teacher Training School down in Brooklyn, and I had spent a couple of years at Stamford, Connecticut, and my first year in high school. A couple of girls I knew from Stamford were going up to Danbury. That was during the Depression. One did not get to go everywhere one wanted. So I applied and was accepted with the stipulation that I would teach for at least two years in Connecticut. In 1934 they added another year for preparation, and I went back, after they closed the Warner's Mill School and took the third year. And then I ended up in Bloomfield for two years."

What was it like suddenly to step into one of these little one-room schools? "At that time you were sent out to get training in rural schools. That's what we called them. There were two in Danbury and they were connected with the Normal School. Highway 84 goes past where one of them stood: Mill Plain. And there was one called Miry Brook. So I had done a month's training before coming here, but they had a coal stove in that school. The first time I ever made a wood fire was down at Warner's Mill school house. But I learned quickly and always had plenty of heat."

What was it like in the mornings when you opened the door? "Well, you walked into that entry. Most schools were similar to mine. First, I had to bring the drinking water. That's another thing. Teachers always brought it out. You did not have apartments like you have today. You did not get paid enough to have an apartment. So I had to bring the water from the house across from the town hall. That's where I boarded. It was Mrs. Mary Barnes' house. I used one of those big insulated jugs. The well that had been down by the school had been contaminated when they built the road as far as the school. The state would not allow us to use it. We could only use it for washing our hands. But you could not drink it.

"The kids had rows of hooks, and at the end of the entry was a big box that we kept the wood in. The oldest boy who could have built a fire was brought to school by car from the other side of town. There were six kids, who could have built it, but half the other kids would have been there, before they got there, so I had to get down early and build the fire. When it was really cold I could sometimes go down at ten o'clock at night and pile it up with some wood. I had a car, at first the Whippet and then a Ford Coupe."

Lewis then asked her to tell the story about the trouble she had making it to school one day. She said, "You'd go down a hill. There was a young boy. I taught his sister. And the boy went up to the high school, which was then the Booth School. Those people had a chauffeur. The chauffeur dropped Anne off at school and started up the road. After a little while he came back and asked, 'Did you stay here all night?' And I said, 'No, what makes you think that?' He said, 'I can't see you up the road, and I can't see your tracks coming down.' I did not realize how bad it was. In those days there was no snow plow. Everybody had chains. I had slid down, you might say. I had the chains in the back of the car. The state road men came down after lunch, around one o'clock. They saw I had no chains on the car, and they stopped and came in and wanted to know if I wanted to have my chains on. So I said, 'Sure, go ahead.' Otherwise I never would have made it up the hill again."

But how was it that some children were driven to school by chauffeurs in those days? "Well, not all were. There was a polio epidemic in New York City at the time. And the Murklands were going to stay up, because they did not want to take their youngsters back into the city. Then there were some other people from New York, I forget their names, but they lived just across from Clayton Squire's house. They had two youngsters. They did not want to go back to New York, either. It was in 1931. So there were four extra youngsters right in that area. I had about twenty in the class. They went from seven to fourteen in their ages. Fanny was 15 but she was really over age. I had no five-year-olds. I had second grade, but no first-graders."

At the age of 19 how did she manage to control a room full of children. "You know," she said, "I'll tell you this story. You never had too many problems. They were there from nine in the morning to three-thirty in the afternoon. And in the wintertime you really did not go out." Lewis interjected, "She had the older kids teaching the younger kids. So everyone was busy," to which Mary Pokrywka added, "They felt responsible." She said, "I still say that if the kids today had the same back-up as we had, you would not have so many problems." What she meant by back-up was, "The parents would say, you know, 'You just do what's right.' Mrs. Wagner told her boys that the new school teacher had red hair and they better watch out.

"Here's one story: The second year, I was there at noon-time in the early spring. There were some big rocks. The children would climb up and jump off. One youngster was Fanny Pierce, who lived up above Mrs. Wagner's house. These were very poor youngsters. They lived in the garage."

Lewis recalled that her mother's name was Clara Pierce. "Yes, and she had some relatives who came up from Bridgeport. They were really very poor. Father Day used to help them out with some food. So this youngster jumped and fell on her arm. When she got up it was bent. I thought, 'Now, what in the world?' I had no telephone, no lights except one oil lamp. There were no houses near. The closest was Clayton Squire and he was almost a mile away. This was at the end of South Street, where River Road goes off. So I did not know what to do. I thought I had to take her some place. So I told the youngsters to come in. I was going to put assignments on the board. They were to write the stuff out and then put the papers on my desk. Of course, Fanny was about 15 years old. She was the oldest. I took this youngster over to Dr. McIntyre at the end of Squire Road on Route 67. Mrs. McIntyre was also Treasurer of the School Board, and her son was in the class.

"So I went in with the girl and she said, 'That's the Greentree fracture. That youngster has not had the proper nutrition. If she'd had the proper nutrition it would have been broken.' But it was bent. She said, 'I have to take her over to Woodbury to have it x-rayed. Do you want to come with me?' I said, 'Dr. McIntyre, I left the kids all alone in the school.' And she said, 'Oh, that's all right.' I said, 'No, it's not.' I was more afraid of my supervisor coming around. When I got back, I never had so many papers to correct as I did that night. They did just what they had been told. That's why I've always thought they were a good bunch of kids in Roxbury.

"There was another one. Repkovich. He lived at Tschauder's house. He was the only one to go home for lunch. One day, after it had snowed, I guess he just wanted to scare the other kids. He made a snow ball and threw it. It did not hit the side of the building. It went through the window right by his seat. He just stood there. He was petrified. I went to the door and said, 'You tell your father to come back with you and measure the window and put a new one in.' I had a new pane in there that night. Another kid would have run."

Lewis asked her whether being so young, was she not frightened when that grim-faced superintendent came and sat with her. "Well," she replied, "Mr. Johnston was pretty good. Miss Snyder was his assistant. I think I was more afraid of Miss Snyder than I was of him. She really spent much time with you. He didn't spend that much time. She would sit in and really supervise. I felt good, because he came once in the winter time and said, 'You really have it warm in here.' And he stood there for a long time warming up. Miss Snyder, on the other hand, had been taking courses down at Columbia in the School of Education, and they were implementing the modern education at that time. It was changing a little bit. You really had to work a little bit harder. When you made projects, you had to co-ordinate various subjects into a project and not just have it cut and dried. It was more difficult."

Most of the children ate their lunch at the school. "The Wagners would bring a couple of quarts of milk. The father's name was Richard. They had a farm. Roy Isakson and Billy Isakson, they had two farms on Squire Road. Billy's father's is the one Dr. Sherman bought. They would also bring a quart of milk. So I made cocoa."

In fact, she devised her own school lunch program. "That's right," she said, "And nobody thought anything about it not being pasteurized, either. Of course, on the stove it was, once you boiled it." But she did not supply the food. "They'd bring sandwiches. And sometimes they'd have dessert in a glass jar that something else had come in, peanut butter or something. The lunch break would last about an hour. In the summertime we'd go outside and eat. There was no other recess between classes. If someone wanted to go outside, because we did not have any bathrooms in the school-house, they'd go outside, one or two of them. For the younger ones: they could do quiet games in the corner of the room, because the whole room was not filled up with desks. Six feet in front, the room had nothing in it except the teacher's desk. One time we had a party and program in the evening, and we had a curtain drawn across, so it was like a stage."

She also remembered how they dealt with eight different classes at a time. "There were spelling bees: you'd have four grades and they would realize that some of them would have harder words than the others. The same with multiplication tables. Even though a person was in sixth grade that particular person might not be that much ahead of a fifth grader, who was as good as a seventh grader. They all were not of the same ability. That's where it made it better in a one-room school. The youngster got through some of his or her written work, and then he could sit and listen to what the grade above him was doing, and he'd pick up a lot more. In that way some of them progressed faster." She added, laughing, "In effect, you could eavesdrop on what you were going to have next year and decide you didn't like it."

"We also, at the end of the year, had achievement tests. These were to show how much improvement the youngsters had made. Many times they would show a year and a half of improvement, which proved they had gained from listening to other classes being taught.

"We, the teachers, also had to do some music and some art work. But then we also had a music teacher, who came twice a week. She'd spend about half an hour with us. And those youngsters learned to read music as well as sing.

"Ordinarily, until 1933, the graduation classes of all the one-room schools had their ceremony at the town hall. But the last year, they did not do it, because the town wanted to save money. I had three boys who were graduating that year, and I felt they ought to have some kind of ceremony. So we had it in a class room and Dr. McIntyre gave the diplomas out. From there they would move up to the Booth School."

That was the end of the one-room schools in Roxbury. "The reason they closed them down," Mary Pokrywka explained, "was that there were only three schools left (out of formerly eight.) The population had gone down so far that in 1935 Bill Hodge said, 'You know, the only people buying houses in Roxbury are retired New York school-teachers and retired couples. We don't need any more schools.' The school population had dropped so far, and farmers were even going out." But Lewis had another idea. He said, "You see, the population at one time was 1,800. In 1935 to 1940 it dropped to about 600." Did that mean that in the late 1930's the only children in Roxbury schools were farmers' children and a few, whose parents did not want to send them back to New York?" "That's right. The New York children finished out the year, and then they stayed for a second year," she said, "What was really also bad was that so many of the youngsters, after they graduated from high school, would leave town. Take the Wagners. There were four boys in the family. Only one stayed in town. They were all good students. In fact, Mrs. Wagner was quite upset that Richard did not want to go to college. He was the oldest one, but he wanted to work the farm, and he felt it would be better to stay right here. That's just one example. How about the Orzecks? There were at least four in their family and only one stayed."

Mary Pokrywka, still a young woman, also had to move. "I went to Bloomfield in my third year," she said, "It was supposed to be an advancement. But I got less money than I had in Roxbury. Small towns like Roxbury and Bridgewater were getting state aid. So they could not cut your salary. Bigger towns that were paying their own way, they cut back. A friend of mine was getting $1,000, but the year I started, they cut it back to $950. She was not the only one. All of the teachers were cut back for two different years, because of the Depression. After Bloomfield, I went back to New York for a while. I was not making enough money. I spent it all for room and board. You could make it only if you were living at home. So I went back to New York, where my family was. I worked in the printing industry for a while. It was a small shop in Manhattan, south of Canal Street. Then they opened the Training School down in Southbury (a special school for retarded children), and they knew that I wanted to get back to teach in Connecticut. I applied and taught there, and then I married and had my own youngsters."

Her husband was one of the Roxbury Pokrywkas. Mary's maiden name was Billyou, an Anglicized French name from northern New York state. She met Albert Pokrywka, when she first started to teach school in Roxbury. He brought wood to the school. But they were not married until 1942, a year after Mary had returned to teach at the Southbury Training School. It was not a continuous courtship, however. Mary had bought a little house near Booth School. It was her house and her family would come up from Brooklyn for the summer to live in it with her. The following year she and Albert were married.

He had a small business hauling milk from the farmers to the dairy. His people had sold the farm. By that time, none of the old one-room schoolhouses were left. "They had closed them in June 1941," Mary recalled, "and they opened Booth Free School in September 1941. Frank Johnston's wife was teaching, and Mabel and Madeleine. The three of them were teaching in the three rooms and came down to my house to have coffee." But, as Lewis explained, "Before that, it was all high school. Then it went to high school with the seventh and eighth grade, and then they added three rooms to get those three teachers for the lower grades." But, Mary added, "Once they had three more rooms for the lower grades, they sent the high school kids to Washington." From that time the Booth Free School was the grade school of Roxbury.

Later, Mary taught there, too. "I did quite a lot of 'subbing' in 1948 and 1951," she said, "before my second son was born. I also had two girls in the meantime, so I did not teach much at all for about ten years. Later, I went back to teach the upper grades in Social Studies and Math. And in 1967 I went over to New Milford." And what were the changes she encountered compared to the old one-room schools? "Of course, in the first three rooms you had two or three grades to a room," she said, "they put additions on so you could cut down mostly to one grade to a room. By that time all the youngsters were being bussed to school, except for those who lived in the center. They all stayed for lunch, however. You ate in your classroom. Only when they put the first addition on, which had a kitchen, then they also had a lunch room. The hot lunch program did not really start until the government had a lot of food that they wanted to dispose of. The different school districts would be able to get it at very little cost. That is really what started the hot lunch program. It made a difference. You had a longer lunch period and in many places it was better for the nutrition of the youngsters. Not so much in Roxbury. By that time no one had to worry about nutrition in Roxbury the way we did during the Depression."

Did that mean the children had to sit still for eight hours in the old schools? Lewis seemed to recall that they had at least one 15-minute recess, which was the longest of the day. But Mary said, "Oh, they got to walk around. They did not really stay quiet. We had activity areas. One was for math. You had books for reading. Some of the youngsters would be off in one corner, helping each other."

And how would a typical day pass for a teacher in the old school rooms? "We'd be sitting down by 9 o'clock. But first we'd have the salute to the flag. We always had to have the salute. Then I had them file into the school house. I always figured that children would have to learn to get in line at various times. Before they had come I had put various things on the board. Either I had done it the night before or in the morning. For instance: 'Fourth Grade is going to study spelling, page such and such,' explaining, 'You are to study the words. There are sentences at the end of the page, where you are to match the correct spelling. Write the whole sentence with the correct word.' And, 'Eighth Grade: We are going to read pages 400 to 420 in the Reader, and we will discuss that. Find the answers to the questions so that we can discuss the reading.' And then perhaps Third Grade would study the three times table. The hardest subjects, reading and math, we would do in the morning. The afternoon would be for subjects that were more discussion. Some children learn these things better through ear than they do through the eye.

"You generally started with the First Grade for their reading. They were liable to sit quietly for that. And the others would turn to what they were going to do and open their books.

"After 15 minutes I would call the Second Grade up and go through their reading, in another ten or 15 minutes, the Third, and sometimes the Third and Fourth together. So that possibly by 10:30 a.m. we had covered most of the reading. Then we got started on arithmetic. Then you would let youngsters, who wanted to go outside, go out one at a time. They knew that. But they did not always want to go out.

"Next we'd have arithmetic. On Fridays there would be a spelling test, just before ten o'clock. We had a clock in the front, and they knew what times were, and they would be ready, more or less, for what you were going to do. Then we'd stop and have lunch. Then they would go out and play until one o'clock. All played baseball, boys and girls together. I also played baseball."

Lewis said, "All the teachers got so they could do that," and Mary Pokrywka nodded, "Yes, you were supposed to do that," and then said, "we had a good field. I guess we had one of the best fields to play and my youngsters, like the Wagners, were very good ball players. So we had a very good time out there on Erbacher's field."

Lewis, a little mischievously, then asked, "Did people go out to smoke pot?" But Mary Prokrywka ignored him, or else she did not know what he was talking about. "Of course, they could go out any time," she said, "but there was not that much they could do outside. The street was so quiet that whenever a car or something did go by, everyone would go to the window to see what it was."

Did she ever give them home work? "Sometimes," she said, "but not many times." Lewis explained that "many of the people here were needed by their fathers for work on the farm in the afternoon." Mary added, "Take, when the Wagner boys came home. One of them had to bring in the wood for the kitchen stove. The other one had to go out and bring the cows in. Then the other had to bring the calves in. So they all had work to do." And Lewis said, "It was not the same in later years. Some of the First Grade could count to 50 and would know the full alphabet. But some others had not even started. It took a while to get these two up to the same level."

Mary gave an example. "Anne Murkland was very bright, for instance." Her family was one of the first to come up from New York, and her father was with Western Electric. "She was practically Fourth Grade level," Mary said. She would help the Pierce youngsters, one of the very poor. And Anne would bring beautiful sandwiches, while the Pierce girls would sometimes have just plain bread - but home made bread. One day Anne said: 'Could I have some of her plain bread?' And I said, 'Sure, Anne.' Wanda, the other girl, was not naturally slow. She just had not had the advantages.

"Now the Pierce boy. I had him in 1933 and 1934. In 1943 Joyce Davenport, who lived across the road, came and said he was visiting her and he recognized 'Billyou' on the mail box. He was in the Marines, and in those years, '42 and '43, the Marines were taking the best fellows, better than the Army and Navy were getting. He was a handsome boy. You would never have thought that he would have had nutrition problems as a youngster." She also recalled that two brothers, nephews of the boy's and girl's aunt, where they had lived in Roxbury during the Depression, had done time in jail during that period. They were caught breaking into a house in Trumbull. One of them was allowed to live in his aunt's chicken coop, the other in the garage. They were only in Roxbury a few years, and then went back to Bridgeport. What she meant to say is that Roxbury had its Huckleberry Finns, too.

But we also wanted to know how she graded her youngsters. "Well," she said, "you'd have written tests. You would also have them work on the blackboard lots of times. When you started to do multiplication with two figures, for instance. You'd have two or three at the board. You could check them, if they did happen to make an error, you could correct it immediately. Then you gave them assignments, which they could either do in school or at home. You would also pay attention to their attitude. A youngster who was really trying hard but had a hard time learning, I'd give him extra credit for that. I had a couple of youngsters who were very, very bright, and sometimes they'd sit on their laurels."

Who were they? Of course, the Wagner boys. They must have been her favorites. They also had to walk a ways to get to school, Lewis offered. "But the Pearces had to walk even further," Mary said. Their home was about 2 miles from the school. "Dr. McIntyre would transport them in a car, part of the way. Besides the Wagners there was another girl from that end of town, and the two Isaksons. She got paid for doing it. Harry Larson did the same thing at the other end of town, towards Washington, and brought them down to the Center School-House." Then they mentioned Albert Brown and all his family, who all had to walk all the way from Botsford Hill. Later, they had to walk all the way to the high school, and that is why a lot of the youngsters did not finish high school. Those who did finish - like Madeleine Beigneux - would live at the Hurlbuts. After school, she would wash dishes and help out, just for four days and four nights, so that she could be there at school.

Lewis, having attended the old one-room school in the Center, also remembered the paper they used. He said, "It used to burn me up that we used to have to go over to Johnston's office in New Milford to pick up the paper. And when we'd be given the first test in the middle of the week, we'd cut the paper in half. Sometimes you'd cut it into quarters. Twenty years ago, when I'd see kids write their name and throw the paper away, I got a shock. Because of the Depression we had to save on everything.

Mary agreed. "For instance, we had studied the American Flag from the time of the Revolution and its change. So I thought, 'Oh, just to make a little decoration of the room, I'll have the kids paint various flags.' So I went to Danbury and I bought some paints and I came back and we painted these pictures and put them up. Miss Snyder came in and said, 'Where did you get the paint, Mary?' I told her, 'I bought it.' She informed me, 'Well, the school board will not give you any money for paint. And they won't give you any paint, either. Don't spend what little you have.' In those days the kids bought their own crayons, which today they don't, and their own pencils. Of course, we also had steel pens with ink wells.

"Mrs. Will Minor called me after a couple of weeks, after I had begun teaching, and said there were some books at the old school house which, if I wanted, I should get them. She also had some of what we call 'busy work.' It was types of games or things that children could do by themselves. They were a learning process that took time and kept them out of trouble. She had a big box that she gave me. The books were ten or 15 years old. We learned from them. I also had some new books on Social Studies, because they were just coming out then. But at that time they did not have modern math, yet. We were still doing the old-fashioned math."

But the students would arrive as they do now with their books under their arms. "Yes, but I do not remember seeing any school bags," Mary said, "They'd have a lunch pail and the books, but not too many. The teachers themselves brought a lot of stuff in."

Did anyone ever present her with the proverbial apple. "Oh, yes," she said, "And if you asked for a cake, you'd get so much. I remember that our Rural Ed teacher at the Normal School in Danbury, May Sherwood, had said, 'Never let them know that you are afraid of anything.' If they knew you were afraid of toads, they'd have a plague of toads in the school house. I'm not petrified, but I'm not crazy about mice and things like that. Anyway, Roy Isakson used to do a lot of trapping, and he caught a skunk and brought it in saying, 'Miss Billyou, feel how soft it is.' It was dead, of course. I felt how soft it was. It almost killed me to do it. But I never let him know.

"The girls would pick flowers and sometimes bring them in. At Christmas time you'd always get a lot of cookies."

Did parents come to discuss problems they had with their children with the teacher? "No, not really. We saw each other at night sometimes, when I put on parties, halloween parties and things like that. It was with the parents and the youngsters, and they'd put on a little entertainment. In the middle of spring we'd have something else. And then we'd have the graduation. Or else you would see the parents in church. Often I'd take a youngster home, too. I went to the Wagners quite a bit, because I was personally friendly with Mrs. Wagner. And there was Mrs. Valentine Rebkovich who made beautiful cakes."

It must have been a lot of fun. "Well, yes, it was." But Lewis thought it still must have been something of a culture shock to come from Brooklyn into this backward rural setting, where you were expected to make the fire in the school house and clean the toilets. "When you're young it does not bother you that much," Mary said, "I'll tell you another thing. You were glad to get a job. There were possibly ten young women after the job I had. They hired me in the third week of August to start in the third week of September, because they had just decided. I drove up - because I had my own car - and Frank Johnston from the School Board met me and then he brought me over and they were working on the outhouse of the new school."

How could she afford a car in the Depression? "In a way it was not quite my own car. Nobody knew how to drive in my family. The year I graduated my family rented a cottage down on Lake Zoar. And in order to get there I learned to drive and get a license in two weeks. So I got to drive the family car. I used to drive down after 3:30 p.m. and drive to New York. It would take me three or three and a half hours to get to Brooklyn. You drove on Route 7, not on a four lane highway. But you did not have the traffic you have today, either. In the winter I would go down only once a month. Otherwise it was only on weekends. Of course, you could also use the train from New Milford. But then I'd have to drive from here to get over to the station, anyhow."

160

And were any of her students still around? "I think they're all gone," she said, "Only some of the younger boys I taught at the Booth Free School in the past 15 or 20 years are still around."

What happened to the old school house? "It was empty for a couple of years. Then they decided to change the location of River Road, and they moved the school house closer to the river. Then a woman from New York, I think it was Mayor Wagner's secretary, bought it and built a first addition on one side of it. Then somebody else added another. Then Carl Reeker bought it, and now it's really a nice place. They left the blackboard up. The last time I was there, a couple of years ago, there was an opening, where you could go up into the attic. They had left it. This was now their living room.

"It was really well situated. I used to love to stand by the window and watch a storm gather. They would come right up the river. They moved the school house so it would be in the same position, so you could still watch the storm come up the river."

Lewis concluded the memory session with Mary Pokrywka, saying, "All the schools were made use of. Mary Skedgell lives in one on Painter Hill. Russell Montgomery took the one in Burritt District, and one down in the Weller District near the station is a house. There's only the one on Gold Mine Road. I think that was the first one that was empty."

In 1952 Nellie Beardsley Holt wrote down some memories of her own of what it had been like a little earlier, when she attended and later taught school in Roxbury:

"I lived in Bridgewater," she said, "but attended the Weller District School at Roxbury, and later the Booth Free School at Roxbury Center. There were no school buses and the walk to Booth's was long and lonely. During the winter the snow was apt to be deep (roads were not plowed the way they are now), the thermometer hovered around zero, and for a bit of exercise we often took our skates to use during the noon hour. I now marvel that we are to tell the tale and smile about it.

"In the Spring of 1896, the Booth School Fund was so low that it was necessary to omit the spring term. The last day of the winter term the teachers of the district school were at the Center School taking their examinations. Beulah Dickinson and I decided to take the test just for fun. They were not hard and from then on we forgot about it. Later, she was given the opportunity of teaching a small school, and I was offered a still smaller one - Painter Hill. We had not planned for this - 16 years of age.

"I had never travelled as far as Painter Hill, in that direction of town. With nothing to do all spring, and the chance to earn $5.50 a week, why

161

not? Five-fifty a week for ten weeks looked like a fortune. The distance from home was no stumbling block, only five miles down and up hill in the morning. This could easily be made in an hour by pedaling the bicycle fast; and coming home it was down and uphill again. Part of the way was walking and pushing the bike, but the gold at the end of the rainbow was $5.50 a week.

"As for knowing anything about teaching, my knowledge was only that acquired from having been a country school pupil myself, and a knack for imitating the teacher. The uppermost thing in my mind (having attended the Weller School) was having a good sturdy hickory stick handy.

"The first morning of the spring term was my introduction to the 'Little White Schoolhouse' on Painter Hill, which was easily found. There it stood on the knoll at the side of the road with the stone wall, the fields, and in the distance Good Hill with white farmhouses dotting the landscape. Not a sound to break the stillness. Not even a bird.

"It was a small building, having but one door which opened into the entry where the children were to hang their coats and hats in one end, the other end being filled with wood, kindling, a broom and shovel, a box with a water pail and dipper. The entire place had had a spring-cleaning.

"From the entry, one turned to the left to enter the schoolroom, which was well lighted with windows on three sides, all placed high enough to prevent the children from seeing the road. This precaution was unnecessary as the traffic was about three milk teams a day. At the right of the door was the teachers's desk and chair, facing the room of desks for pupils. On the wall back of the teacher was the blackboard. There was an extra chair for any caller, and once during every term the 'School Visitor' came to spend a few hours to see if the pupils were making any progress. This one was G.S.P. Leavenworth.

"Near the door the 'station agent' stove was always ready to furnish an abundance of heat, no matter how cold the weather. Before long the children came shyly walking in - one, two, three, etc. As I remember, there never was an attendance of more than ten, which differed from the Wellers District, where the average was eighty, ranging from the ages of five to fifteen.

"It took but a few minutes to realize that the hickory stick would never be needed; we used it to kindle the first fire built on a cool day. I well remember the people of this district, many of whom I seldom saw, but how they took an interest in the school whether they had children

162

who attended or not - the Pickett, O'Brien, McKeever, Leavenworth, Haggerty, Tracy, Dooley, Edwards and Seidler families.

"I thoroughly enjoyed that spring term, but fully realized that to make teaching a success more training was necessary. During the summer, when asked to teach the school again the following year, I accepted with the feeling that I wasn't worth $5.50, but possibly I was doing as good a job as anyone and the experience would be beneficial should I ever plan to make teaching a career; there was also the urge to return to the place I had so much enjoyed. To teach there for a year meant making the arrangement for a place to stay during any inclement weather. This was easily done, the price was fifty cents a day for room and board. During the spring and fall I often was in the Pickett household which consisted of Father and Mother Pickett, their son, Michael, his wife and their baby boy. During the winter months I stayed with Mrs. O'Brien whose daughter, Mary, was home that winter.

"I always spent the weekends at home and well recall one Sunday when it started to snow and indications looked like a bad storm in the offing. Father decided to take me back that afternoon. He hitched the old horse to the sleigh and away we started. The travelling was easy until we left the Center, and by the time we reached the Seeley house we had to leave the road and go through the fields. The sleigh tipped over a few times, and father had to make a path for the horse a few times. We finally reached the Pickett home where they were glad to take me in, and father reached home safely. Mother Pickett gave me a nice hot supper and at the same time heated a couple of bricks to warm the bed. Up the stairs we went to the guest room which hadn't been used all winter (this was not unusual as the majority of country rooms were cold). I will never forget that bed, it looked so high and had a lovely quilt for a coverlet. Still being cold, I hurried to undress and jump into it and sank almost out of sight in a soft downy feather bed. Mother Pickett piled another one over me. The sandman was there in a minute, and the next I knew someone was shaking me to say it was time for school.

"Will O'Brien was the only person to have braved the storm. He had a team of horses and a sled, taking his milk to the station. On his way back, about eleven o'clock, he stopped to give me a ride to the school house. It took but a few minutes to have a brisk fire and in no time the room was cozy. No pupils appeared and by way of the stonewall it was easy to get to Mrs. O'Brien's where I spent the rest of the week. I went to school the next day, but no pupils came until Thursday; if the teacher was present, but no children, that day did not have to be made up at the end of the term.

"Days when the weather was bad, and hours could be shortened, I was alone in the building with plenty of time to practice the two-step, waltz and polka, which were being taught at the dancing class in the Town Hall at the Center in that winter - up and down the aisle and around the stove, with a broomstick for a partner, and by the end of the season I was always sure of not being a wallflower at a dance if Fred Lendeveg, Lev Castle, or Nate Beardsley were there.

"The year was a happy one and the last day of school came too quickly. Plans were made for the usual picnic, and a surprise for the children had been planned. Mother was to bring a large freezer of ice cream, cake and lemonade.

"I said nothing, but was getting nervous waiting for them. Finally, around the bend in the road, came our old white horse with a sort of sheepish expression on its face. It had been up to its same old trick. That horse was gentle and reliable 'till it decided to rest; then no amount of coaxing would make it move unless, occasionally, it would look at you, then easily turn in the harness and lie down, but was thoughtful never to break the shafts or harness. When the spirit moved, up it would get and travel along.

"The picnic was a success, and one of the bright memories of my life is Painter Hill."

Booth Free School in 1903.
Now part of Consolidated School
at 14 South Street, Roxbury.

Hervey Booth, an
eccentric benefactor of
Roxbury education.

Typical one-room school, circa 1900.

VII
The Dairy Farm

George DeVoe, the most successful realtor in Litchfield county, managed Judds Bridge Farm from 1933 to 1947, beginning in the Depression and right through the turbulent era of World War II and its uncertain aftermath. The farm was then one of the largest dairy operations in Northwestern Connecticut and straddled Roxbury, Washington and New Milford land along the Shepaug River.

DeVoe remembered that there were thirteen farm houses in the valley, when he first started buying for Raoul Metcalf, who wanted to become a gentleman farmer. "In the first part of 1932 Raoul bought nine properties," he said, "and before he got finished he bought a total of 2,300 acres. But that included the land up on the hill toward New Milford."

Charles Hartwell's house, John Hensl's, and the Ingersoll houses were among those he bought. Hartwell's, which came with 297 acres, was the largest farm. Metcalf paid $12,000 for Hartwell's place. He paid $18,000 for the Ingersoll farm. "Yet, when I took over the management of the farm, Metcalf was losing $6,300 a month," DeVoe said. He had bought 300 head of cattle of which about 25 were Brown Swiss. He also had 25 Ayrshires, and about 125 to 150 Jersey cows. The Jerseys were mediocre, the Swiss were terrible, only the Ayrshires were excellent cows. "But I had to get rid of the Ayrshires, because they could not stand the pressure of the combine milkers in the milking pound, which was one of the first around here."

"I came out of New York and Wall Street in 1929," DeVoe explained, "I had told my partner George Pratt to sell all of his stock, but my broker did not execute my order. So I lost my shirt. I bought this land--on which my office still stands--in 1929 with 12 acres of land. When Raoul told me he could not afford to keep the farm on which he had spent $150,000 by that time, I asked him to let me run it for a month. I told him that nobody but a crook or a genius can lose $6,300 a month on a farm, and I had not seen any geniuses. In the first month I cut $2,500 off the expenses. Every salesman that came asked me how much I wanted. I told them I was working for the farm, not for DeVoe."

After five months the loss was down to $900 and he told Metcalf, "I'm going to college at your expense."

DeVoe knew little about cows or dairying before he began. But he had studied chemistry. "So the first thing I did was to go into the barn to watch the milking of the cows. Knowing nothing about cows, this was a milk factory to me. They were driving the cows into the washing stalls and then putting them into the milking parlor. They'd strip them and then put the machine on, milk them, and take the machine off. I watched the boys and said, 'Listen, boys, you're doing three operations here. It's taking three hours and 40 minutes to milk the cows twice a day.' I suggested we take the fore-milk and strip them in the barn. It worked. We cut the time to an hour and a half.

"Anyway, we lost a hundred quarts of milk a day, so I got out a book on veterinary medicine to learn how a cow made milk. I decided what we were doing wrong was starting and stopping the flow of milk three times. So I had the cows taken to the wash stall, and after each cow was cleaned and dried then, when the stanchion opened, the man in the wash stall would take fore milk and then we'd put the machines right on. I did not want to take the time to strip, so I had weights made to put under the DeLaValve, four pounds for the Jerseys and six pounds for the Swiss, and that did the stripping. It was very amusing to me, because the following day Col. Adams, the father-in-law of the owner, brought a very famous doctor to the farm, and he assumed that I knew everything about cows. But I'd been there a week or ten days only."

The doctor asked DeVoe, "How does a cow give milk?" Luckily, this is just what DeVoe had read up on the night before. So he said, "Sir, it's an involuntary act induced by some stimuli, the bleating of a calf, the rattling of a milk pail, or the sound of a milking machine, whatever they associate with the let-down of milk. This produces a hyperemia of blood in the lombar plexus..." and he went on talking like that for about half an hour.

The next problem he had to confront involved bacteria. The count was supposed to be less than 10,000 colonies per cubic centimeter, "But to my amazement it was 300,000. So I went down to the milking parlor in Washington. They were rinsing the warm milk out with cold water and hyperactive soda in hot water, and that made an insoluble salt. I said to myself, if I had cold milk in a glass, I would rinse it out with cold water, and if I had hot milk, I would rinse it out with hot water. They were rinsing out warm milk with cold water, hardened the fat, and then they were baking it on with steam. So we put in some valves to get 100 degree water, which was about the temperature of the milk from the cows. And then I put the water at 185 degrees to sterilize it. The bacteria count dropped to under 10,000 colonies. But in addition to this the men were spending two or three hours a day to clean out the milk stone that we had in the long pipes from the milking parlor to the coolers. These were just a few of the side issues."

"We finally made the farm profitable, but it took me years to do it. I turned it back with a $168,000 a year profit."

The farm was bottling 400 to 500 quarts of milk a day, which were delivered to neighborhoods in the region, schools and hospitals. "We were shipping as far as Greenwich," DeVoe said. But the milk was too expensive to be used for making cream, butter, or cheese. Cream cost the farm $1.80 a quart to make, and it was very heavy (55% to 60% butter fat content) cream. "And we were in competition with Walter Gordon for baby milk. I was very proud that we were lower in our leukocyte count." The leukocyte count relates to the condition of a cow's udders. The cows were tested every month by health officials. DeVoe started testing them himself every week at a time when 180 were being milked.

The general decline of dairying in Connecticut owing to growing competition from the larger spreads in upstate New York did not appear to have made much difference to Judds Bridge Farm. "When I started, we were getting three or four cents for our milk," he said. "In order to make the place profitable, we had to develop a market." Once they had some steady customers, they were able to charge 14 to 16 cents wholesale. Besides Greenwich, where they supplied the hospital with milk, they also had a market in Bridgeport. Instead of using the rail the way most other farms did, Judds Bridge Farm had its own delivery truck. "Only in the hurricane of 1938, we shipped it down by rail," DeVoe said. "Back in the 1920s and 1930s this was the 26th dairy county in the United States." The smaller farms were shipping their milk all the way to New York, using the creameries as their intermediaries. There were four creameries in Connecticut then, but Judds Bridge Farm was producing 2,400 quarts of milk a day on its own (including the 400 to 500 quarts it bottled), which was almost as much as all the other Roxbury farms put together.

DeVoe eventually gained national fame for having raised the finest herd of Brown Swiss dairy cattle in the country. "I had 29,000 index cards giving the records of all the Brown Swiss cows,." he recalled, "and I took all of their records and correlated them under the sires and dams. I took the best cows of the best families. In 1935 Raoul gave me $40,000 to buy the ten best Brown Swiss and the ten best Jerseys in the country. I came back with nine cows. Raoul asked me how much I spent. I said I had spent $2,700. 'I told you to buy the ten best in the country,' he complained. I said, 'I did.' We broke one world record three times: the four-year-old, twice-a-day milking.

"I was very much interested in the Jerseys, when I started, and the Ayrshires, but at the end of the year I suddenly realized the Brown Swiss

- even though they were a mediocre herd - had given me more milk with fewer problems than any of the other cows. The Ayrshires were high-strung. When we sold out in 1947, we sold 158 head for an average of $1,228, which then was the highest ever." In between the herd had been first or second in the United States, year after year. "They all started from the cows I bought in 1935 and in 1936."

From the start DeVoe enjoyed managing Judds Bridge Farm so much that he neglected to pay himself very well. One day Raoul Metcalf asked him, "What are you paying yourself, George?" This was the first time they discussed his remuneration. DeVoe told him $200 a month. This seemed to come as a surprise to Metcalf, who remembered paying him $1,000 a month in real estate fees. So DeVoe told him. "I know what I'm doing in real estate. But I've got too much pride to charge you more than $200 a month, when I don't know what I'm doing."

Few of the farmers, who had sold out to Metcalf, stayed to work for him. Charlie Hartwell was one. He stayed for five years on a rent-free basis. Another farmer, Will Sissky, bought himself another farm and continued farming on his own. Lester Ingersoll gave up farming alto-gether. DeVoe remembered that it had not been easy to separate these men and their families from their farms - all in one year.

"When I went to a place to buy, I had to park my car on the hill and walk to Judds Bridge. The roads were frightful. You couldn't drive a car into Judds Bridge. First I bought the Sissky farm. Raoul got very impa-tient. He kept saying, 'I want to buy that farm,' or 'I want to buy this farm.' I told him, 'Let me buy them.' I went to the Ingersolls. I knew his wife was anxious to get out of the valley, because she got stuck every time she went to town. I said to Raoul it was worth $15,000. He would have paid more. But if I had given in on one, I would have had to pay more for the rest of it. I was buying. Normally, our obligation is a little more to the seller. In this case I was buying. Those barns were not for sale, a lot of them."

"It was interesting. Raoul had a friend, Roger Edson. He was in real estate. And he came up. He offered Raoul $50,000 to horn in on my job. Raoul called me up very irate and said, 'I thought you said that was worth only $35,000?' So I said, 'Is that what you want to pay for it?' Afterwards, I went over to see Charlie (Hartwell), and although Roger Edson had of-fered him $50,000, I came away that morning with a deed for $35,000. I said, 'Who is buying for Raoul Metcalf? Roger Edson or George DeVoe?' He said, 'George DeVoe.' So I said, 'Okay.'

169

His son Joe Hartwell wanted to sell his farm, too. He offered to sell it for $10,000. I told him that I did not want to hurt Raoul Metcalf, but I did not want to hurt Joe Hartwell, either. So I offered to buy it for $12,000. He had 80 acres right in the middle of the valley."

* * *

Joe Hartwell, who never held a job for very long after that, moved to the center of Roxbury, where he still lived when we interviewed him in 1986. He refused to have any more to do with George DeVoe after he left the valley and looked back at selling his farm to Metcalf with considerable bitterness.

He recalled that the valley took its name from a farmer named Judd, who had built a toll bridge across the Shepaug river, "but that was before my time." The farm he sold to Metcalf covered land in all three of the neighboring townships: Roxbury, New Milford, and Washington. But because his house stood on Roxbury land, he was considered a resident of Roxbury. "My dad had around 400 acres," he said, "and I had my farm right next to it. There were 60 acres to it." Although he was born in New Milford, his mother had lived in the valley even before her marriage. (He did not recall from whom his father had bought the farm.) Certainly, there had been Hartwells on the land before. One of the roads was called Hartwell Road.

"My father had a store right on the side of the station," he explained as he rummaged in a drawer and fished out an 80-year-old photograph of the tiny, wooden station. "There was a regular little industry there. They had a car-load of feed every month, sometimes two." He worked in the creamery at first. It did over 100 cans of milk a day, which were shipped to Bridgeport from the tiny station on the Shepaug Valley Railroad. His father also ran the Post Office. The train picked up the mail without stopping. "They just put out a hook and grabbed it," he said.

There was an ice house to store the meat his father butchered, and two meat carts. Sometimes quarters of beef would arrive on the train. "The man from the train would bring it over and lay it on the kitchen table." Joe's job then was to fetch some cider from the cellar for him. "We always had two or three barrels. I used to hate having to draw it as a kid. But we never paid any fare riding on the train." The ice for the ice house came from the river. "We had plenty in those days. You didn't have to worry about it. After a while, they cut it on a pond I had on my land."

170

The train, of course, would stop for the milk cans from the creamery. "I got so I could whirl them through. Nowadays I could not lift one of them." Each can had 85 pounds, or 40 quarts of milk in it. The milk also came from Painter Hill, which lies above the valley. "All that end of town brought their milk to Judds Bridge," he recalled, and in Bridgeport, where most of it went, the Mitchells, who owned the creamery, had another farm. They also made cream sometimes, spilling the skimmed milk into the river. And they made casein, the protein constituent of milk.

He could no longer remember how many houses there were in the valley altogether. Right around the little station there were six. His own was among them. It was an old house. "Selling it to Metcalf was the biggest mistake I ever made. I hated the place, when I came down here. I was out of my element." Then why did he sell?

"In the first place, my wife did not like it. She was a city girl." Her name was Irene, and she is well remembered in Roxbury as one of the best school mistresses the town ever had. Like Mary Pokrywka she had grown up in Brooklyn, and Hartwell admitted that, "to get a wild Indian like me was quite a change-over for her. She went to church twice a day, and once on Sunday," using their Model-T Ford to get back and forth.

The way Hartwell remembered it all the farmers knew that Metcalf wanted the whole valley. But how did he manage to persuade every one of them to sell? "With money," Hartwell shouted, "Hell, if I had not sold out, they would have squeezed me out. I would have had to give it away. What the hell could I do, a little nothing there. When I bought the place there was nothing on it. When I got through I had 1,000 laying hens, and I had 16 head of cattle. I had three horses. I had a car. And I started with nothing."

He did not remember how much Metcalf offered him for his farm. "I guess it was $15,000, or something like that. It was a good price for those days."

But there were a lot of other things he remembered about living in the valley as a young man. To get started he worked as a timber cutter. "I was not proud. My brother and I got $36 a week. The rest of them got only $24 a week. They would not let us cut more than 1,000 feet." The timber went to the saw mill. From his earnings he bought the old house in 1923. He paid $1,500 for it and the 60 acres of land. (The house in Roxbury, which he bought from the proceeds, cost $7,500 and included ten acres of land.) "I had one field with a load of hay on it. When I sold it, it had ten loads. I brought it up. I bought lime and the field was about six or seven acres. I would take two acres. I would lime it and fertilize it the way it should be. Of course, we had the manure. Chicken manure makes things grow. The next year I would go from there and then start back again. You should have seen the corn I grew up there. That was good land. There were no stones."

He worked for Metcalf for only four days. "I was not accustomed to being a serf," he said. "They had a foreman there, and I asked him that I should have a contract like some of them did." He could not help quickly adding, "they were stealing him blind. Even the foreman did. He came down one day and said, 'You're going to do what I tell you.' I turned around and said. 'You can go right plumb to hell. I'm through right now.' Then they came back and wanted to pay me off. I said, 'You can keep it. I don 't need it.' And I told him then that he was going to get fired. He did."

What did he mean by stealing? "They would send you to buy stuff. And when you got back, the foreman would ask, 'Did you get ten percent?' Then there was this chicken farmer in there. He got so much out of it. They'd go down and buy a cow for $2,000 and get a big cut out of that. I don't know how much the foreman got, but they were all doing it." Joe Hartwell saw Metcalf one day, who told him that he should not have quit. Hartwell remembered asking him, "What future was there for me? If I had stayed there much longer, I would have killed somebody." Another farmer, Joe McGovern, worked there for a week, before he also quit. "That's what happens to big farms. They bring in these men, who ruin the country. They brought in the foreman from Vermont. He brought in his friends. They made it so damned miserable, you can't stay. That's how they do it. Of course, that's their privilege."

In the end not one of the old farming families stayed in the valley to work for the new farm. "It makes me sick to look at it now. Some of the fields have trees on them that big. I had it all clean," Hartwell complained. The talk moved on to other things, but something had been stirred in the old man. It suddenly came out as if from a deep well. "When I was a kid, how I used to chase them cows all over the field up there," he said, and then gasped," Oh, God!"

* * *

DeVoe, on the other hand, clearly remembered how the farmers were all ready to sell. "They wanted to get out of the valley. Metcalf originally wanted only 200 or 300 acres. I sold him 2,300 acres. He wanted to be on a dirt road, in a valley, with a river, and a railroad. He wanted to bring his food in by rail and ship out by rail. I looked it over on a topographi-

172

cal map and chose this valley. It was a natural. Finally, there were 15 or 16 farms he bought."

Of course, the dairy market was far from booming. In fact, "it was very poor," DeVoe granted. "We were in a very serious Depression. At that time Guernsey milk was very popular. It had that yellow color. One of my Brown Swiss friends took the Guernsey market away with an ad, which I thought was one of the dirtiest tricks I'd ever seen. He put a full page ad in the paper that said, 'Our milk is guaranteed not to turn yellow in the bottle.' He took the market from the Guernseys.

"Brown Swiss milk, let's face it, is very healthy milk. It's a soft curd milk. It's very digestible. But so is Holstein, and so is Ayrshire, and so is Short Horn. But the Brown Swiss is very easy to digest. We sold it to people with ulcers. They could digest it without that heavy fat. Remember, the cows originally came from the British Channel Islands, which are called Jersey and Guernsey. They were shipping their surplus milk to London. But because it was so difficult for them to ship it out, they shipped cream and butter.

"You can do anything with animals in breeding. By selection they bred the animal that gave the highest fat. Brown Swiss runs to only 4% or 5% fat, while the Guernsey milk runs to 6% and 7% fat. People got sick, if they lived on just Guernsey and Jersey milk. The Brown Swiss milk, on the other hand, was used for cheese. They wanted the protein. Brown Swiss is therefore higher in protein. Brown Swiss does not quite have the flavor and palatability that some of the other milks have. I experimented a great deal, and I decided to use Guernsey and Jersey combined, which make a very palatable table milk with about 4.5% or 4.6% fat. Today, Guernsey and Jersey are not as popular, because people do not want the fat.

"The one thing that made our area dairy country was the market. I mean the distance to the market. In those days they had to cart it by truck. And it was easier to truck it for 30 miles than to bring it in from New York 100 miles away."

Here Lewis Hurlbut demurred. He thought that before the railroad came to Roxbury, there really was not much of a market for anyone who kept, say, ten cows. It was only after the railroad came that the creameries were built. "Yes, in 1932, they were still going to the creamery," DeVoe agreed, "You had to be big to be on your own. There were a lot of little peddlers in the local area. People like Bill Griggs. He would make about 100 bottles of milk a day and bottle it in his own little plant. Also, back in 1932 we still had some tuberculosis in cattle."

Yes, but did not most farmers have a little spring down by the road, where they kept their milk cans cool? DeVoe laughed, "Sometimes the lid fell off. I remember one of the Mitchells shipped a can of milk down to Bridgeport and it had a trout in it." He visited Art Mitchell's farm once with an inspection team of the American Certified Milk Association and found it to be, "one of the dirtiest, filthiest farms I'd ever seen." On the other hand, Norm Magnuson, the man who worked for Mitchell, was a top cow man. "I never considered myself a great cow man. I was a breeder of dairy cattle. I was never a man to get under a cow and get the last drop of milk out of it. "It makes a difference, if you have a top notch milker or just an average milker, especially when you have to test cows. You can get one man, who can get 800 pounds of milk a year out of a cow that only gave 400 for another man. There's a difference. The attention they pay to the animal. They know exactly how much to feed." Magnuson was such a man.

But it was not lack of hygiene which made it difficult for Roxbury's dairy farmers to survive, although DeVoe agreed that, "they could not compete with the Western dairy farms. In New York state they'd have 1,500 acres and a hay field. Here we'd have two or three acres, five acres. When it became cheaper to transport, they started to bring it in. I was always a little outspoken about it. The dairy farmers in the county were fighting among themselves. They were fighting the big dairies. I said, 'Listen, you want to protect the big dairies. They're your market. Don't fight them. Play along with them. Or they'll go to New York state. They can buy it cheaper there.' Litchfield county lost a great deal that way. Again, of course, you had the situation where you could not farm 10,000 acre land. (What he meant is that there was no one who had farms that size in the Litchfield hills.) Now the land is bringing so much money, who can farm it?"

He mentioned a farm, which had changed hands in Washington recently for $300,000. "You know darn well you can't raise corn on a $300,000 piece of land." Again, that was not quite the way Lewis Hurlbut saw it. He reminded Devoe of the standards which the Milk Association had imposed, such as pre-cooling and minimum daily production, as well as a quota on how much milk could be brought in from New York. But at the mention of the Milk Association DeVoe's mind came up with something else. "They had a lot of problems. During the war, three men were sent down (to Washington, DC) from Connecticut: Morton Pierpont, and someone representing the Jersey breed, and I. We went to Washington, and they had a panel to set up a code for the dairy industry.

There were eleven labor people on it and one farmer. They were telling us that we should give our men eight hour days. We should work them five days a week.

"I finally got up and said, 'Gentlemen, a cow gives milk for love of its calf. You can't expect a cow to give milk to its own calf five days a week, and two days a week, give it to a strange calf. These men take the place of the calf. The cow becomes used to the calf. If he's changed, there is a drastic reduction in the milk flow. And once it goes down, you can't get it back again.' When I took over Judds Bridge, the men were working every day in the month. They were working 12 hours a day. I said that no one could work more than nine hours for me. We worked a nine hour day, and I gave them two days a month off, which meant a little change, but it's not as bad as two days a week off.

"It's amazing. The first month I was there, we had 31 men working for us. The next month we had 18 men. Raoul came through and said, 'George, I went through the barns. They're sitting down. They're not doing anything.' I said, 'When you came in, did they run around and make believe they were working?' He said, 'No.' I said they did not, because their conscience did not bother them. The reason they were sitting down was that they were waiting for the cows to come back from the barn. I said, 'We have 18 where we had 31. Don't complain.'"

And what happened to the creamery and the Post Office at the old Judds Bridge station, Lewis wanted to know. "The old Post Office was still a station," DeVoe recalled, but trains rarely stopped there, anymore. "They stopped for feed, but not for passengers. We had a cook named Jim Berry. We fixed up the old station house and made a nice quarters for him. He fed the men. He was the chef for the single men on the farm. Jim would generally use the toilet in the main house. But there was a privy up at the railroad. He would walk up the tracks to this privy. Every morning. One day the train came along. He was much more deaf than I am. (George DeVoe, 84 at the time of the interview, was on a hearing aid.) The train had to stop, because Jim did not hear them. He turned around and blew the living daylights out of the engineer for sneaking up on him. Another time, we had a pet turkey, who would not get off the tracks. So they had to stop the train for the turkey."

In a way it is curious that Roxbury's and much of Litchfield's growth as a retreat for people from New York came after the railroad ceased to be the most efficient way of getting back and forth. Although few people contributed more to the change in the county's character than DeVoe, even he was sometimes struck by the speed with which prices in real es-

175

tate had escalated. "I sold a house a week ago. I bought it in 1932 to live in Washington. On eleven acres of land. I decided that I was living at Judds Bridge and I had two other houses. It was ridiculous for me to own one up there. So I never went through with the purchase. Thirty years ago I sold it for $45,000. Ten days ago I sold it for $512,500. When I bought for Raoul Metcalf, we bought most of Judds Bridge for under $200 an acre. The going price at that time was $100 an acre.

"A hundred-acre farm was worth $10,000 and that included the house and the barn. Today, you pay $750,000 for the same farm. We just sold one with 105 acres. Golden Harvest (part of which was later zoned for a dozen new residences) got $2,900,000. I sold that in February 1980 for $3.5 million. The appraiser thought I was crazy. So he had this woman come in, and she appraised it for $7 million - the year that I sold it for $3.5 million. He listed with me for $750,000. He sold it in April 1984, he said for $3.5 million, but I think he got $2.9 million. My buyer (of Judds Bridge Farm, Arthur Carter, a man who had made a fortune on Wall Street in the 1970's and early '80s and settled in Litchfield county to become the publisher of the 'Litchfield County Times') had signed off that for 15 years he would not split off, or sell any land. And he agreed to not to give use of the house as long as the seller lived in it."

The rise in land prices was not only because of inflation. "They see an attraction. It always means a great deal, when you have people like Arthur Miller coming in. They bring in their friends. Dustin Hoffman will bring in his friends. He bought the Lilly farm (on Good Hill Road) for $550,000. The more that is sold, the more will be sold. You can't mix success. You take Roxbury, Bridgewater, Washington, Sherman," he continued, "These are the places where people now want to buy land and build their country retreats." DeVoe seemed less worried than most about what they might do to the environment - not to mention turkeys on the road.

"Don't sell Litchfield county short," he said. "As long as we have our rocky hills, there will be a limit to how many houses can be built. We are going to soil-based zoning. The Federal government and the U.S. Farm Bureau have cooperated in establishing the soil pattern of the country. You've got soil, where half an acre is enough for a septic tank. Here very few towns are going to put less than an acre or an acre and a half. Roxbury now has only three acre zoning. Bridgewater has one, two and four. Washington is one, three, and five. Roxbury is not soil based yet, but it's the coming thing. It's the only way we can protect ourselves."

Arthur Carter, the present owner of Judds Bridge Farm, who agreed not to sell any piece of it for 15 years, now has 1,100 acres and is still working the farm. The rest of the land was sold off in bits and pieces, after Raoul Metcalf's death in 1965. Most of it was sold to his friends and people, who lived on adjacent properties.

* * *

And what happened to Joe Hartwell, after he moved into the center of the town? His new property stretched from the junction of Route 67 and Route 317 to the Catholic chapel and into the hill behind it. But all of the ten acres still lie fallow. He was never permitted to farm them. He sold much of the land to the Catholic chapel, which today uses part of it as a parking lot.

For a while he worked as a carpenter. Then as a mason. "I also worked nine years in a lime quarry for my brother. I made a mistake there, too," he said, "but what are you going to do? When you're hooked, you're hooked. It don't pay to work for a relation. What used to help me here was that I was a substitute mail carrier. I carried from November through April. That would give me a boost." He even ran for First Selectman once and held the office for a term. "Allen Hurlburt tried to get rid of me," he remembered, "But I'm Sexton down here in the cemetery. I buried the bastard."

VIII.
A Local Politician

For most of its history Roxbury was spared political strife. With a few exceptions people were neither rich nor poor, and they were always ready to help each other. They wanted little help from either the State or the Federal government. Republicans won most elections, although Democrats often held office, too. Public service was regarded as a responsibility rather than as a way of gaining power.

Just how casual the selection of a candidate for the State Assembly could be is described by Jerome Beatty in an 'American Magazine' article he wrote in 1949. Beatty had just been elected on the Republican ticket. "Apparently, I shot off my big mouth too much," he wrote, "For a good many years I had been talking and writing about how a citizen is to blame for the bad state of politics, because he doesn't take an interest in government. I've dulled up many a man's evening by arguing that honest men ought to make sacrifices and run for office. Then one day all my words got together and exploded in my face. Somebody stuck a finger into my chest and demanded, 'All right. How about you?'

"So here I am in the House, which is Republican, 180 members to 92. We have a Democratic Senate, 23 to 13, and Chester Bowles, a Democratic governor. There is so much party conflict that sometimes it looks as if we wouldn't have any government at all -- good or bad.

"At the end of two months my constituents, who had sent me up there expecting me to do right by them and to take a vigorous attitude on such questions as housing, taxation, and education, began to ask me with some impatience, 'What're you doing up in Hartford? When are you going into action?'

"'Well,' I would say, 'it takes some time to get in all the bills and for the committees to take considered action. You don't want us to go off half-cocked, do you?' They said, 'Better half-cocked than not at all,' and I said, 'We're moving. We're doing things.'

"Roxbury happens to be one of those rare and admirable towns that does not want anything from the state. Not a soul wants a political job. It has only 521 registered voters - mostly dairy farmers - a strong and active Farm Bureau, a comparatively low tax rate, good roads, a new fire engine and a cracker jack volunteer fire department, and a good school. The P.T.A. wants a gymnasium for the school (which they eventually got) and our Town Hall is a bit too much of a lovely old antique (in 1988 it still was. To the chagrin of many a newcomer and most weekenders a new one, or at least an extension of the old one, costing about $1 million to build, was in the works), but we have one of the prettiest towns in Connecticut - one of the few in this part of the state that is zoned. No billboards and no tourist homes.

"After election, all the successful candidates were asked to speak before our Monthly Forum to tell what they intended to do. When I spoke, I confessed that I would be a freshman, but I said I would do my best to see that Roxbury got what was coming to it.

"After the meeting, Norman Hurlbut, a farmer, one of Roxbury's great gentlemen, came to me. A Democrat, always endorsed by both parties, he has held many town offices. He said quietly, 'What you said about doing things for Roxbury in Hartford -- I don't think the folks here are interested so much in that. What they'd like is for you to work and vote for just one thing -- what's best for the state.' Would there were more like him in every town and city in the nation. So I have introduced only one bill. It has to do with collecting cash from husbands and fathers, who have skipped out of the state, deserting wives and children, and who won't send money back to support their abandoned families. I was inspired by the 'Fugitive Husbands', an article by J.B. Griswold in the January 1949 issue of the American Magazine.

"Evidently there are no sleuths who check to see whether legislators are earning the money the tax payers pay them, because even through those idle months, my pay checks were delivered regularly. I get $120 a month with $1.60 deducted for Federal income tax, until I have been paid my entire salary of $600. We have one regular session every two years, ending the first Wednesday after the first Monday in June, unless I am confused and it is the first Monday after the first Wednesday. We meet three days a week in the early part of the session and four days a week when business picks up.

"During the campaign, taking my cue from other candidates, I mentioned at every opportunity that I was seeking a job that paid $600 for two year's work. I began to believe it myself and feared we'd have to mortgage the house and get along the remainder of our lives with the 1939 Studebaker. Then I heard about 'mileage.' Mileage is the most beautiful word that ever falls upon a Connecticut legislator's ears, unless he is so unfortunate as to live in or near Hartford. We get ten cents a mile, round trip, for expenses, each day we serve. I live fifty miles from Hartford and collect $10 a day, so my total take for the five month session, mileage plus salary, will be around $250 a month.

"Some of the blame should be placed upon John Pickett, a farmer, who had served three good terms in Hartford and decided he could afford no more, so the Roxbury Republican committee had to find a candidate. One morning in September, Mrs. George Devoe, whose husband is an insurance man and one of the nation's leading authorities on Brown Swiss cattle, called up and asked Mrs. Beatty and me to come up that afternoon for cocktails. Mrs. Harry Ripley, president of the local garden club, whose husband is a New York banker, was coming, too, Mrs. Devoe said. And since Mrs. Ripley lived next door to us, would we please bring her.

"There were only five of us, including our host and hostess, and something was cooking, but I couldn't figure out what it was. The fact that George Devoe was chairman of the Roxbury Republican Committee never entered my mind. He asked me to come into the kitchen to help mix the drinks, and when I got out there, he said suddenly, 'How'd you like to run for the Representative?'

"'Representative for what?' I asked.

"'Roxbury, to go to Hartford.'

"'George,' I said, 'you must stop smoking opium. It's driving you nuts.'

"'I mean it,' he said.

"'Me? That's the craziest idea.'

"I stopped. I'd lived only eight years in Roxbury, a New England town; and in New England, if you and most of your ancestors weren't born there, you can live there 50 years and still be an outsider. This, I realized, was the greatest compliment that had ever been paid me. I kind of choked up and swallowed a couple of times. Call it hammy, if you will, but that's the truth.

"'Thanks, George,' I said gratefully, 'but I can't do it. I couldn't afford it.' I meant it, too.

"'Anyway, I wouldn't be any good.' He nodded in what appeared to be instant agreement and said, 'You carry that tray, and I'll take this one.'

"'Hm-m,' I muttered to myself. 'He might at least have given me an argument. I guess he did not want me very much, after all.' I started my campaign the next day -- by waving at every car that passed, whether I was driving or in my yard spraying poison on the weeds. Some of the folks in New York cars appeared to be a bit startled, but I overlooked nobody. Beatty was everybody's friend, and besides, Roxbury is only 70 miles from New York, and sometimes its voters rode in New York cars.

"I was nominated, with the other Republican candidates for town offices, at the official caucus at the Town Hall. About 60 persons were

180

there, most of them my friends. There was a rumor that a revolt against the town committee had been organized and that the committee's ticket would be opposed, but the steam roller operated, and we were all nominated unanimously. I had prepared a speech of acceptance, but before I could rise and deliver it, everybody else was on his way home.

"Roxbury has seldom elected a Democrat to the Assembly, and my election, the committeemen said, was in the bag. I wouldn't need to do any campaigning. However, about three weeks before the election, one after another, Republican committeemen approached me with an air of uneasiness. Mrs. John Dickinson, wife of a dairy farmer and one of our best friends, who started the 'Draft Beatty' movement, hinted that I'd better get out and meet the folks. The Town of Roxbury covers a lot of territory. I live in Roxbury Station, at one edge, and knew most of the people who gather in Roxbury Center in Hodge's store, which houses the post office, but many citizens, who vote in Roxbury, live far away and don't come into the center. Allen Hurlburt, First Selectman, and John Pickett said maybe they'd better take me around and introduce me, particularly to the farmers over in Tophet, Judds Bridge, Good Hill, Painter Hill, and the folks down on Southbury Road.

"My Democratic opponent was John M. Dooley, Roxbury's Democratic leader, a farmer, head of the Grange, and an old and respected citizen, who had served in the Assembly some years back. Roxbury is a farming community and somebody--not John Dooley--had started a whispering campaign against this Johnny-come-lately, who was a Midwestern city fellow, who knew nothing about dairy farm problems. Besides, it was pointed out, I spent a lot of time travelling around the country, and it was charged I probably wouldn't go to Hartford very often.

"The 'New Milford Times,' published by Fred Tisdale, seven miles away, in Column One, Page One, carried a story headlined, 'Beatty-Dooley Contest stirs Roxburyites. It's Farmer versus Writer in a battle for Representative.' For a fellow who really didn't want the job, I certainly was scared. Now I did want it very much. I tried to think up arguments that would swing votes to me. John Pickett thought it best not to emphasize my manner of making a living and carry no magazines. The folks were always glad to see us. We made about 50 calls, met wonderful, good, sound citizens, and it is not political oratory when I say I had a good time and made a lot of new friends. My only disappointment was that, after I had prepared for political discussions, we talked about the weather, the roads, who had died, who had had babies, gossip of the town, but nobody asked me one question about my attitude on political questions. I never was able to bring up the subject.

181

"I mentioned that to John. 'These visits don't seem to be doing much good,' I said, 'I don't get a chance to tell them how I stand.

"'They don't care how you stand,' he said. 'They just want to get a look at you.'

"There were no babies to kiss, and if there had been, promiscuous osculation would have cost me votes. These farmers raise cows and chicken scientifically and know about germs, and wouldn't like to have politicians spreading goodness-knows-what. A few days before election somebody quietly mentioned. 'What about your election night party?'

"'Well,' I said, 'four or five people are coming in to listen to the returns on the radio.'

"'But John Dooley always has open house, whether he wins or not. And so did John Pickett.'

"'Holy cats!' I said. 'Thanks for telling me.'

"So Dorothea quickly ordered ham and asked Mrs. Axel Rehn and Mrs. Audrey Walker to come and help, and I ordered a keg of beer, and found out that Bob Kuhn, an artist, knew how to handle the pump and coil, and he promised to supervise that. I had three or four bottles of liquor on hand, so we were all set. I thought. We told the folks at Hodge's store and others to pass the word around about the open house.

"The day before the election, somebody told me, 'I hear you're planning on beer.' News gets around Roxbury. 'Yes,' I said. 'We'll have enough for forty or fifty people.'

"'These folks don't drink beer,' he said. 'They want high balls.' And what do you mean about forty or fifty people? Everybody in town is coming. You'll have a hundred and fifty!'

"That knocked the breath out of us. Pandemonium proceeded to reign in the Beatty family. Dorothea frantically got another ham and two turkeys, while I drove into New Milford, cancelled the order for beer, and brought out three cases of whiskey and four of soda. Unlike my fellow politician and running mate, Mr. Dewey, I was mighty jumpy on Election Day. My condition became worse when, on my way to vote, I saw a truck carrying s huge sign reading, Vote for Dooley. What a fool I was! What a blithering amateur in politics! There wasn't a single sign in Roxbury asking anybody to vote for Beatty! Why hadn't I been smart and hired a calliope? Things looked bad.

"The folks began coming to the party about 8 o'clock, and I realized I had a narrow escape from being disgraced forever in Roxbury. We would have quickly exhausted the food and liquor, if we hadn't had the warning. More than 100 came.

"About 8:30 P.M. Allen Hurlburt called up and said the straight Republican ballots had been counted and were enough to elect the entire ticket. I was congratulated, and I relaxed. Later, the official count showed me a winner, 301 to 131.

"The hosts had a swell time at the party, and I think the guests did too. Republicans and Democrats came in and out until about midnight. The news about the victories of Truman and Bowles came in too late to spoil the party for the Republicans, not to startle the Democrats into a Bacchanalian celebration on my liquor."

* * *

Politics was not always as chummy as John Beatty made it out to be. Four years later, running for the office for the third time against John Dooley, Beatty got into a real slugging match with him. Senator Joseph McCarthy, a Republican from Wisconsin, had arrived with his Communist scare tactics, and Roxbury was not spared the national fever. Beatty fanned it himself in a letter to the Waterbury Republican in which he accused Governor Chester Bowles, a member of the liberal Americans for Democratic Action, of being "soft on Communism," because they supported freedom of speech for everyone. The Dooleys, on the other hand, were ardent anti-McCarthyites.

John Dooley replied to Beatty's article with a letter in which he charged him with resorting to "scare, smear, and diatribe," and "personal vilification and hysterically wild accusations."

He wanted no part of Communists himself, Dooley wrote, "But it's not our way to use our anti-Communism as vote bait."

Beatty quickly replied with another letter in which he said Dooley was a "blind" supporter of Governor Bowles. "Like Bowles, I gather from the letter, Mr. Dooley hates Communists, but believes it would be proper for Paul Robeson or any other pro-Communist to speak before Roxbury students, and for Communists freely to spread their propaganda in Roxbury." He then put it to Dooley that, "Down deep in his heart, John Dooley doesn't believe in full freedom of speech for Communists any more than I do."

Dooley never took him up on that. In a second letter to 'The Republican' to answer Beatty's, he merely enjoined him to "stop yelling 'Communist' at everyone who disagrees with him," and left it at that. Paul Robeson died without ever singing or speaking in Roxbury.

IX.
History Buffs Debate

Roxbury's official historian is Elmer Worthington. Like all Roxbury historians, whether amateur or official, he has his own view on Col. Seth Warner's demise, which haunts the town like a bad conscience to this day. Worthington disputes the legend, often repeated in earlier histories, as well as in our chapter 'History Revisited,' that George Washington personally came to Roxbury to visit Warner's destitute widow and paid the mortgage on her house.

"Washington never came anywhere near here," Worthington maintained in a conversation with Lewis Hurlbut in 1985, "Stratford is the nearest place he came to, after he was president. But Washington apparently met with William Samuel Johnson, and Johnson came up to Roxbury and gave Mrs. Warner money, and gave her a horse. I imagine probably a trooper with Washington came along with Johnson and the kid (Seth Warner's son), who was only twelve years old, thought 'Gee, this is Washington.' He had a uniform on." Anyway, that's his hypothesis, and he is sticking to it.

We also asked him about Roxbury's oldest house, the two-story gambrel-roofed structure on the bottom of Sentry Hill Road, which had recently been given special landmark designation -- and which Norman Hurlbut mentioned in his account of Roxbury's 'men of renown.' "It was the Remember Baker House," Worthington said, "built by John Baker in 1733. John Baker had several children, and one of them was Remember Baker, who was born in this house. He was killed in a hunting accident by a friend of his. His son, Remember Baker Jr., was three years old when his father was killed. He grew up in this house, and he went with his two cousins, Ethan Allen, whose house was a little further up Sentry Hill Road, and Seth Warner, who lived down on River Road, to Bennington, Vermont, in 1763. They were all in the Green Mountain Boys, a regiment founded before the Revolution, when they were fighting with New York state. The house continued in the Baker family until 1796. Then it went through several hands up to the present owner, who is Dr. Leon Root.

"The Baker family," Worthington continued, "was an interesting family. Remember Baker Jr. fought with his two cousins for the capture of Montreal. He was killed by the Indians just before the capture, beheaded, had his head put on a pole, and the British soldiers bought it. And they returned it to America and buried it on the side of the Richelieu River. His family continued to stay in Vermont, and his son, Remember Baker III, moved to Stratford, New York, where his son, Lafayette Baker was born. He became head of the United States Secret Service during the Civil War by appointment by President Lincoln. He got the appointment because his father, Remember Baker III, served under General Winfield Scott who, at the beginning of the Civil War, was at the head of the American Army. He later wrote a book on the history of the Secret Service. I have that book. The book also tells about the family and its New England roots. His grandson was Newton Baker, who was Secretary of War during President Wilson's administration from 1913 to 1921. But Roxbury saw the last Baker in 1790.

"But there are still some Roxbury families related to them. Remember Baker married a Hurlbut, and his father was killed by a Hurlbut in the hunting accident."

Worthington said, "There were two more killings in Roxbury. One, and that was the first one, was during the War of 1812. The Christ Church Rectory was then a village inn. A recruiting officer went to the tavern and there was a draftee, who had refused to come with him to serve in the army."

At this point Lewis Hurlbut interjected, "The book says the killing was at Knapp's house," but Worthington insisted, "No, the killing took place at the tavern the way I read it. Not far from the tavern is a stone giving the name of the officer and it says who murdered him."

(According to William Cothren's history of Woodbury, the source of practically all local historiographical efforts since 1876, Lt. Thomas Weller was killed by Archibald Knapp May 16, 1814 at Knapp's home in New Milford. Weller went to his house as Knapp had enlisted in the Army but did not show up. Lt. Weller's gravestone in the Roxbury Center Cemetery has the following inscription: "Lt. Thomas Weller, an officer in the United States Army, who was murdered by Archibald Knapp.") According to Cothern there was another fatal shooting in 1787 in the town's tavern in which David Downs, a local resident, was killed by accident.

From there the conversation drifted to cemeteries. Elmer Worthington mentioned that none of the Baker family's graves could be found in any of Roxbury's cemeteries. "Where they were buried, I have no idea," he said, "because I wrote a book on the cemeteries of Roxbury and could not find them buried there. There was a house that was just sold on Church Street, and it has an old grave stone right in the backyard." Lewis Hurlbut affirmed, "there are a lot of houses that have them. Over in

Bridgewater there are two houses with grave stones. But these stones are old stones, which they took from the cemeteries when they put new stones in. We had two in the cellar, too."

Asked whether there might also have been a tradition of burying people on their own grounds, Lewis said, "No, not very much. Our cemeteries were large enough. The only places I know, where they have little family plots, are up in New York state. The one up at the Leavenworths (a house on Gold Mine Road now owned by Thomas and Nancy Tafuri) has two revolutionary soldiers in there. They were not Leavenworths." Worthington pointed out that, "one of the stones is not where the Leavenworth's cemetery was. They were moved. They were down in the field. When they started plowing the field, they pulled them up."

Lewis said that it was his father, "who pulled them up to the wall. But that's the only place I know. The cemeteries were kind of sacred, and we had enough cemeteries to take all the dead people in Roxbury."

To which Worthington added, "don't forget that you could not be buried in Roxbury until 1743. Woodbury would not allow anyone to be buried here, until it became a separate parish. The earliest grave in Roxbury is dated 1745. It was one of the Warners down on the Castle Street cemetery." Hurlbut replied, "There were a lot of objections when Allen Hurlburt put down Squire Road." Worthington, "Yes, there used to be a sign saying Castle Street Cemetery. I don't know whatever happened to that sign."

The interviewer asked them whether any more was known about other people who lived in Roxbury's oldest house after the Baker family left. Worthington answered, "In 1796, when the last of the Bakers lived there, Roxbury itself became a town. Since then all the records are in Roxbury. The deeds would indicate who owned that house over the years. It was all ordinary people." Hurlbut added, "But the records of the town of the early 1800's are all lost." Worthington did not contest that statement, but continued, "the only one, who was somewhat active in the town was Davidson. He lived there. I think his first name was Todd. He was very active in mineral activities." Hurlbut said, "I think the one you mean was Treat Davidson. Another, who was there for a long time, was Allen Philbrick." Worthington agreed.

Over the years the house also underwent some architectural changes. "It has windows twelve over twelve," Worthington said, "But they added dormer windows on the roof. They still have some of the original glass in those twelve by twelve panes. Some of the doors are the earlier plank construction, two planks thick. And the old hardware is still on the doors.

"Treat Davidson was a man of importance for many years. He was Selectman. He also owned a grist mill." He then asked Lewis Hurlbut whatever happened to the fort his family and other early settlers built on Sentry Hill. Lewis told him, "I think it was taken down for the wood." Today, said Worthington, "it is the foundation of Horace Gillette's house." Again Lewis Hurlbut remembered it differently. "That was Peace Minor's house, and that goes back to pretty near that time. The only description of it anywhere is in Cothren's history. He says how many yards it is from the Remember Baker house. In fact, we're putting a historic stone there."

Worthington then suggested there are other records at the Beinecke Library in Yale University, which contain the plans of the first Roxbury Church. But all this goes back to a time which no one remembers, and the interviewer had to remind the two men that what they were after was not what was in historical documents but what people themselves remembered or had heard in their families about happenings during the last 100 years. They had both mentioned Treat Davidson. Who were some to the others?

Worthington's first nominee is Col. Albert Hodge. "I knew his son Charles Hodge," he said, "Col. Hodge was the paymaster and bookkeeper of the Roxbury iron mill at Mine Hill. His title was probably honorary, because he was never in the army. He was in the local militia. His son, when I first started in the banking business in 1928, was the president of the First National Bank of New Milford, which is now a division of Colonial Bank and still later part Bank of Boston, Connecticut. We were always having a lot of fights, because I was in the New Milford Savings Bank and Charley was in the National Bank. But he was also a Director of the Savings Bank. So any time we discussed raises in the Savings Bank, Charley Hodge would be against it, because he claimed he was getting only $1,000 a year as president of his bank. But everyone said he was getting more in dividends on the bank's stock. So he did not need any salary. He was a bachelor. He had no family. He really ran the bank as a one man institution." Still, Hodge was not the richest man in town. Allen and Everett Hurlburt were probably richer.

"I would say the two of them," Worthington said, to which Hurlbut added, "I think George Hurlburt's family really got their name through (starting) trade between here and New Haven. He had a brother in New Haven, and his business, handling farmers' goods before the railroads, really gave them a start in financial stability." Although the Hodges eventually bought Mine Hill, "this did not give them any money," Hurlbut said. "The ones who got the most out of the mine," Worthington offered, "was lawyers with their fees." Hurlbut joked - perhaps because the interviewer was born in Germany - "They had a German in there that got a lot of money out of the mine." (This was a reference to an early account that a German silversmith, who had been brought in to look for silver, was discovered with silver bars in a chest which, legend has it, broke open the day he left town, after years of failing to find any silver in the mine.)

The talk about mining reminded Worthington that, "many of the family names in Roxbury go back to the Welsh miners, who worked in Mine Hill." Hurlbut added, "and the Polish names came in through the silica factory. They came in as single men, and when the silica mine closed, they stayed on as farmers." Worthington recalled, "In New Milford, when I was in the bank making loans to farmers, more than half the farmers in New Milford in the 1920s were either Swedes or Poles. The old Yankee farmers had begun to die out. One reason was that the Yankee farmer may have had two or three children. The Polish farmer had half a dozen, and they all worked on the farm. I think the last Polish farm in New Milford was just sold the other day. They were better farmers than the old Yankees."

As an Old Yankee farmer, Lewis Hurlbut was not about to take that statement lying down. "I'm not so sure about that," he said, but Worthington quickly amplified, "for the Polish farmer, machinery was something he really protected. They would have their machinery in the barns. They would not leave it out. I can say that, because I'm a Yankee, and my family ran a farm for hundreds of years in Connecticut, and they would not think anything of leaving it out. To the Poles that was valuable property. You did not leave that out to rust." Hurlbut said he could name a few really good Yankee farmers, "for instance, Ben Seeley and Edward Seeley, who were probably two of the most outstanding farmers in this town." In 1986 their farm was still producing, although as a 'gentleman's farm' owned by the Diebold family. "The Dickinsons were good farmers, too. And Nate Beardsley. They were all Yankees."

Elmer Worthington nevertheless insisted, "You'd go to these Yankee farms, and you'd find equipment all over the farm. You went to a Polish farm, and you'd find that at the end of the day that went into the barn to be protected." Asked whether newcomers did not always work harder, Worthington said, "It's true that to own land and not to be tenant farmers was new to them and gave them special motivation. The Yankee had been on the farm for generations. He did not worry about being the first one, and he did not have so many children to run the farm, either. And I do not think the Yankee farmer had the feeling for the farm as the Polish or the Swedish farmer. This was his land. This was the first generation that had owned land."

Hurlbut then said, "Well, the good Yankee farmers got smart early and went west. I don't know why my family didn't." Perhaps they stayed. because they were happy in these hills. But Worthington had another idea.

After the War of Independence Connecticut insisted on at least a part of its original title, which went back to a royal grant to the Earl of Warwick's corporation known as the Council of Plymouth. This title assigned to Connecticut, 'All that part of New England, in America, which lies and extends itself from the river there called Narragansett river, the space of forty leagues upon a straight line near the sea shore, towards the south-west, west by south, or west, as the coast lieth, towards Virginia, accounting three English miles to the league, all and singular, the lands and heridaments whatsoever, lying and being within bounds aforesaid, north and south in latitude and breadth, and in length and longitude, and within all the breadth aforesaid throughout all the main lands there, from the western ocean to the South Sea.' Before the war there had been bloody battles, because Connecticut claimed land in what had become the states of New York and Pennsylvania. The claims were settled in court. After the war 'Horizontal' states were declared ungovernable, and most gave up their Western territories. In 1786 Connecticut was nevertheless awarded a 120-mile long Western Reserve along the southern shores of Lake Erie between its own parallels in what was to become Ohio. So Connecticut farmers, when they went west, could and did create a new Connecticut in rich bottom land.

Worthington explained, "the Western Reserve in some respects was a scam organized by Connecticut people. The land in Wyoming Valley, Pennsylvania, was absolutely that. You know that Connecticut had the Wyoming Valley, too? And the same way with (Moses) Cleaveland and the group that went out to the Western Reserve. They were selling the farmers in New England. I think one reason is that the oldest son took over the farm, and the second would go out to the Western Reserve. In eastern Texas the farmers, who settled there, also came from Connecticut."

Hurlbut said, "But the land was so much better than in Connecticut. There was good reason for going there. You know why they call them 'swamp Yankees.' They were down by the river, and they never got up enough guts to go west."

Worthington again disagreed. "They called them 'swamp Yankees,' because they lived in the poorer section of the state. They're like the 'red necks' of Georgia."

Hurlbut allowed that, "the name is not very definite. But they were people who never had much gumption, who never went west."

The interviewer recalled an old ditty from Massachusetts, which went something like this:

"There was a young man in Boston,
Whom this dilemma was tossed on
Whether 'twas to go off and become rich in the west,
Or stay poor and respectable in Boston."

This fired Hurlbut up to say, "They heard stories of what beautiful land lay in the west."

Worthington, "It was all advertising."

Hurlbut, "But it was worth advertising, Elmer."

Worthington, "The people that made the money were people like Cleaveland and those, who ran the various land companies. The people did not buy the land from the state. They bought it from the land companies."

But how much did they pay for it?

Worthington, "It was unsettled, and it was terrible along the Cuyohaga River. Some of them got discouraged and came back. It was the land companies that kept pressure on the second sons."

Perhaps the question of why they left will never be settled. It can be argued that the more ambitious left, just as it has been argued that America was settled by the risk takers of Europe - and other continents - while it can be just as easily argued that the more successful ones stayed home, because they already had what they wanted.

"That's what I say," Worthington concluded, whereas Hurlbut reminded him that "you forget one thing. People do have adventurous characteristics. The ones who went west were not the riff-raff."

One of Hurlbut's grandfathers and two of his cousins went west. As he recalled, "they were seeking better opportunities."

Worthington, on the other hand, reminded Hurlbut that most of the people who went west came from eastern Connecticut. "You did not have too many families from this section of the state. The land companies were in eastern Connecticut, the poorer section, the textile section of the state." A lot of people from western Connecticut had gone to Vermont, but that was a century earlier.

In fact, Roxbury had enough industry around that time to provide a livelihood for everyone. "In the last hundred years a lot of people were making beaver hats," Hurlbut said. "They did not make the whole hat," Worthington added, "just the blocks." Even in Danbury it was mostly blocking. "But then you had the collapse of the beaver hat. The beavers were not coming in from the west, and the style changed." This occurred in the late 1800's. "Don't forget that the main industry in the Housatonic Valley up until Depression days was tobacco." Hurlbut also thought the hat shops were quite small. "They were less than 20 feet square. And in 1850 there were ten of them in Roxbury."

Another source of industry was the plentiful water power. All along the Shepaug River there were factories. "There were a tremendous number of factories," Worthington said, "Iron factories. All sorts. It all depended on the water power." They recalled that an old saw mill remains in New Preston, just below the lake. Worthington said there were three such mills in New Preston.

The highest level of industrial activity and population growth was at the turn of the century, Worthington pointed out. "I would say that Roxbury from 1810 to 1820 was the largest, until you got up to the last decade. When I moved to Roxbury from New Milford in 1946 it was 600 and New Milford was 5,000 people. New Milford is now 20,000 and Roxbury 1,500."

Hurlbut thought the biggest population was when the granite mine was being worked. "There were 140 workers in the quarry,"

Worthington countered, "I don't think that was the biggest population." And he proved his case by producing the figures. His statistics show that in 1800 the population was 1,121, in 1850 1,114, and in 1900 it had sunk to 1,087. Then, by 1950 the population had dwindled to 740, before it started climbing back to 1,500 again.

Reminded of how many people pursued pre-industrial activities in their homes then, Hurlbut said, "many was the house that had a loom right in the attic, when they built them. They made cloth for everything, blankets and clothes."

The conversation then returned to talk about prominent families. Worthington thought that from about 1920 to his death in the mid-40s, Charles Hodge was certainly the most prominent businessman in town. "He owned the mine," he said, "when only the granite quarry was being used."

Hurlbut praised Hodge for the way he ran his bank during the Great Depression and for bringing it out in very good condition, although thousands of others all over the United States failed in that period.

Worthington: "I can't quite agree with you there. I was in the opposing institution. Besides, none of the banks in the small Connecticut towns failed. There was not a single bank in Litchfield county during the Depression that failed."

He explained, "I'm not saying that he was not a good banker. It's just that all the banks in the county were conservative." Nor did Worthington consider him very astute as a banker. "Here's an example," he said, "Up until the Depression you paid on mortgages twice a year. And you never did anything about reducing the principal. If you bought a house or a farm, you assumed the mortgage. The mortgage may have been from 1880. The only thing you had to be careful of was that they changed the dollar in 1890. In 1933 the Home Mortgage Loan Corporation came in and said we had been handling mortgages the wrong way for 100 years. The interest rate may have been 6% in 1870 and in 1930 it was still 6%. During the Depression they went after some people that had not owned their house for 20 years or more. Now they insisted that you reduce the principal in monthly payments over a period of 20 years. I had more arguments with Charley Hodge about that. He thought it was ridiculous. He was the old school."

Perhaps these old-fashioned bankers knew when they had a good thing, namely 'evergreen loans' that worked like perennial annuities for them, which could be paid back only in full. But interest rates must not have changed much for 100 years, at least until the Depression, if they remained happy getting their annual 6% from one generation of borrowers after another.

The change in mortgage financing had far-reaching consequences, of course, especially during the Depression when the value of the collateral was collapsing all over the country, including and above all the value of farm land. If one could not repay the principal, a new loan would exceed the value of a property after a few years. Luckily, and probably partly thanks to the new regulation, there were very few foreclosures in Litchfield County. Neither man could recall a single one in Roxbury. But paying interest year after year without being able to repay a loan was the bane of generations of Hurlbuts.

"Of course," said Worthington, "one of the things that happened was that when you grew tobacco, you got paid once a year, in November. If you had a good crop, you got a good check. If you had a bad crop, you were out of luck. So when the Depression came and people were not buying tobacco, and the prices fell out of bed, the farmers went into dairying. The dairying gave a check once a month."

192

Lewis Hurlbut also recalled that at first farmers relied on small out-croppings of silica for their cash, before tobacco became their cash crop. "My grandfather had a crop of tobacco," he said, "but it was only just a small piece. It gave him a little cash money at the end of the year to buy shoes or something. With milk they first made butter and changed it for something else at the grocery store. But all that changed with the rail-road. Then they could ship their milk. Then the North Pacific Railroad came through, and everything went flop again. Then the creameries got started. There were four of them in Roxbury. The farmers had a place to go to again."

Worthington thought the big change from tobacco to dairying came in 1934, right in the midst of the Depression. Roxbury had never had much tobacco, except just along the Shepaug River, below Mine Hill. Also, "as I recall along Wellers Bridge Road that was all tobacco land," he said. Later, a lot of the milk went to Goshen, which for a time was one of the biggest makers of cheese not only in Connecticut but the entire United States. Millions of pounds of cheese were produced there every year. Then why didn't the local people think of making their own cheese? Lewis Hurlbut said there had been one cheese factory in Roxbury. "The wall is still there right at the beginning of Painter Hill Road. The man's name was Nate Smith," but he had never eaten any of it, because "it was before my time."

X.
The Established Church

The Congregational church was Roxbury's first and goes back to 1732, when Roxbury, which was part of the Woodbury Society, was given winter privileges. The winter services went on thirteen years, before Roxbury was made a separate parish. Until 1744, people living in 'Shippauge' had to trudge nine miles and more to attend services in Woodbury, except during those winter months.

The first minister, Thomas Canfield, preached in the first and second meeting houses for as long as they stood - until 1794. In 1746 a larger building was constructed 44 feet south of the first one. There were three more long ministries. In fact, for 120 years the church had only four ministers. During the next 120 years, from 1864 until 1984 it had 32 more, few of them staying longer than five years. It is not clear why so few stayed for any length of time. If recent history is any guide, the congregation did not look so much for leadership as for compassion in the man at the head of the congregation. His pay was meager, and while enough money was found to build four meeting houses, the last one in 1838, the secular management of the church and its independence hardly guaranteed a preacher unquestioned authority over the members of the church.

In the beginning there was no other church, because the Congregational church was the established church of the state. It was wedded to the state's government, which established the bounds of the Congregational parishes, provided that the local parish tax inhabitants for the support of the church and minister, and mandated that all residents attend services. For many years, eligibility to vote and hold office in Connecticut was based on church membership.

Although the Federal Constitution of 1789 guaranteed that Congress would make no laws restricting freedom of religion, the document did not prevent the state from religious discrimination. In fact, Connecticut was the last state in the Union to guarantee complete religious freedom to its inhabitants.

Roxbury's official historian Elmer Worthington likes to recall that, "up to 1818 we were in a church state. The Congregational church was the state. We had an Ecclesiastical Society that ran the church and the town. In 1818 western Connecticut voted practically overwhelmingly not to divide the church from the state. Roxbury delegates to the Constitutional convention voted not to change it. They came back to Roxbury and had a town meeting, and the town wanted to separate church and state. So they were overruled. Right up to 1965, when we got a new constitution, we were a Christian state. We had one Jewish governor, Abraham Ribicoff, who swore to uphold the Christian state of Connecticut."

"By law, you had to support your church," he recalled, "up until 1818 the only way you could get out of it was by sending a letter to the town clerk and to the clerk of the Ecclesiastical Society stating that you were now a member of, say, the Methodist church. That got you out of paying your dues into the Congregational church."

The local Congregational church assets were in effect owned by the town's Ecclesiastical Society. One of the things that caused a lot of trouble only a few years ago was the question that if we ever dissolved the local congregation, where would the assets go? One of them argued they should go to the Connecticut Conference. Another group wanted them to go to the town. It was a very bitter fight. It was also ridiculous, because there were no plans to dissolve the church. Only recently it was decided - without any opposition - that they would go to the State Conference.

The Ecclesiastical Society did not run the town directly. The Selectmen did, but one can easily imagine who did the selecting. "The Society had the real power in the town," Worthington said, "they were something like a town council. It was just called 'the Society,' and it was made up only of members of the Congregational church. Before you had a town, you had the parish."

Roxbury was a parish for 53 years, from 1743 to 1796, before it was incorporated as a town. So for more than one generation the Society was the only authority. The town later collected the tax for the Society and eventually for the other churches. The rule, more custom than law, remained in effect until the Second World War. In addition to the required contribution, which was adjusted to the financial need of maintaining the church and its minister, "what you did is you paid for your pew," Worthington explained. People also owned the sheds behind the church in which they tethered their horses and wagons, while attending services.

The last of the original "four pillars" of the church was the Reverend Austin Isham. The end of his ministry coincides with the beginning of the Civil War. The issues leading up to the war had caused a deep schism in Congregational churches around the state between those who favored the abolition of slavery and the anti-abolitionists, among other things. In the end it appears that some people could not countenance the stand of their church. They left, and later most of the dissidents joined the Methodists. It is not exactly clear what the immediate cause of their departure was, but it seems that the people who broke away were followers of Abraham Lincoln, whereas the majority in Roxbury were for peace (with the Confederacy) and did not feel very strongly about slavery one way or the other.

The way the story has been handed down in the Hurlbut family is simply that, "one Sunday a fiery minister came and the people in the church who subsequently became Methodists walked out of the church and vowed never to return," Lewis Hurlbut said. "We know there was a strong division here, because Lincoln had lost out here in Roxbury." Unfortunately, there is no record of this walk-out in the church books. Elmer Worthington said, "I have been going through the books from 1743. They're all in our library here. And going through the materials of the period, I don't recall anything in the church books that indicated any particular fight over abolition or the Civil War," as was documented for the Congregational church in neighboring Washington. There a conservative minister made a strong last-ditch stand against abolition, until the congregation ousted him. Such battles often raged around one strong personality. Col. George Hurlbut and Mr. Preston withdrew in 1863.

Worthington did find some interesting trivia such as that when the third church was built in 1795 everybody who brought stones for the foundation received half a pint of rum, while "one hundred years later the church was leading in prohibition." So Roxbury, despite its remoteness from the center of political power, went with the times.

The 1864 school essay by Jeremah Decker with which we began this memoir made no mention of the war. But the Hurlbut family has a few more school essays, written in 1862 and 1863, in which one A. Francis Squire expressed a despair that must have reflected the general discontent - and confusion - with the politics of the day. He seems to have considered partisanship the sole cause of the war. In one essay he described the country as being "in the midst of one of the most unjust and (un)called for wars...and all of this for the sake of party." In another essay, Squire found himself alone and surrounded by Democratic opponents who "say the ministers preach Abolisionest (sic) till old John Brown went down to free the niggers and this caused the war," and argues, "I do not think John Brown done right in going down there but he received the penalty of it and it was settled on the spot." He then threatened to "defy any of my learned friends to prove that the Republicans had anything to do with this war."

He upheld both slavery and the Republican party, which, as every school boy today should know, under President Lincoln fought against the Southern Secessionists in the name of the Constitution. "Another one of my opponents," he writes, "says that the president does not abide by the constitution. He nor any other man cannot prove an instance where he has violated it. He says his (Emancipation) proclamation does. I will deny it. The constitution upholds it in every respect. It says that any state that rises in rebellion, the property shall be confiscated to put it down." But there is a curious kicker. He adds that "...niggers are as much property as our old black horse is..." To him apparently the issue was that Lincoln was right in depriving the south of its property, especially its slaves, whom it had forfeited by seceding from the Union.

Of course, the writer was very young, but his confusion must have come from the talk he heard at home and among his neighbors. In the last essay, written in February 1863, he states, "I am afraid we have seen the best days that we shall ever see as far as a nation is concerned...I am sorry that the inhabitants were foolish enough to cause a war for the sake of party." What to our minds has become the real issue of the war consistently escaped him. But his confusion is forgivable. The year 1863 was a tumultuous one in Connecticut history. The traditional parties had been split into abolitionist and anti-abolitionist wings. The Free Soil party, the Know-Nothing party, and the Temperance party had thrived on divisive single issues, and a pro-Southern Democrat was running for governor against the incumbent Republican. He was only narrowly defeated.

Also, although Connecticut had abolished slavery in 1848, this did not mean that it had become very tolerant of Negroes, who continued to be barred from schools, work, and were relegated to 'African corners' in churches and communities. Besides a Negro slave after whom Jack's Brook is named, Norman Hurlbut in his historical sketches mentions only one other Negro resident. At the foot of the Woodbury Road, opposite Painter Hill Road, where Jonathan Hurlbut built a house in 1730, "on the south bank of the brook, just north of the foot of Ranney Hill Road and west of Painter Hill Road, one can see part of the foundations of the Bradley house, whose last resident was one Negro, Caesar Broadhead."

Lewis Hurlbut's grandfather was among those who left the Congregational church during the Civil War, and "he was a strong supporter of President Lincoln," Lewis said. Norman Hurlbut was brought up as a Methodist. Other Hurlbuts remained in the Congregational Church or

197

became Episcopalians. Lewis himself returned to the Congregational church, after the Methodist church was closed down in Roxbury because of the dwindling population. Roxbury has had five churches, the Congregational, Episcopalian, Methodist, Catholic, and Baptist. By 1940, these had to be supported by no more than 600 people. Even the Congregational church was nearly dissolved. "The population was so small that it could not keep up its budget, and we were in the Depression," Ethel Hurlbut recalled. Lewis added, "Allen Hurlburt had to pay for painting the church." Lewis' father never did become a full member, although he attended Congregational services.

The Methodist church, which stood near the town hall, was torn down in 1940. In the last four years only about twelve or fourteen families still worshipped in it. Its last minister was William E. Stone. "They were older people closely related to the people who broke from the Congregational church," is all Lewis remembers. A 1924 document in the Hurlbut's possession states: "In about 1847 in the ministry of the Rev. Way was organized a Methodist church. Unsuccessful efforts were made to build a church and the organization became practically extinct. In 1862, however, the Methodists had every four weeks preaching in the house now (i.e. in 1924) occupied by Henry Trowbridge. Soon after this Sheldon Leavenworth bought the old shop since owned by Mr. Trowbridge and now torn down and services were held in the upper part. These continued until in 1867 the present (1924) church was built. The Society at its organization had 55 members."

The existence of these two churches divided the town and its families. George Hurlburt, for instance, forbade his two sons, Allen and Everett ever to set foot in the Methodist church. "They used to talk about how couples walking to church would be going in opposite directions and pass each other without speaking. They were Congregationalists and Methodists," Ethel said. This was no longer true in their days, however, only in their parents days. "We knew what the divisions were," Lewis said, "My mother's father was a good Methodist, and his wife was a very strong Episcopalian. So he went to the Episcopal church. Here was us going to the Methodist church and Henry Bronson, my grandfather, who would have liked to go, was probably taken by the arm and his wife saying 'Come on, Henry, we're going up the street.' My own mother remained a strong Episcopalian. But I also know that my grandfather was a very strong backer of that Methodist church." Despite all this fervor, little is known about what philosophical, moral, or religious differences had driven the churches apart.

Several disturbing episodes occurred in Lewis Hurlbut's own time. One had to do with about 20 horse sheds next to the Congregational church, which had been owned by the town's most established families. The land included a strip that connected them to the main road. Selectman Allen Hurlburt had bought all of these sheds in the 1930's and moved them to build the town garage, leaving open the land around the church.

Later the growing church needed more space for its activities. Plans were developed to move the chapel to the open space east of the church and build an addition between the two buildings. Some older members felt strongly that transplanting the chapel and building a structure on the green would be a mistake. A move was made to stop the project by buying up a strip of land that still belonged to heirs of the former horse shed owners and blocking construction on that land for at least 15 years.

The beautiful historic house west of the church (between the church and the chapel) was bought by the church for their needed facilities, and later also used as a parsonage for their minister. The garage apartment became a temporary home for a succession of small families in transition to new homes.

In 1983, the parishioners decided to sell that church house and most of the grounds on the west side and buy the smaller house on the east, realizing a nice profit for the building fund to move the chapel and make the dreamed of addition. A strong building drive followed with promises to make the rooms available for community activities.

The church's autonomy, administered by an Ecclesiastical Society made up of lay parishioners, was eventually challenged. Like all other Congregational churches in Connecticut it had been only loosely associated with others through a state conference. "We had some terrific fights about 25 years ago," Elmer Worthington recalled, "when they wanted to merge with the E and R (Evangelical and Reformed) church. This is a German church. A lot of people, not necessarily in this neighborhood, did not want to merge the English with the Germans. They also said they were afraid that we would have bishops and become more like the Episcopal church or the Methodist church, if we joined the E and R. Its government was a lot stronger. There was a big feeling that we were losing our independence, which had not happened, when they joined the Christian church. It was very similar in its government. There were a few people who dropped out of the church then."

"Now we are in a little tighter organization, but it is one from which we can withdraw, if we wish," Ethel Hurlbut said. "When I was quite young the congregation voted to join the Association of Churches through the Ecclesiastical Society," Lewis added. Through the association it became a member of the State Conference. Roxbury was part of the Litchfield South association which grouped 14 churches. But locally it was still run by the established families. "Allen Hurlburt and his family had more to do with the ministry than any organization," Lewis said, "he'd say so-and-so is coming next Sunday, and if we'd like him, he would settle here. That's the way it worked in the years, when I was young. He thought he knew what was best for the village." Eventually a growing membership became strong enough to be more self-governing.

Eventually, the Evangelical and Reformed Church, or E. and R., as it is called, merged with the Congregational church. The Roxbury Congregation, keen to keep its independence, had at first voted against it. They said, "of course, this meant we would no longer be in the Litchfield South association. We would have to start another conference of our own. That helped us have another meeting. The E. and R. were becoming the United Church of Christ. There was so much feeling that night that Everett Hurlburt's son, Bud, had himself brought to church on a stretcher, because he had recently had an operation. That night we voted to join the United Church, even though he was opposed. Charles Russell, one of the parishioners, later said, "Sometimes even the majority can be wrong."

Becoming part of a larger, national church organization made less difference than many parishioners had feared. "We still choose our own ministers," Lewis said, "and we still control our own property." The congregation could select one, but the Roxbury Church was not really strong enough any longer to support one. So it was "yoked" to the Congregational church of neighboring Bridgewater shortly before its 1944 Bicentenary.

A Struggle with Conscience

Then, in 1963, a hundred years after the Civil War, after Dr. Charles Gerlinger who had then been 'settled' as minister in Roxbury and Bridgewater for six years, the town again faced the divisive issue of racism. "This was at a time when such disruptions were beginning," Lewis said. It was the time of sit-ins in the south, of Civil Rights marches and Freedom Riders, and of Martin Luther King preaching his dream. "A black writer wanted to buy a place here," Lewis recalled. His name is Ralph Ellison, who had won national fame for writing 'The Invisible Man,' a novel about a black man who had gone underground in New York, because he did not feel tolerated above ground. Ellison was a friend of William Styron, another well-known novelist who had been living in Roxbury since 1955, and was finishing "The Confessions of Nat Turner," a novel about the rebellion of a black slave.

"My sister Dorothy was involved in this," Lewis said, "but quite a few people we knew in the church would not sanction a black man coming to live in Roxbury. There was an unspoken law. A petition was circulated, but he was never allowed to settle here." That was all he remembered. Together we made some inquiries and the story that emerged was one most people in Roxbury would rather have forgotten. The way Roxbury and its ministers dealt with the petition showed that the town, like much of the nation, was far from ready to take the step of inviting black Americans into their midst. Here is how Jean Murkland who, together with Dorothy Miller drew up the petition, remembers the incident:

"I saw Dotty Miller briefly in front of the parish house and she was quite upset over a story she had heard that a black writer had wanted to look at property in Roxbury, and had been taken by the real estate agent not only outside of Roxbury but to the worst district of downtown Seymour, an industrial city. I agreed. I thought that was absolutely terrible. I asked Rose Styron what the real story was. She told me that Ralph Ellison and his wife had visited them on occasion and they had suggested he look for a house here. She telephoned the agent Malcolm Bray to ask whether there was anything he could show them. He said there was, but once he got Ralph and his wife in the car, he said, 'Of course, you understand I can't show you anything in Roxbury.' When they came back Rose was surprised they left so quickly.

"Subsequently, Ralph Ellison was interviewed in TIME Magazine in the course of which he said something about some of his friends in Connecticut, who did not know how dearly they paid for their rural seclusion and security. Rose went 'click' and called him, but he said, 'No, no. I was not talking about you. I was talking about Elmer Rice.' Rose smiled and said 'I'm sure he reassured every other friend who called that he was talking about the Styrons.' That was as far as Rose had gone with it.

"Dotty and I got together and I said, 'Why don't we write a letter.' This is it:

"MAY BE PUBLISHED IN LOCAL PAPERS
"To whom it may concern:
"We have just heard that a few months ago a man and his wife asked to see property to buy or rent in Roxbury. They were shown property by

a Roxbury Real Estate agent, but they were not shown any property in Roxbury, though there were at that time houses available here. The agent was later quoted as follows: 'You know I can't show property in Roxbury to Negroes. There is too much feeling against it here.' We don't know whether this incident is an isolated one or one that occurs often, but we are shocked to find that Roxbury in 1963 can be characterized by anyone as a town that refuses to sell or rent property to anyone on the basis of skin color, religious beliefs, politics, hair style, diet habits, or any other aspect of his personal qualities as an American citizen. Are Roxbury's property values dependent upon its zoning laws, the beauty of the land, and the caliber of its citizens, or are they in truth dictated by the unhealthy and unreal standards of prejudice? Is this town a real piece of the land of the free and the home of the brave, or are we just pretending?"

And this was tacked onto it:

"The above incident really happened. If you have trouble verifying it, check your local real estate agent or any of the top signers. If you too are shocked, please add your signature to the letter. If you are under 21 please list your age."

"After us it was also signed by selectmen Joseph Hartwell and John Pickett, Dr. Charles Gerlinger, Robert Eipper and Frances Munson. They were the original sponsors. The other signatures I have here are David Krieger, Frank and Gertrude Russell, Regine Krieger, Marie White, Donald Barr, Louis and Ann Ogden, Don Sibley, Edward Murkland, William and Rose Styron.

"We decided we would ask every business establishment in town to post it. Munson's grocery store had just opened. It was about two weeks old. We had not mentioned the name Malcolm Bray on purpose because we knew that every agent was doing it. This was the only specific incident where we could prove that it had happened. Our point was to go around to all the ministers and all the Selectmen to have them sign it, before we posted it in the store. But we did not think it was fair to post it only in the store. We wanted to post it in all the churches and all businesses. Roxbury had Hanny Dickinson's egg stand, Pinky Carlson's produce stand, the garage, and the Mabel Bernhardt (Smith) meat market. (Hurbuts' stand was not yet in operation.)

"Joe Hartwell, then Third Selectman, said immediately 'Of course.' John Pickett was Second Selectman. Allen Hurlburt was First Selectman. I left the letter for him to sign. I went to Hannie Dickinson. She said she'd like to read it and consider. I was to come back. She was a staunch Republican. When I went back, she took the time for a long, gracious visit detailing personal experiences that kept her from wanting to sign or sponsor the petition. Pinky Carlson said of course he would post it. Then I took it to Mabel and her husband Sanford Smith. Their meat stand was opposite the school. I went to Munson's store, and Bob (Robert Munson) said 'Sure' and the petition went up. Allen was not home, so I left it for him to consider. I went to the Episcopal Church and it was up. Rev. Tillson said 'Sure.' He was going to sign it himself. A lot of people were going to sign it. But he didn't. It was also up in the Congregational Church and had Dr. Gerlinger's signature.

"Everything happened within a matter of days. We started on a Wednesday. By Thursday or Friday phone calls started coming. Mabel and Sanford were the most realistic. They had thought it through and knew what the town was going through. They knew exactly what was going to happen. But they said, 'Yes' they would back it. Friday morning Rev. Tillson showed up here. He said they had called a special meeting of the Planning Commission. I kept some notes on this, and he said, 'the sense of the Planning Commission and other people there thought the intentions of the statement were of the best, but that it should not be circulated in public, because reputations and business of real estate men and women could be damaged by said piece. If picked up by outside news sources it could be blown up, exaggerated, interpreted as being fact that Roxbury citizens as a whole might be falsely seen as actually having these prejudices, which we do not have and never have had. In its present form it should be withdrawn."

Lewis said, "I do not remember any decision being made at the meeting, however."

Jean said, "Tillson gave me the impression that he had been appointed by the people there assembled to talk to me, because I was an Episcopalian. And I believe the reason he brought up your name is that he knew we were both Democrats. He thought that would reach me. Elinor (another Hurlbut) was appointed to see Dotty Miller."

Lewis replied, "I can't see all the working of it, but at that time I was on a Committee in Waterbury working against racism. And so I did not go there with any intent to..."

Jean interrupted him "Lewis, were you really? Because at that time this was just beginning to ferment. Maybe it was a little after 1963 that you were on that Committee."

Lewis, "I was on the Planning Board. That was organized in 1962. In 1963 it did not have much status. It had hardly started working yet. And I do not know by whom or why I would bring it before that meeting."

They agreed that the meeting itself had been called to discuss the enlargement of the town hall.

"I can't remember bringing it up to the meeting, unless I just automatically spoke there."

Jean: "My hunch now in hindsight is that by this time there were letters to read at the store, at the meat market, at the garage, but by the time I went back to Pinky to find out whether signatures were accumulating, they had been down to him and he was furious. They, I do not know who, had visited him. First they got to John Pickett, who called up to have his name withdrawn. John was part of the group that went to Pinky to put pressure on him. And Pinky said, 'You know, Jean, people around this town are wondering why you and Dotty Miller aren't at home scrubbing your floors, where women are supposed to be. And I wonder that myself.' That's what he said. He not only said that. He was upset. He was in a poor position. I was very upset by it. I did not have anything like the toughness I have now. I was talking to Bill Styron on the phone and told him what Pinky said. Bill said, "For heaven's sake, what does Pinky matter?' I said, 'Anybody matters.'"

But we still did not know what really happened at the Planning Board's meeting. Lewis tried to explain: "The only thing that I can say is that there was nothing much that I could do or anyone else, because there was an unwritten law that nobody spoke about. There was not any regulation or any law about what we were doing in this town concerning black people, but it was understood that a man came to look for a place here.

"If I said something at the meeting it must have been that I knew of the petition. I just don't recall. I must have just heard from Dorothy. I knew it was working. But I had not seen the petition, at all."

But it was his sister. Had she not shown it to him? Lewis: "It was only beginning. This happened very suddenly. There were only a few days there."

Jean interjected, "I think it might be helpful, if I read from my notes."

"On November 3rd, 1963 Dotty asked me to verify the Styron-Ellison dealings about buying or renting land in Roxbury. November 6th: Verified story with Rose Styron. Reported to Dotty Miller, Joe Hartwell, who happened to drop in at Millers and said he would sign letter to be drafted and approved by Dotty Miller, Jean Murkland, possibly edited by my husband Edward to post and offer for signature around Roxbury, and subsequently published in local papers.

"November 8th: Dropped first draft by Jean Murkland with Dotty Miller and for verification Rose Styron.

"November 10th: decided to use the first draft.

"November 11th: Decided to change heading from 'Should be published in Local Papers' to 'May be published.' Miller agreed to type copies.

"November 12th: Miller and Murkland signed twelve copies. Murkland got Eipper and Hartwell signatures on five copies. Munson, Carlson agreed to post. Pickett to take copies from Roxbury Market home for perusal before signing.

"November 13th: All copies signed by Pickett, Eipper, Hartwell, Miller, and Murkland, and Gerlinger. Carlson agreed to post.

"November 16th: At 10 A.M. Mr. Tillson showed up at the Murkland house. At that point there was a copy in Roxbury market, in the vestibules of the Congregational, Catholic, and Episcopal churches. Copies left for decision at O'Brien's garage, Bernhardt's and Hannie Dickinson's egg place. Library, and Booth School still to be approached. 11:15 a.m. a copy delivered to school and put up at Bernhardt's. Dotty Miller was called by Malcolm Bray. An hour conversation. Murkland called by Bray. An hour and ten minutes. Styron phoned by Bray. Two hours and ten minutes. Stated among other things to Murkland that he had no prejudice. Agreed with all the letter, except the top incident. Maintained accuracy should have been checked with him. But said it was accurate. Said he felt he could sue for libel. Said he would have helped us phrase a letter that could have helped him and all real estate men to combat prejudice. After repeated requests offered no objections to accuracy of statements. Said he had taken clients to Oxford, not to Seymour, to non-industrial property, and white, of Philip Evergood. Said he felt he could be taken to court as a result of this letter.
"My final word to him was, 'If you agree with everything, sentence by sentence, come sign it. Then you're in the clear.' He still insisted it should be taken down. So on the 16th Rev. Tillson came down and said the sense of the Planning Commission and other people here was that it should not be circulated. All those people were invited to the town hall enlargement discussion meeting. The letter came up, brought up by

Lewis Hurlbut. Told Tillson I would not take the letter down. There was no other form or idea offered in its place. And the two reasons given were in my view already obsolete.

"That same morning Dotty Miller was visited by Bob Eipper and requested to withdraw. She refused the request. She visited the agent to convince him the statement was not against a person but against a prejudice.

"I finally called Allen Hurlburt to see whether he wanted to sign it or not. We were relatively certain that Allen would not want to. But we certainly wanted to offer it to him. He was very gracious, and very sweet, but positive that he did not only not want to sign it, but that he was really sorry that he could not return it to me. I heard later that Everett, his brother, had visited him and been so angry that he had ripped it up and thrown it in the fire. So that was why he could not return it."

Bob Eipper was part of the loyal crew. Jean said, "Yeah. John Gerald and Dr. Gerlinger then moved in on Dotty Miller. They met her at the agent's house. Dr. Gerlinger said he was now convinced the statement could be of harm to one person. Therefore he wanted his name withdrawn. He made the statement that 'a ball has been started rolling. Beginning of week I will get together with Father Rooney and Rev. Tillson and see what we can do about this problem.' When I went down to see, if Bob Munson wanted more sheets of paper, because people were really convening there, he said he had to take it down, because crowds were forming. One name was constantly being mentioned: Malcolm Bray. And he could not have controversy in the store. I sympathized with that. He said, 'nobody is buying. They're just standing on the steps talking. And it's just a whole controversy. And I can't handle it.'

"After the Gerlinger influence, Dotty called me and said, 'They have persuaded me that this could cause harm to Malcolm Bray, and as a Christian woman I cannot do that.'

"They really pressured her. I had just read a feature in the Reader's Digest about what had happened to a little town in the south, where two brave women had gone door to door and found prejudice, and the whole town had blown wide open. And it had been a wonderful forward step for blacks. But it had destroyed the town. I was aware of that. I was talking to Styron and feeling terrible. And he said, 'Well, to hell with that. We'll go do a Martin Luther. We'll pound the thing on the front door (of the church). I've got a photographer and a friend from Time-Life, who will come up and take a picture.'"

Lewis asked: "Yes, but did he or Rose, or you or Dorothy approach the Committee? "

Jean: "They signed the paper."

Lewis: "They did not go any further than that."

Jean: "I lay awake nights a long time. And I'm still not certain whether to call myself courageous or cowardly. But when Bill spoke, it pulled another picture in sharp focus for me. And I knew it was very important to me to help change what was going on in Roxbury and have people live together in harmony without that kind of regard for race and prejudice. But I knew that I did not want Roxbury to become the town that had the whole nation's cameras on it."

Certainly, with Styron involved it would have attracted a lot of attention. She added, "Not only media attention. Bill knew exactly how to use it. And from one point of view it was precisely the way to do it. But I wanted us to live together in love, peace, and harmony. We did not want to set neighbor against neighbor.

"One of the hardest things I ever did was to go to Bernhardt's and take the petition down. They asked, 'Why?' They knew exactly how much courage it had taken for them to put it up. They had thought it through and they knew that was what they wanted to do. I said, 'I can't ask you people to be the only people to do it.' In front of them I felt like a real coward, as if I had not had a stiff enough backbone. It was really hard. We did not have words like 'polarize' then. I wanted us to grow. I had gone down Squire Road with it and got somebody to talk about it. It was a very dear person and a very nice person, and suddenly there was this hard, contorted face saying, 'why don't you go up the road and ruin the real estate values of your friend Bill Styron.' And here were the Bernhardt's saying the Diamond place is for sale. Now anybody that could afford to buy that, I don't care what color they are, they'd be fine neighbors. They were unusual in Roxbury. People were either outspoken, getting contorted faces, or keeping quiet.

"Mabel Bernhardt had been through a lot. She was a one room school marm, then a teacher at the Booth Free School, then principal. And she did not marry the man she loved until after she retired."

* * *

And that was the end of the story. To Jean it was obvious how she had been stopped. "I realized only two weeks later that the haste was based on getting it down before the weekend. What if all those weekenders came up and saw it and signed it. They were absolutely determined to get it out of the churches, before people came to church."

Sometime later some of the young parents organized a series of meetings under the heading 'A Town Wants To Know!' Even members of the Black Muslims were invited. Their leader Malcolm X was still alive then. They refused to take part, so a non-Muslim student presented their case in the forum. "It was amazing for our little town," she recalled, "to have the Muslim literature distributed in the lobby of our school." It was not the sort of meeting Allen Hurlburt would have called or attended.

Dorothy took the whole thing quite hard. She still refused to be interviewed about it even 25 years later. Lewis said, "This really bugged her. She used to take a great part in the church and in the town. She just withdrew from everything after this and other distressing events. She just divorced herself from having anything to do with public affairs."

To this day no black family owns a house in Roxbury. Some people recall a black family living on Bacon Road early in this century. Later, New York Mayor O'Dwyer's secretary briefly occupied a house on River Road until her neighbors' hostility became too unpleasant for her. Since this incident, Jean said, "My son and his wife, Carolyn, and my grandsons lived here in this house for a year and a half. She is black. But that does not quite qualify. Nobody knows whether Carolyn would have been allowed to buy property here."

When we asked William Styron why he had not made more of a fuss by himself, he said. "After Jean backed down, I was also afraid it might create more of a tea-pot tempest than one wanted at that time. I did not want to be at the heart of a controversy like that. I'm a writer. I was doing a book that was going to demonstrate this horror, and the categorical imperative did not apply to me. I had something else on the fire.

"I had spent all of my youth and childhood in the south, in a very heavily segregated part of the south, during a time when segregation was the status quo. And I chose to live up here in the north for various reasons. I always resented deeply that there were many northerners who looked down their noses at southerners for the way they mistreated blacks, but who themselves, when forced to the wall, behaved just like red necks in Georgia.

"The point is this. It was the early 60's. Within a decade it was made clear that some of the most despicable racism was in Boston. America as a nation is racist. It's not just the south. We are a racist nation. Abraham Lincoln was racist. White people are racist."

XI.
A Writer Remembers

The hilly country of northwestern Connecticut appeals to people who need some isolation to work, but who also like to feel an intimacy with their surroundings, almost as though they were seeking its protection. It has therefore always been an ideal place for artists and writers. Arthur Miller came to Roxbury in 1949. In 'Timebends,' his autobiography, he revealed that he first built a cabin in the woods behind his house with his own hands, as if driven by instinct, before seeking its shelter to write "Death of a Salesman." The play had taken shape in his mind while he was hammering together the planks.

William Styron, who came to Roxbury in 1954, found a cottage ready-made for him, next to the house he and his wife Rose bought on Rucum Road. He wrote three of his best-known works there ('Set this House on Fire,' 'The Confessions of Nat Turner,' and 'Sophie's Choice'), and still uses it for that purpose today. "I really love that cottage," he told us. Like many other people who chose to live in Roxbury, it did not take him or Rose very long to make up their minds. But let him tell the story of how he came here himself:

"Rose and I had come back from Europe. We'd just got married. And we were fed up with New York, which was dirty and noisy, and all the other things that cause people to be unhappy with the city. I had an agent, Elizabeth McKee Purdy, who had a house on River Road, right on the corner of South Street. It was a little cottage. She asked Rose and me to come up for a weekend in late summer. We just immediately said: 'This is where we want to live.' It was love at first sight. And even today, despite all the development, it's still pretty rustic. You can imagine what it was in 1954. It was just bliss. It was remote. It took two and a half hours to get here from New York. We just fell in love with the town. We spent a couple of weekends here, and finally in the fall, we spent a long week here with the intent of buying a house.

"We heard, quite coincidentally that the house of Arthur Styron was for sale. That surprised me, because Styron is an unusual name. I had heard of this much, much older cousin - all Styrons are cousins - he was from North Carolina and had written a rather good biography of President Monroe. The house was the house that Ed Tierney now owns, you know, on Apple Lane. Rose and I went to see it one Sunday afternoon. I remember we heard Wagner being played at high decibels. It was one of those hot autumn days. The windows were wide open. But we could not find anybody. We had made an appointment, but only Lohengrin was blaring through the windows. We finally looked through the window and there, stretched out on the floor, was this elderly man, white hair, and near-by, also stretched out, in perfect bliss, was his wife, a younger woman. They were both listening to Lohengrin. Both were dead-drunk, just plastered - about noon of a Sunday.

"We knocked on the door. They staggered on their feet and got themselves slightly together and showed us a little of the place. But you could tell they were just plastered. They were very nice, and he said 'I've heard of you,' because I had written something by then, and I had heard of him. We shook hands like all Southerners do, and called each other 'Cousin.' But the house was not for us. It was too small, for one thing. We bade them good-by, and we never did see them again. Just a couple of years later, he died of alcoholism."

William Styron is still a little puzzled about the co-incidence. "I never meet a Styron in a hundred years, travelling anywhere, except right here in Roxbury." The house he and Rose eventually chose is the one in which they still live today. "It has a remarkable history, because it was owned by the heirs to a Russian doctor, named Dubrowsky, who had for many years been the head of the Russian Red Cross, which acted as a kind of connection between the old country and thousands and thousands of emigre Russians, who came to the United States during the '20's and '30's. In fact somewhere I have a picture of Kerensky (the last Russian parliamentary majority leader ousted by the Bolsheviks) seated in one of those old-fashioned bathing suits over by the pond."

When the Styrons took it over, "it was just a broken down old hulk of a house. But the little house, the cottage over there, we just fell in love with. The two structures, plus fourteen acres, including the beautiful little pond, and the wonderful shrubbery and landscaping he had created over 20 years, it came to a total of $29,000, which even in those days was not a huge sum. It seemed a little high, but we could scrape it up. We thought it was a bargain, because the little house came furnished. And it was nicely furnished. The reason was that it was way, way out."

Roxbury had not yet been discovered as the haven for weekenders it has since become. There were no Interstate Highway connections to link it either with Hartford or New York. "You had to go through the back road to Danbury," Styron recalled, "then you wound your way through Danbury. Several stop lights in Danbury. And then you'd go down Route

6/202 to Hardscrabble Road, past a reservoir in New York State, and Goldens Bridge. And then you'd end on the Saw Mill River Parkway."

Robert Munson had not yet taken over the town's only store. "I remember Hodge's store had a lot of cockroaches in it," Styron said, even though the building was only about ten years old. For the next three years, the Styrons were in transition. "We lived in the little house. For a couple of years the old house just lay here. Then it was remodeled and rebuilt. Suzanna, our first child was born in the little house. We decided to move, when our second child, Polly, was born. It was getting a little crowded over there." Rose chimed in, "We also had a huge Newfoundland." The little house then became his studio. "A substantial part of all my work was done here - right in that little house."

At the same time, he said, "I suddenly saw what an ideal country community could be. It still does despite the explosion of people. It was what someone like me who had been born on the margin of a city had always wanted. To me the idea of living in a city is anathema. I know some people can do it. I could not."

To Rose it was "like having died and gone to heaven, because it was exactly the kind of community...I loved the farms. I spent a lot of time out, either fishing with Carl Carlson, or when the sheep were born, I'd go down there with him." Among the Styron's neighbors were two working farms. "So when we lived in the little house I would wake up in the morning, and the cows would be peering at me over the wall. It's what I had always wanted. I knew from the time I was five years old that I wanted to live in New England and in farm country. And that's what happened." She met people in Roxbury mostly through her children. "We saw the Crabtrees, the Carlsons, the Howards here, then the Murklands. I took the kids to church and was very briefly in the choir, and knew the women in the Episcopal church choir. I worked at the polls and got to know Doris Squire and people that way."

Styron himself was less successful, but also less eager to fit in. "I remember, pretty soon after I arrived, I was quite naive about certain things," he explained, "I said to myself, 'O God, I guess it's a duty to join the volunteer fire department.' I learned almost immediately that it was the 'closed society' of the entire town, and it would be a cold day in hell before I could just go down there and get into the fire department."

Rose, on the other hand, turned down an invitation to the Garden Club, because it sounded too much like the sort of elite social organization she had been trying to get away from in her native Baltimore. "I did not realize that this was a wonderful compliment from the women here.

I've always regretted it, but it sounded too much like the Junior League to me."

Living and working in relative solitude is what William Styron had sought and found. "The place merged perfectly with my needs and what I feel I wanted in terms of domestic life. If I had been really gregarious I would have stayed in New York probably." He did get great pleasure from daily walks in the country, along dirt or paved roads on which automobiles were about as frequent then as planes landing on the stubble on top of Good Hill. Although traffic has increased a great deal since, the Styrons and their dog can still be seen promenading along Tophet Road or the Upper County Road, especially in the spring and fall. Their summers are now spent at a second home on Martha's Vineyard. "We like to go along Welton Road, which I think is beautiful. Upper County we call the Gavel Road, because it runs along their land. It's a long, dirt road."

No one knows what will happen to that land once Henry Gavel, the last of two brothers, who farmed it, when they were young, is gone. "If anything happens to that property," he gasped, "it will be like another heart by-pass. If that got developed, it would be disaster." Lewis mentioned that it had come up at meetings of the Land Trust to which substantial amounts of former farm land as well as woodland have been deeded to keep it out of the hands of developers. But, he said, "the Land Trust can't buy a piece of property like that. We have so many preservation groups in this state. Somebody has to head it up, or it will go just like Golden Harvest in Bridgewater. They're building estates on it." Everyone agreed that "it would hurt like the devil," as Lewis put it, if the 200 acre Gavel farm went the same way. Rose said, "Of course, what we remember from our walking is that our favorite walks, which used to be the Old Roxbury Road, up past the cemetery and then back down through Carlson's land and here, used to be totally unoccupied. Now houses are built there. The same thing has happened on Rucum Hill. We used to walk up in those woods and then to the pond. A lot of the walks have gone."

A few years after the Styrons settled in Roxbury, Norman Mailer, who had been a close friend in New York, established himself as Bridgewater's writer-in-residence. An attempt was made to create a coterie if not a colony of writers, but nothing came of it. Here is how Rose Styron remembered it. "When we first moved here, not knowing anybody, except Bill's agent, she introduced us to Malcolm Cowley, who introduced us to Van Wyck Brooks ("The Flowering of New England"), who belonged to an older generation of New England writers, and they kind of took us under their wing. We also met Robert Penn Warren, whose wife had grown up in Roxbury. And some of the writers we had known in Rome and Paris came to visit us. Lou and Jay Allen from the South, who were our friends, bought a house up here. Bill and Norman Mailer had been friends, before I ever met Bill. But then they had a falling-out and did not speak for 20 years.

"Mailer lived here for only two years," she explained, "Arthur was the first, but we did not know Arthur. We got to know him only after we'd been here several years. Bill, and Norman, and James Jones were best friends in New York. Norman became very jealous of Bill and Jim's friendship. But we had some very funny times, after Norman moved up here. A critic named John Aldridge bought Arthur Miller's house. He had an idea, because he had written a book, "After The Lost Generation" about Bill, and Norman, and Jim and a lot of the other writers who were young and of that age after World War II. He would start a sort of literary salon and community here, and that he would be 'best friends' with Bill, Norman, whoever else was around, and that they would have breakfast together in the morning, and discussions together in the evening. And Bill and I did not like that, at all. So Aldridge and Norman became good friends.

They had a thing which we stayed out of as much as we could. Norman was then married to a very nice woman named Adele. We saw them occasionally, but at that period Norman was into drugs, pills, he had an orgon box in the silo over there, but he also persuaded his wife, who was a lovely Hispanic earth-woman, that she had to be very hip. She had to take painting lessons. So she studied with Hans Hofmann, and their houses were filled with these great bright, unobjective paintings, and the painters and the group to go with them. So we gradually did not see much of the them. But he and Bill had a terrible falling out, and it was only because Norman was on all this stuff."

Eventually, Norman moved back to New York. Aldridge moved "wherever he moved out West. We've never seen him again," she said. Lewis Hurlbut asked how the hospitality they encountered in Roxbury differed from the hospitality of the South. "The New England Yankees are a little hard to know. They look at you twice before they might say hello," Lewis offered. William Styron replied, "I've never felt any coldness in this community - in any real, stand-offish way. It's not the truly outgoing thing that they have in the South, which is a sometimes almost embarrassing friendliness. You know, it's more than you can handle. I've always felt that people here in Roxbury were people who even if you did not know them, at all, would respond immediately to any kind of need that you might have, or any kind of emergency. There is a basic, very warm friendliness in the town."

He admitted to being something of a loner. He was known as such even among his friends who were writers. "In the South it would have been tougher to keep your distance, as I do. They would consider it a hostility. The Southerners I grew up amongst are so desperately in need of constant stroking and friendship that if you stay too far away, they consider it a kind of anti-social act. A good example is Faulkner, who lived in this small town in Mississippi and kept his complete privacy, and they resented him for it. They don't do that here. The Yankee attitude is that if a man wants to be alone, let him stay alone. If he wants to make gestures in our direction, fine, and they'll meet him half-way. All that I find very civilized. I think one of the lesser virtues of the American way of life is this desperate need for pal-ship, you know, buddyhood, all of which is admirable up to a point, but which can be overdone."

On the other hand, he granted, "the other side would also apply. You can be a perpetual stranger down there. I never felt that here. Certainly, after ten years, I never felt I was a stranger. Now, after thirty years, I feel I have a right to say that I'm a member of the community."

He felt less happy about a so-called personal business tax the state of Connecticut imposed on writers for about three years in the early 1980's. "It was preposterous," Styron exploded, "It was the most discriminatory tax you can think of. The idea that some director of publicity at Union Carbide over in Danbury could be making $400,000 a year and not pay any state income tax, and then a writer had to pay it, because..." he stopped, then finished the sentence, "it was one of the most despicable taxes, I think, that any state ever tried to foist on writers. I remember bitterly having to pay those big hunks of money every year."

Before the state's legislators ever thought of 'soaking' them, writers had flocked to its northwestern hills. Styron thought, "it's the beauty of the countryside. New Jersey is not nearly as attractive. In New York, almost from the moment you cross the state line, it begins to look different. It gets tacky. And any normal person would go crazy out in the Hamptons (of Long Island.) The umbilical cord with New York City is too strong. They're people, who really do not want to get away. They want to stay with their own kind all the time. Living up here is a distinct removal from the environment of New York," he concluded, "Long Island is not."

As to his own preferred way of life, he added, "I have never been in touch with more than a handful of people, anyway. For instance, only a few days ago, I ran into Barbara Howar ("Laughing All the Way") in the Washington market. She said, 'I live in Roxbury.' I said, 'Isn't that interesting. How long have you been living up here?' And she said, 'a year.' She has a house on the intersection of Painter Hill and Painter Ridge. If this had been the Hamptons, she would have made her presence known within an hour. I'll probably give her a call, but I might not."

The oddest people turn up in this corner of the state, or should we say world. For instance, few people know that George Schaller, the world famous photographer of leopards and gorillas in the wild, has been living in Roxbury for years. "I've only met his wife," Styron said, "although I knew he lived here from Peter Mathiessen's book on the Himalayan snow leopard." Colin Turnbull, the British anthropologist who described the life of pygmies in the Central African rain forests, is another unlikely denizen of these hills. Styron maintained, "the reason is simply that it is a beautiful part of the world. It's near a metropolitan center, one of the great ones of the world. What else do you need? Most important, however, is that there is no sense of a writer's colony. You can be up here and if you wish, you can see some other people, or if you don't, forget it. And that to me is the beauty of the place. I've never felt in the slightest obliged socially. And that's what I've wanted."

Roxbury writers, William Styron and Arthur Miller, discussing the risks of literary life with townspeople. 1989.

Courtesy of New Milford Times

XII.
Neighbors

Everyone finds something in Roxbury. My wife Barbara and I found a home here and some good neighbors. We came here toward the end of the time frame we chose for this memoir, after having lived in such different places as Bonn and Munich, Paris and Prague, Kinshasa and Lagos, and London. We were foreign correspondents . Both of us were born in Germany with roots in a region not unlike the hills of northwestern Connecticut. Because of its tall, dark pines and spruce trees our native region is known as the Black Forest. But along its southern edges, where it shares borders with Switzerland and France, there are a lot of mixed forests of oak and ash and even some maples. I still remember vividly Barbara's shouts of joy, when we drove down Painter Hill Road for the first time on a fall day in 1973. "It looks so much like home," she kept crying. Well, not quite. The road was strewn with leaves so yellow that they looked more like the petals from some late blooming flower. Few forests anywhere, and certainly not those of the southern Black Forest, blossom into such strong color in the fall.

For two years, before coming here, we had lived in a cottage in Calvados, a department in the French province of Normandy, where thanks to generous subsidies from the European Community a dairy farmer could still make a living on a herd of no more than twelve cows. We used to watch our neighbor there every evening standing and chatting with his wife while she was milking a cow. He would pour the milk from the pan into a ten-gallon pail, which he set on a small cart and then trundled off toward their house, where it was picked up the next morning together with another two, or at most three pails to be taken to the dairy for pasteurizing and bottling.

They did this every day, spring, summer and winter in a cycle of life that had not changed much for centuries. Our neighbor also made his own butter from cream he skimmed off the top and kept in a cool shed. He skimmed only as much as he needed to churn a few pounds of butter by hand each week. This he would take to the market in Honfleur on Sunday mornings.

He did it, he told us, to keep from having to go to church with his wife, but mostly, I am sure, for the entertainment he found on the market. A Normandy farm market on Sunday mornings is the place where more gossip is exchanged than produce. He always had two or three pounds of his rich, yellow butter on a small table. The butter was decorated with a florid pattern that was pressed on with a wooden mold. Norman butter is as prized in France as fresh goose liver from Alsace or les Landes. For this farmer it was a ticket to take part in the fun of a Sunday country fair. In the afternoon, he rarely came home having sold both loaves, but he never looked or felt the slightest bit ridiculous standing behind his tiny market stall.

All of his neighbors stood around him behind similar stands, some larger none smaller than his. The talk was of weddings, and births, and funerals, and of who had lost a calf that week, or how the government was trying to take back their ancient right to distill liquor from the fruit of their trees. The Calvados region produces the world's finest apple jack, and the very best and most aged is found in farmers' homes. It is drunk with every meal, where it fills what they call a 'trou Normand,' the hole a Norman discovers between courses of food that is often rich in sauces made of fresh, heavy cream.

In listening to Lewis Hurlbut talk about what life was like, when he was still a boy, I often compared it in mind to what we had seen in Normandy and in our own native region. Sometimes I thought how much luckier farmers in Normandy and the Black Forest were not to have been exposed as rapidly and rudely to the economic changes of the last hundred years. Many of the refinements that European farmers have been able to bring to their produce were not to be found here, whether it was the process for a particularly delectable cheese or making a liquor with a taste peculiar to only one region, or a special way of smoking sausage, of air-drying ham, or raising lamb on the salty grass found along a certain shore. Nothing like that had developed here. Perhaps it was because Connecticut farmers were not given the time it takes to hone a single skill to a point of uniqueness. Nor were they compelled to do so. The memory of country life in most of New England is of pioneers, whose economic choices were far greater than those of European farmers. The gray-green, lichen covered stone walls they left behind attest to more than a century of back-breaking labor today. These stone walls are as distinct to this region as gnarled olive trees are to the hills of Tuscany. And they continue to draw people, who like to live among old stones.

Living in the country still calls for some special skills: as we were to discover soon after buying our home on Cross Brook Road. It was a small house which, according to legend, had been built by a saddle maker shortly before the War of Independence. There was only one other old house on the road, which then belonged to Leonie and Geddes Parsons, both of solid Yankee stock. They gave us our first lesson in Yankee neighborliness. One morning, after rain had turned to sleet and then formed a filigree of ice on the branches of every tree, turning them into glistening silver sculptures in the bright morning sunlight, our car spun like a top on the usually gritty dirt road. A thin layer of hard ice had made the surface so slippery that I was forced to crawl back to the house on all fours - after the car had come to rest in a ditch. As I looked up, I saw Geddes Parsons, enthroned like an Indian on top of an elephant, coming to my rescue behind the chained wheels of a large tractor. He hauled the car out of the ditch by winch and chain. Then he invited us to join him and Leonie for a drink at their house later that day. We had not laid eyes on each other until then. But we became instant friends. Much of what we have learned about living in the country, coping with the quirks and ailments of an old house, we have learned from them. Geddes, especially, like so many Yankees, is a born tinkerer.

Across the road, on the other slope of our small bowl of a valley, stands the studio of the Alexander Calder, the man who had turned the Yankee knack for tinkering into an art form. I used these words to describe Calder's work in an article for TIME magazine many years before. In 1963 I had visited and interviewed him in an almost identical studio in Sache, a small French village near Tours, where he liked to work in the spring and summer. For several decades he had been honing his skill of cutting and bending small sheets of metal into shapes that entered his hands from his mind. He worked at it every day. There was no one in the world who could get more fun out of a piece of wire or tin than Alexander Calder. Once, I watched him snip into a can of beer with his scissors and in a jiffy turn it into a rooster complete with sickle-shaped tail feathers.

By the late 1960's the Calders came back to Roxbury only in the fall, usually just in time for the colors and the local elections. While we were looking for a house to buy, I stopped at his studio and talked with him again. He had built it on a spot, where it received the first rays of sun coming over the hills in the morning. The choice of where I wanted to live was, of course, influenced by the prospect of seeing the panes of his studio light up like fire every day, and having him as a neighbor on the other side of the valley.

Leonie remembers him from an earlier time, fore fame and fortune allowed him and his wife Louisa to hop back and forth between the continents. After considerable prodding she finally agreed to share some of her memories:

"We first bought the house in 1941," she recalled. She and her first husband, John White, came from old Waterbury families, whose fortunes were based on brass. One of Leonie's ancestors, a Frenchman named Henri Midgeon, had been lured to Connecticut by Lafayette to manufacture brass buttons for the uniforms of the Continental Army. Waterbury had become more and more industrial, and especially during World War II it was not very pleasant to live there. "At first we came only in the summer time. After the war we decided to come out on a permanent basis. We wanted the country, really the country. Here we found it. Actually, my mother already had a little house here. She probably spurred us on. Of course, the incredible changes of the last ten years had not begun to happen yet. The house we found was in very poor shape. It was a simple farm house, owned by a leatherman. He made straps and reins used on work horses."

The house had belonged to the Tracy family of whom Arthur Miller wrote in his book "In the Country" that they were so poor they had to sell a piece of land every time someone got married or a woman "needed a new hat." Rob Tracy, one of the two brothers who had owned the house until the Whites bought it, took another plot on Gold Mine Road and built himself a small shack there. "Their mother was a wonderful woman," Leonie recalled, "and she loved flowers. Actually, the peonies we have here came from old Mrs. Tracy. We brought them down from the house, when we moved." (In 1977 the Parsons moved into the center of Roxbury, when the house originally built by Gen. Ephraim Hinman came on the market).

Because Leonie and her husband at first wanted to use their house only in the summer, "we got a builder and decided that we'd do it in very simple fashion. We did not drill a well but lived off the dug well. It was a very simple existence. Later, after the war, we had the land and had the house and the makings of doing things all over." The house was enlarged, a modern kitchen added, walls between rooms removed, and one large window opened the view to the valley and shadeless northern light. One of its distinctions is that Alexander Calder, at Leonie's request, drew a design of a serpent winding its way across the tiles around a sunken bath next to the master bedroom. They left it, when they sold the house to the movie critic Rex Reed in 1977.

"We met Calder the first time, when we were flying kites on the hill between our two houses," Leonie said. "He saw the kites and was curious, and came over. He immediately asked us all to come over. We had friends visiting us. We went, had a drink, and discussed life in general.

From then on, intermittently, we saw a great deal of them. They were here all the time then. The children, Sandra and Mary, were in Booth Free School. He worked here year round. I remember talking to Louisa, Calder's wife, and she said, 'You know, he's just like a businessman. He works from eight till five. He's gone at eight. Maybe I'll see him at lunch.' Of course, people would go into the studio to see him. I went there many times myself. He was always willing to stop what he was doing. It was not until the great Guggenheim show in 1966 that their lives changed, that they began going back and forth, and living in Sache most of the year. We also visited them there. On my son J.O.'s sixteenth birthday there, he gave him this wonderful present all wrapped up in a piece of brown paper. He opened it and it was a piece of cardboard with two pieces of a mobile, and he said, 'this is a do-it-yourself present.' It's a perfectly wonderful mobile.

"The Calder's life was different after the Guggenheim exhibition, because their house was flooded with all kinds of people. I saw the circus many times. I remember when Joe O'Brien's father (a local farmer) came down the hill, because everybody in the neighborhood was invited. He came down, tall, straight, a wonderful looking man, and sitting on the bleachers, eating peanuts like the rest of us, not saying very much. But Sandy loved everyone, and he wanted everyone to be invited. Of course, for a long time he lived simply." He also loved his small pond. To keep it clear of algae he would often strap a copper sulfate sack on his back and swim in it. Louisa would joke, "He's up taking care of the pond." We had very happy, very gay times. There was always a party. People would come and play the drums. Roy Anderson came and was always asked to play the piano. Louisa loved to dance. So did Sandy. Then there was Ken Blanchard, a dentist in Waterbury, who could jitter-bug. He would grab me, and we would jitterbug up and down with a hooting and a wailing. They loved anyone who did this kind of thing.

"My first recollection of Calder's daughter Mary was before the fire. It was in the long, old shed of the house. We were sitting around the table and having some wine, when Sandy said to Mary, 'Get us some cheese.' And here was this four-year old dragging a whole Provolone across the floor to get to her father. Sandra, who married the French journalist Jean Davidson and still lives in Sache, was the quieter of the two. Mary was always the one."

"We also had marvelous picnics together. He had an old LaSalle that had no top to it, and we'd fill it with all the children and all the families and go up a hill near the Shepaug River. One day the brakes did not work. We did not know what was going to happen. Fortunately, Pop knew what he was doing. We always called him Pop, because the children called him that and Louisa did. He used the hand brake and also jammed the old La Salle into reverse gear.

"I think I learned an entirely new way of living from them. (I had never eaten that way.) I had studied all kinds of things in art, but during the war many new artists came to the Calders: Joan Miro, Peter Blume, Arshile Gorky, who was an absolutely delightful guy, Rofino Tamayo, who played the guitar, and, of course, all the surrounding intellectuals, whom everybody knew. The marvelous thing was that we were always included. Time and time again, I kept saying to Louisa, 'What do you want us for?' She said, 'You're gay and we like to have you.' That's the way she looked at it. But it was the beginning of my love for contemporary art, because all of them painted that way. And then, when we saw them in Paris, we went for the same kind of thing."

Leonie became a collector, but some of her finest possessions are early works of Calder, including some very intimate ones such as a pair of gold earrings he made from gold wire, door handles of brass, and small models of mobiles and stabiles, which he had bent in his studio. "Of course, I know I started at the top," she says today.

It was the architect James Slavin's idea to ask Calder to design something for the bathroom's tiles. "So I went over and said, 'Pop, we're doing a new bathroom. How's about doing something with the bath tub.' And he looked at me, the way he always did. If he was not too busy, he would stop. He got a piece of brown paper, almost newspaper, and sketched the whole thing out. And he signed it: Love, Pop. Another time he designed a nose piece, saying, 'Now, remember that you have to wear this one at least one night every year.' And I did at a party."

Alexander Calder is remembered above all as a fine neighbor, one who was always ready to have a little fun.

Frederick Ungeheuer, 1973

Alexander Calder at work in his studio on Painter Hill Road.

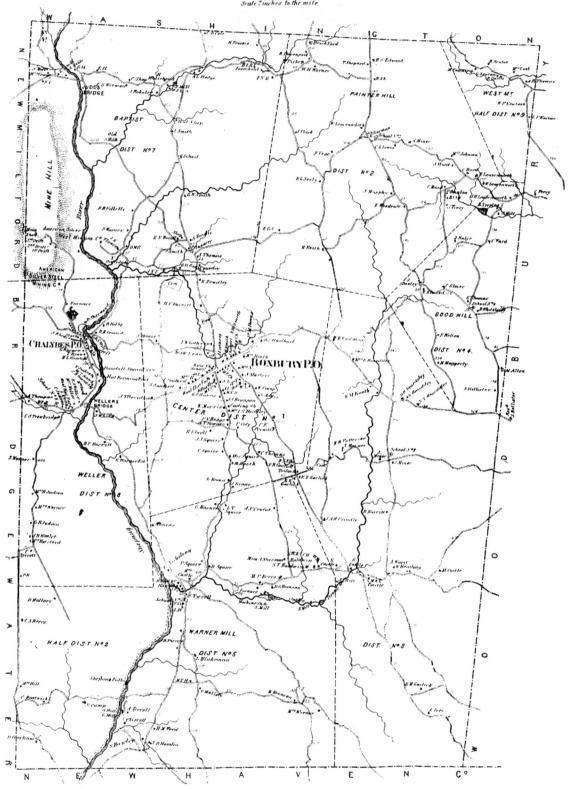

Roxbury, circa 1870

MAP OF TOWN OF ROXBURY, CONN.

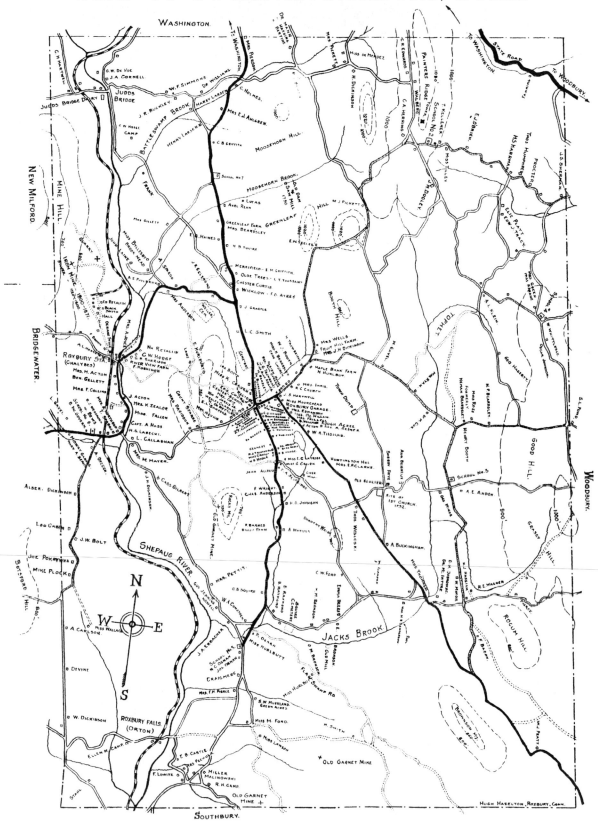

Roxbury, 1934

Roxbury Center, 1876

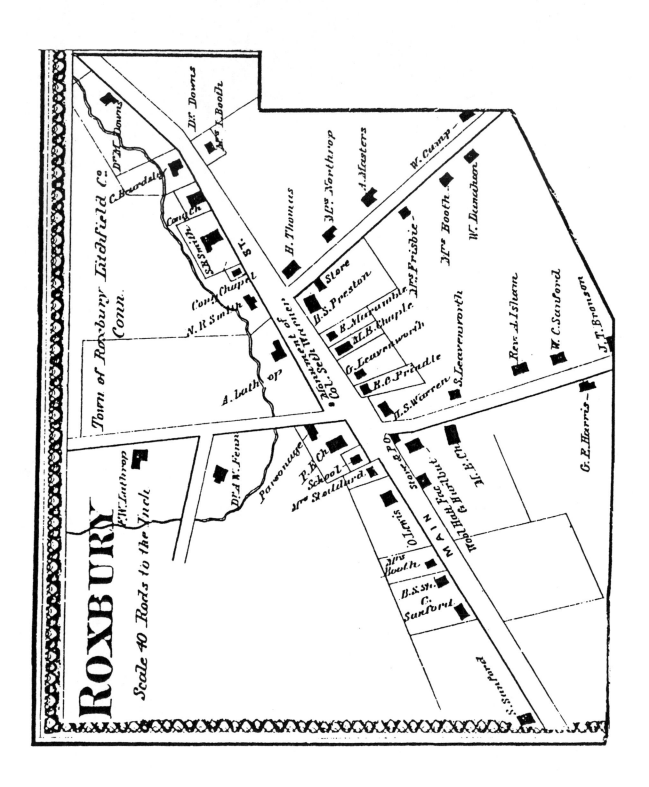

Chalybes, 1874

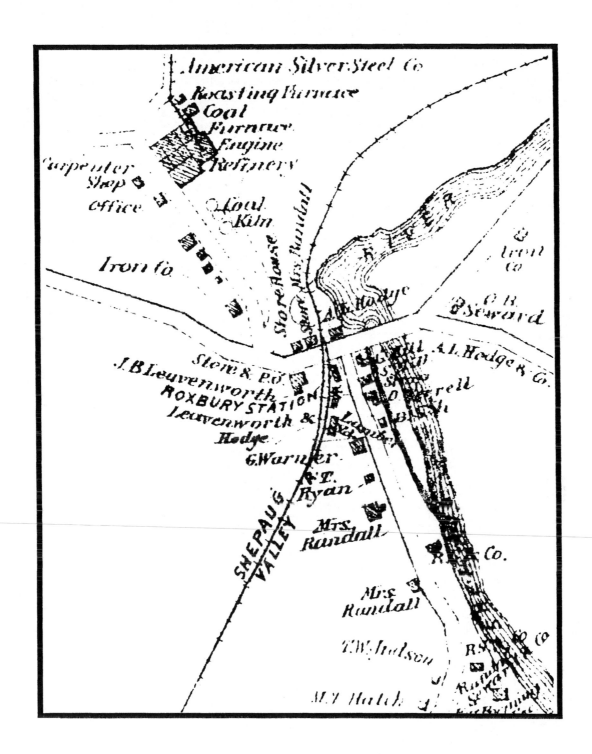

Index

0-595-32940-3

Printed in the United States
R2168100002B/R21681PG47061LVSX00002B/1}